ECONOMIC LIBERALIZATION AND INDIA'S FOREIGN POLICY

ECONOMIC LIBERALIZATION AND INDIA'S FOREIGN POLICY

CHAN-WAHN KIM

PUBLICATIONS

KALPAZ PUBLICATIONS

DELHI-110052

ECONOMIC LIBERALIZATION AND INDIA'S FOREIGN POLICY
[*Economic Studies*]

Rs. 725

ISBN: 81-7835-309-1

Published in 2006 in India by
Kalpaz Publications
C-30, Satyawati Nagar
Delhi-110052
e-mail: kalpaz@hotmail.com

Laser Typeset at: Alphabet, Delhi
Printed at: Salasar Imaging System, Delhi

To my teacher

Prof. Shanta Nedungadi Varma

and my wife

SeongHee

Contents

Preface

The immediate challenge before the Congress government constituted in June 1991 was to overcome the severe economic crisis and direct the economy towards a sustained growth. The challenge appeared formidable because the task was to be accomplished by liberalising the hitherto closed economy, the success of which would determine policies in almost every domain-political ideology, social policy, external policy and relations.

Accelerating economic growth through liberalization and globalization necessitated not only dismantling the stringent rules and regulations but also inviting foreign capital and technology. It also meant restructuring its trade regime to make it more export-oriented so as to prepare the economy for greater integration with the global economy. The far-reaching implications for India's foreign policy were a natural corollary to the restructuring process. Foreign policy of India was suddenly called upon to adjust itself to the emerging new and qualitatively different challenges. India's foreign policy establishment faced the daunting task of manoeuvring economic diplomacy. India had to convey to the world that by liberalising its economy, it was making sincere efforts to overcome the economic crisis and achieve a sustainable growth rate. This process of readjustment in India's foreign policy was further enhanced by the demands of the altered international environment in the post-Cold War era which encouraged globalization, regionalisation and liberalization of economies.

At this juncture, when crucial changes have taken place in India's economic and foreign policy, there is a vital need to understand the basic issues which were involved in this process. The process of interaction between economic liberalization and the foreign policy of India assumed special significance in this period. These years were marked by certain distinguishing features. It was the period 1990-1995 that witnessed major changes in policies. The process of the first generation of India's economic liberalization which was started in mid-1991 clearly slowed down by the year 1995 as a result of factors which were largely political. The year 1990 is included in the study due to the fact that it was a catalytic year, a year that provided a background to economic liberalization. Thus, the impact of economic liberalization on India's foreign policy during the period 1990-1995 deserves a systematic and scholarly investigation, not only for the immense practical importance of this particular aspect in foreign relations, but also in terms of conceptual analysis.

This study makes a modest attempt to reflect on the interconnections between the two policies. It situates the process of economic liberalization in the wider context of foreign policy to explore the interaction between economics and politics in India during the first half of the 1990s. However, no attempt will be made in this study to explore India's foreign policy in its entirety. The emphasis in this work will be mainly on the economic dimensions of India's foreign policy, that is, India's foreign economic policy. This study attempts to examine the changes that have occurred in India's foreign economic policy since the liberalization programme was introduced in 1991. It aims at exploring the political forces, both internal and external that propelled these policy changes. This study aims to understand and to delineate the patterns and shifts in India's foreign economic policy in the first half of the 1990s, underlining the varied global, regional and national compulsions.

This study revolves around two related hypotheses, namely, (i) the economic crisis and the subsequent economic liberalization became the major concern of, and provided a significant guideline to, India's foreign policy during the first half of the 1990s, and (ii) the economic liberalization programme of India increased its dependency on foreign capital, while enhancing the openness of its economy towards the rest of the world. The following points with regard to the above hypotheses will be examined for the period of 1990-95.

This study draws on extensive interviews with major policy-makers and bureaucrats both at the central and state levels. Besides, various documentary and other government sources, books, academic reports, journals and newspapers have also been consulted. Taken together, they provide a wealth of information. An attempt is made to confirm the validity of the arguments raised from these various sources by reference to the interviews conducted by this author. Simultaneously, government and secondary sources are used to corroborate the views expressed by the interviewees.

This study has been divided into six chapters. Chapter I attempts to provide the conceptual basis for understanding the complexities underlining the relationship between economics and politics. It briefly summarizes the different perspectives of political economy, namely, the liberal, Marxist and the realist. While this study does not claim to test any particular approach, it recognises that each of these approaches contains elements which are significant for the present analysis. It uses concepts and models from the different approaches to explain the complex relationship between development and foreign policy. The chapter then briefly discusses the history of India's foreign economic policy and the evolution of its policy of liberalization.

Chapter II discusses the major imperatives of India's economic liberalization in the 1990s. The aim of this chapter is to examine the driving forces behind this liberalization. What were the internal factors that led to the initiation of the reform process? What was the impact of the external situation? The role of the economic crisis together with other domestic imperatives are studied. It also analyses the global compulsions, like the Gulf War, the collapse of the Soviet bloc and the changing international economic environment, which led India towards economic liberalization.

Chapter III attempts a detailed study of the nature of the liberalization process initiated by the Congress government led by P.V. Narasimha Rao. It also attempts to address the problems and challenges with respect to the economic liberalization programme.

Chapter IV explores the impact of economic liberalization on India's foreign economic policy with special reference to its relations with international economic institutions. This chapter focuses on the issue of the vulnerability of the state from international economic institutions such as the General Agreement on Tariffs and Trade (GATT)/World Trade Organisation (WTO), the International Monetary Fund (IMF) and the World Bank, during the economic crisis and during the subsequent economic liberalization process. The positive aspects of these institutions for India's economic growth are also examined.

Chapter-V seeks to study the impact of economic liberalization on India's relations with other powers. It first looks into its effect on India's foreign policy behaviour with reference to changes in the conduct of its diplomacy. It further analyses the impact on India's relations with major states as well as regional blocs.

In the concluding chapter, the major findings of the previous chapters regarding the relationship between India's economic liberalization and its foreign policy are recapitulated in a broader perspective.

CHAN-WAHN KIM

Acknowledgements

This study would not have been possible without the constant help and encouragement of many people who familiarized me with India and helped me in nurturing my understanding of the country, A few deserve a special mention here.

I think it is fair to say that the present study could not have been written without the inspiring supervision of my teacher, Prof. Shanta Nedungadi Varma the Department of Political Science, University of Delhi. The insight she has imparted to this research is immense. Words cannot express my profound sense of indebtedness to her.

I have benefited from the views and comments of many experts on the design and progress of this study. I would like to express my deep gratitude to all the professors of the same department for their encouragement and for their enlightened discussions I had held with them and to Prof. Sumitra Chishti, Jawaharlal Nehru University (JNU) for her valuable contribution in developing my understanding of India's foreign economic policy. Also, I would like to express my thanks to Profs. M.S. Rajan, Muchkund Dubey, C.P. Bhambhri and Manmohan Agarwal from JNU for giving a number of valuable suggestions for this study. I would also like to thank the former Director and Chief Executive of Indian Council for Research on International Economic Relations, Dr. S.P. Gupta for his valuable suggestions in preparing the manuscript.

I am grateful to all the interviewees for sparing their time and providing their views and information on the subject of my research. Since it would take too much space to mention all of them, I must, therefore, limit myself to expressing my thanks particularly to the following, who greatly facilitated clarifying many an issue pertaining to India's economic liberalization and foreign policy: the present Prime Minister and the former Finance Minister Dr. Manmohan Singh; the present Defence Minister and the former Commerce Minister and External Affairs Minister Mr. Pranab Mukherjee; and the former Foreign Secretaries of India Prof. Muchkund Dubey and Mr. J.N. Dixit.

I am thankful to all my friends whose cooperation has helped me to make the study a success. I must mention the heartful thanks to M.M. Alam, R.K. Singh, A.P. Singh, S. Kumar and Sanjay for their comments and suggestions on the draft manuscript of this study. I owe my sincerest thanks to Mr Sasanka Sarmah who took keen interest to read the entire draft manuscript very carefully and to make suggestions to improve the contents.

I would like to take this opportunity to express my sincere thanks to all my professors of the Department of Hindi, Hankuk University of Foreign Studies, Korea for their intellectual inspiration. I am also thankful to Profs. J.H. Beak, K.S. Lee and K.H. Kim for their innovative ideas and encouragement, and C.S. Joeng and J.H. Cho for their friendship and encouragement during the period of my study.

Finally, I am indebted to my family whose support, patience, faith, and love, throughout my study period in India was the source of my strength. This research is as much theirs as mine.

CHAN-WAHN KIM

One

Conceptual Basis and Historical Background

Today, more than ever before, economics and politics are closely interrelated. In fact, the blurring of boundaries between and among various disciplines resulted in the phenomenal rise of interdisciplinary studies in the post war period. The transnational forces which gained immense momentum particularly after the end of the Cold War and the later Soviet collapse, brought economics to the forefront of international policy and interstate relations. Any meaningful study of either economic policy or foreign policy has to take into account the extent to which economic and political conditions influence each other. An interdisciplinary approach has become essential to comprehend the complexities of various phenomena. It is within this context that India's economic liberalization is being studied. The discourse attempts to analyse economic liberalization through a political perspective.

For students of political science, economic liberalization emerges as an important area of study because a government's choice of a particular economic policy is a political decision. It is ultimately the ruling elite of the country who decides what economic policies are to be followed. Moreover, economic liberalization has direct implications for the populace at large and therefore, cannot be divorced from politics and political analysis. During the first half of the 1990s, the process of economic liberalization together with the process of globalization influenced the foreign policy of India. The decision-makers had to take account of this changed imperative, while formulating foreign policy. This study explores the economic imperatives of foreign policy and the political imperatives and implications of economic policy during 1990-95.

This chapter begins by presenting the conceptual framework formatting the linkages between economic development and foreign policy. It examines the different approaches in the political economy analysis, focusing on the liberal, Marxist and realist perspectives. It further attempts a brief study of the historical background of India's foreign economic policy incorporating the initial steps taken towards economic liberalization.

CONCEPTUAL BASIS

Economic Development and Foreign Policy

The main objective of any country's foreign policy is promotion of its national interests. Preservation of political sovereignty, territorial integrity and economic advancement are universally accepted elements of national interest. The economic imperatives, thus, constitute a fundamental source of foreign policy formulation. Within this context, the economic policies pursued by a state acquires immense significance. Economic policy, then, forms a crucial part of any nation's overall foreign policy. In other words, the foreign policy of a country is fundamentally influenced by economic imperatives and by its economic policy. The first Prime Minister of India, Jawaharlal Nehru acknowledged this when he stated in Parliament, 'Ultimately, foreign policy is the outcome of economic policy, and until India has properly evolved her economic policy, her foreign policy will be rather vague, rather inchoate, and will be groping'.[1]

Indeed, economic development is a means of generating a country's potential and its confidence to deal with the external world. It becomes an important element in national security. Without economic development, there can be no real security. Military power alone cannot always maintain territorial integrity. Despite its mighty military power, the former Soviet Union could not avoid disintegration. On the other hand, though Japan and Germany do not have formidable defence in terms of military power, they are able to exert considerable influence on affairs. Thus, economic development has a significant bearing on a nation's international position and relations. Similarly the nature of foreign policy also has important implications for economic development.

Thus, in the contemporary world, an effective foreign policy and the level of economic development has become complementary to each other. As Appadorai has highlighted, foreign policy affects the economic development of a developing country like India in four ways: "It may help to secure foreign aid in its development. It may encourage or discourage the flow of foreign private capital. It may, through its foreign trade policies and trade agreements, promote or retard exports with their impact on balance of payments as well as on economic growth. It may, through encouraging joint industrial ventures with parties in other developing countries, give an impetus to increased production which would form an appreciable part of the contribution by the party undertaking to establish the industrial unit".[2]

During the first half of the 1990s, India was conducting its external relations both bilaterally and multilaterally in a manner that would effectively contribute to attract aid, investment and technology and promote foreign trade and Indian joint ventures abroad, for its economic development. During this period, India's main policy objective was to overcome the economic crisis situation. In order to enable economic recovery and enhance growth, it had to adopt a policy of liberalization which was both internal and external. Since fulfilment of national interest is the major goal of its foreign policy, it would be no exaggeration to say that the economic imperatives and strategy adopted during the period of 1990-95 often decided India's policy options in foreign affairs.

Defining Economic Liberalization and Foreign Economic Policy

Since the main aim of this work is to study the relationship between economic liberalization and India's foreign policy by focusing on foreign economic policy, it will be useful to explain at the outset what is meant by these terms.

Economic Liberalization: Though the concept of economic liberalization has been variously defined by different scholars, it has a body of certain core ideas. According to the World Development Report 1996, "in market economies liberalization usually means eliminating price controls and relaxing trade protection in a few heavily regulated or protected sectors.

Liberalizers in transition economies face an unprecedented and more daunting task, that of freeing not only the terms of market transactions but the transactions themselves: abolishing state orders and procurement, state production and trading monopolies, and the centralized allocation of foreign exchange. Liberalization also means freeing entry into production, services, and trade, including the freedom to open a new business, to expand or break up an existing business, and to change product mix, suppliers, customers, or geographical base".[3]

In line with the above definition some main components of economic liberalization can be described as being:

1. Privatisation of State and parastatal enterprises in order to reduce inefficiencies and government protection monopolies;
2. High interest rates and credit squeeze in order to reduce inflationary tendencies;
3. Trade liberalisation in order to open up the internal market and expose local industry to world market competition and boost foreign trade exchange;
4. Domestic demand management, leading to a lowering of State budgets and decreasing expenditure in the social sector;
5. Currency adjustment in order to improve the balance of payments by raising import prices and making exports more competitive; and
6. Free-market prices in order to remove distortions resulting from subsidised food and fertilisers and from import taxes on luxury items.[4]

The above definition and the underscored components of economic liberalization should not give the impression that it is a purely economic process; it is much more than that. The process of economic liberalization is, in its broadest sense, a process of societal transformation, involving economic, political, social and cultural changes.

In the context of the economic liberalization in India during the first half of the 1990s, the following economic strategies had been envisaged:

1. Greater resource mobilisation through fiscal adjustments and economic review;
2. Reducing government deficit through better investments and lesser current spending;
3. Greater reliance on the market mechanism through reducing price controls, subsidies, etc.;
4. Reforms in trading, financial and banking sectors;
5. Increasing efficiency of public sector and cutting its flabbiness through privatisation and disinvestment;
6. Mitigating trade barriers and protective measures to enable a free flow of capital, technology and services and a more dynamic relationship between domestic and foreign industries in terms of technology and investment;
7. Delicensing of industries;
8. Relaxing the Monopolies and Restrictive Trade Practices Act (MRTP) provisions;
9. Developing an exit policy for sick industries;
10. Rational exchange rate adjustment through devaluation and other methods; and
11. Controlling inflation through the growth of money supply.[5]

The redefining of development strategy under the Narasimha Rao government in the 1990s has been described variously as 'liberalization', 'new economic policy', 'economic reforms'. In this study, the term economic liberalization is used synonymously with the term 'economic reforms', to include both internal liberalization and globalisation.

The term foreign economic policy, sometimes also referred to as international economic policy[6] is usually taken to mean "the sum total of actions by the nation-state intended to affect the economic environment beyond the national jurisdiction. As such it is a hybrid, combining elements of foreign policy in general as well as of economic policy in general".[7]

In a sense foreign economic policy becomes a means to achieving both domestic and international political objectives. The need to pursue both sets of goals, namely the internal and the external, creates a situation whereby domestic economic policy objectives and foreign policy priorities are continuously meeting at the intersection of international economic policy. The latter is therefore intrinsically concerned with the nucleus of the other two policy areas. Like domestic economic policy, it is responsible for determining the allocation of scarce resources relative to insatiable demands, as well as influencing employment and price patterns. At the same time, this policy is concerned specifically with national security, that is, preservation of the state's physical integrity and political values. In general, it is concerned both with contributing a more prosperous domestic economy and to a more harmonious and prosperous global political environment.[8]

Thus, in sum, a government's foreign economic policy is really an umbrella term under which a variety of efforts are included: broad statements of principle; bilateral or multilateral negotiations with foreign governments; legislation; unilateral use of executive authority; interactions with domestic companies, workers, and lobbying groups; votes in an international organisation; administration of various programmes; and the adoption of defensive countermeasures.[9]

Keeping the above definitions of foreign economic policy in mind, Sumitra Chishti has broadly defined India's foreign economic policy as "that part of government policy which monitors and develops economic relations of the country with the rest of the world to meet its national requirements on the one hand, and responds to economic developments in the world in accordance with India's overall economic and other objectives on the other".[10] In other words, India's foreign economic policy has been largely shaped by its domestic developmental needs and priorities as it aimed towards providing economic growth internally and economic and commercial cooperation externally. Whichever definition of foreign economic policy one may adopt, it is generally agreed that a country's foreign economic policy is determined not only by national, domestic-level political and economic progress, but also by the global environment. The foreign economic policy of all countries is constrained by both international and domestic factors which contain political and economic dimensions.

Perspectives in Political Economy Approaches

Economic liberalization and foreign policy in a country can be studied in many ways by using different methodological approaches and perspectives. We can best conceptualise economic liberalisation and foreign policy by using political economy approaches. There is no single unequivocal meaning that can be assigned to political economy. For some, it refers primarily to the study of the political basis of economic actions and the ways in which government policies affect market operations. For others, the principal preoccupation is the economic basis of political action, the ways in which economic forces mould government policies. The two focuses are in a sense complementary, for politics and markets are in a constant state of mutual interaction.[11] Political economy is not merely a perspective, it is much more: it is a concept and a method as well. It is the combination of these three aspects which gives political economy its particular relevance as a mode of enquiry into social phenomena.[12]

In international parlance, political economy connotes the following: (a) the relationship between the State, society, and the economy; (b) the cause-effect relationship between technological change and the process of development; and (c) the economic relations among the different nations of the World.[13]

Some like Shaw and Aluko[14] distinguished a political economy approach from an orthodox analysis of foreign policy in at least four crucial categories. First, its *level of analysis* is substructural rather than superstructural. Second, its *mode of analysis* is critical and analytic rather than just descriptive. Third, its *method of analysis* is materialist rather than behavioural, concerned with modes and relations of production, with internal and international division of labour, and with the identification of inequalities, contradictions and prospects of any new synthesis. And fourth, the *implications* of such analysis are basic; radical change rather than reformism is considered to be essential if a history of dependence, underdevelopment and vulnerability is to be transcended.

The study of economic liberalization and India's foreign policy can be undertaken from different perspectives of political economy. These different approaches greatly affect the conclusions drawn as well as the nature of the studies themselves. The use of different perspectives has largely been responsible for differing interpretations. Three basic perspectives of political economy can be identified: studies in liberal political economy approaches; Marxist approaches, including both orthodox and neo-Marxist schools; and realist approaches. These are briefly reviewed below.

The liberal political economy approach believes that the economic role of the government must be constrained. According to this perspective, various forms of government intervention in the economy, intentionally or unintentionally restrict the market, and thereby prevent potentially rewarding trades from occurring. Pure liberalists generally support the provision of certain "public goods" by the government, namely those goods and services that make society better but that would not be provided by private markets.[15] The government, for example, plays an important role in ensuring external security, preserving internal order and the sanctity of property, establishing respect for contracts and regulating a common currency. In other words, the state, like society, is seen to be nothing more than a functional, voluntary and conditional creation of free individuals.

At the level of international economy, liberals assert that a fundamental harmony of interests exists between as well as within countries. They argue that all countries receive maximum benefits when people, commerce and capital move freely across national borders with minimum government interference in mutually rewarding exchanges. If universal free trade were to exist, all countries would enjoy the highest level of utility and there would be no economic basis for international conflict and war. Thus, international economic relations is a positive sum game where everyone can gain in absolute terms.[16] The International Monetary Fund (IMF) and the World Bank also favour this approach in general.

However, this *laissez-faire* concept of the classical liberal approach to economy has been challenged by the issues of equality and justice among the people within a nation-state, and externally, among the different nations. Hence, the concept known as the compensatory liberal approach evolved which demanded equalizing opportunities both within and among nations. Compensatory liberals permit a limited extension of state activity to enhance the opportunities of those who are unduly disadvantaged.[17]

The Marxist political economy approach holds that the individual's consciousness is seen to be profoundly conditioned by the ideologies generated by and for the dominant interests within the prevailing socio-economic system. The effects of the current state of development of that system further impacts on the consciousness.

Marxists believe that classes are the dominant actors in the political economy. According to them, states are largely the creation of the dominant economic classes. Marxists see the political economy as necessarily conflictual, since the relationship between capitalists and workers is essentially antagonistic. Because the means of production are controlled by a minority of dominant classes within society, labour does not receive its full return; conflicts between the classes is inevitable because of this exploitation. Once the economic, social and political system has been transformed through the revolutionary use of state power, then the state will be encouraged to 'wither away' and give way to a new, more libertarian, communist order.

Other Marxists, known as "dependency" theorists, extend the class analysis to the level of the international economy. According to them, the global system is categorized into the two different kinds of countries: a small group of wealthy areas, which forms the "core" or referred to as the First World, and a much larger group of dependent peripheral countries constituting the Third World. The latter mainly produce raw materials for exports which reduce further prospects of their internal development. International capitalism, in this view, exploits the periphery and benefits the core, just as capitalists exploit workers within a single country. This relationship has become all the more entrenched in the era of globalisation as it resulted into increasing dependence of developing countries for their economic gains, consequently jeopardising their foreign policy autonomy. From this point of view, economic dependence and foreign policy compliance have a causal interrelation namely, that an economically dominant country can exact foreign policy compliance from its dependent economic partner.[18]

Noam Chomsky, a world renowned political philosopher, criticising the basics of globalization, points out that the economic results of this process would inflict a "terrorising" impact on the poor and the downtrodden. According to him, the real model of development would be possible only by giving more autonomy to the people. He also emphasises all round individual empowerment through people's participation in micro-level planing and development.[19]

In the context of India, C.P. Bhambhri argues that the political economy of the Indian state in the 1990s is determined by the interests of the exploiting classes who did not want to grapple with the basic crisis of accumulation in India, and who want to cushion this crisis by inviting transnationals.[20] Another leading scholar on Indian political economy, Pranab Bardhan has provided a modified-Marxist paradigm with the neo-Classical public paradigm explaining the Indian state policy as the result of conflicts within the dominant class coalition of industrial bourgeois, rich peasants, and the professionals including white collar workers. He puts the blame on such a dominant coalition which leads to the patronage politics of subsidies, grants and rentseeking against the rate of growth of public investment in infrastructure, the growth of nondevelopment expenditure, and inefficient fiscal management, which ultimately prevented overall economic growth in India.[21]

While rejecting the dependency theory on India and the argument of the dominant socio-economic classes, Lloyd I. Rudolph and Susanne Hoeber Rudolph argue in their well known book, *In Pursuit of Lakshmi: The Political Economy of the Indian State (1987)*, the Indian state is not only relatively autonomous but also self-interested and self-determined as the 'third actor', which is able to resist the pressures from social forces. In other words, the state as third actor plays the principal role vis-a-vis the two other actors of the organized economy, namely, private capital and organized labour. They argue that "the self-determining state is in a position to serve itself and, like other self-interested actors, to be a source of exploitation or injustice".[22]

The realist political economy perspective contends that every nation-state tries to maximize its power and shapes the economy to this end. They believe that nation-states are the principal actors within the international political economy.[23] The most fundamental feature of the international realm is anarchy, or the absence of central rule, a condition under which nation-states are sovereign, the sole judge of their own behaviours, and subject to no higher authority. If no authority is higher than the nation-state, then all actors are subordinate to the nation-state.[24] While private citizens can interact with their counterparts in other countries, the basis for this interaction is legislated by the nation-state.

According to the realists, "political values and security interests are crucial determinants of international economic relations. Politics determines the framework of economic activity and channels it in directions which tend to serve the political objectives of dominant political groups".[25] Therefore, realists allow for circumstances in which nation-states sacrifice economic gain to weaken their opponents or strengthen themselves in military or diplomatic terms. Thus, trade protection, which might reduce a country's overall income by restricting the market, may be adopted for reasons of national political power.

Realist political economy is primarily concerned with how changes in the distribution of international power affect the form and type of international economy. The best known realist approach to this question is the "Theory of Hegemonic Stability", which holds that an open international economy- that is, one characterised by the free exchange of goods, capital, and services- is most likely to exist when a single dominant or hegemonic power is present to stabilize the system and construct a strong regime. For realists, then, the pursuit of power by nation-states shapes the international economy.[26]

It is recognized that each of these perspectives have variants within them, however, these variations are not dealt with here in detail. The three perspectives, the Liberal, the Marxist and the Realist, differ on the inevitability of conflict within the political economy. Liberals believe that economics and politics are largely autonomous spheres; Marxists maintain that economics determines politics; and Realists argue that politics determines economics. On one issue they (the liberal, Marxist and realist approaches) are, however, relatively united, namely that of doubting the simple and rigid distinction traditionally drawn between the domestic economy and the international economic system. Indeed much of the renewed interest in political economy, in whatever form, has been prompted by the apparent permeability of the modern national economy and the growth of competitive pressures within the international economy.[27]

While this study does not claim to test any particular approach, it recognises that each of these approaches contains elements which are significant for the present analysis. While liberal perspectives are relevant while dealing with market efficiency in the context of India's economic recovery, the Marxist critique attains validity with reference to the impact of economic liberalization on the weaker sections of the society, and the vulnerability of the state. In any analysis of India's relations bilaterally and multilaterally, the realist paradigms based on the interest factor cannot be overlooked.

HISTORICAL BACKGROUND

The impact of economic liberalization on India's foreign policy cannot be properly understood without an adequate understanding of the historical background of India's foreign economic policy.

The Early Years: Focus on Nehruvian Approach

One of India's main objectives soon after gaining independence was to achieve self-sufficiency under a planned economic system. India adopted this strategy on three grounds-political (the fear of crippling dependence on external forces), economic (preferring a middle-of-the road development strategy) and ideological (toward a socialistic pattern of society).[28] India's developmental strategy, as Rajni Kothari noted, was to pursue four more or less well defined goals: independence of the economy from its reliance on strategic imports and foreign aid (the goal of "self-sustained growth"), resource mobilization and capital accumulation leading to increasing rates of saving and investment (the goal of a high "rate of growth"), reduction of sectoral and social disparities (the goal of "equality") and the simple concern with providing minimum conditions of subsistence and survival (the goal of equity and "justice").[29]

To attain all these goals, India could hardly escape international economic interaction, especially foreign assistance in the form of machinery, technical equipment, capital, etc. For seeking such assistance India adopted the twin policies of diversification and bargaining with major centres of global power. These policies were pursued with the help of its non-alignment both as policy and strategy.[30] As an independent approach to foreign policy, "Indian non-alignment was as much a response to global conditions as it was an indigenous policy for her development".[31]

As a result, India could get technical and financial assistance from the two major centres of global power. From the Western side, India mainly obtained agricultural and infrastructural assistance. Among the capitalist countries, the US was the largest donor. Much of the US aid including the PL 480 programme was mainly in the field of India's urgent food needs and the expanding agricultural production.[32] Some private foundations in the US also contributed in this direction. For instance, at the behest of the Ford Foundation, India adopted high-yielding wheat, maize and rice varieties which were sources of the Green Revolution in India. In addition to that, the US also provided India with technical aid under the Indo-US Technical Cooperation Programme established in 1951.

However, apart from a few cases of financial and technical aid from the UK and France for building steel plants in the public sector in Durgapur and Rourkela, the capitalist countries were generally reluctant to support India's industrial sector, specially its public sector industries. It was the Soviet Union from whom India obtained both financial assistance and the technology transfers which laid the foundation of its industrial infrastructures. This included heavy metallurgical and mining machinery, oil exploration and production, steel mills, heavy electrical projects, petroleum refining, and pharmaceutical and surgical instruments. Without doubt, in the field of industry, the Soviet Union was the most important source of external assistance to India.[33] It contributed to placing India among the top ten industrial nations of the world.[34]

By the seventies, India was able to establish "a solid heavy industrial and agricultural base"[35] as a result of external assistance from the two ideological blocs. Therefore, it may be considered that "undoubtedly, this was a major achievement for India's economic and political diplomacy, since she was the first developing country to benefit from a cold war situation, obtaining meaningful assistance when the other developing countries, which had allied to one bloc or the other, should have been logically the greater beneficiaries of the bipolar system".[36]

However, it must be mentioned that the attainment of foreign assistance from the two ideological blocs was facilitated mainly by the geo-political understanding between India and the two superpowers.[37] In other words, the attainment of external aid from the two rival blocs did not mean that India emphasised its economic aspect of foreign policy. Foreign policy continued to be centred around the independent approach which lay at the core of its non-aligned perspective.[38] The emphasis on economic dimension of foreign policy was negligible, despite Prime Minister Nehru's observation that 'ultimately, foreign policy is the outcome of economic policy'.[39]

It is, therefore, important to note that Nehru himself did not put such a pragmatic policy in practice. For example, when the then Japanese Prime Minister Ikeda visited India in 1961, it was reported that Nehru did not respond adequately to Japanese economic diplomacy. According to one source, 'the Japanese delegation left India somewhat disappointed with Nehru's advocacy of non-alignment to them while paying little heed to their economic cooperation proposals'.[40]

An important aspect of India's foreign economic policy during this period was that while India tried to maximize the inflow of foreign aid without sacrificing political and economic independence, she did not favour the liberal economic order of foreign investment. This was evident from the fact that the 1948 Industrial Policy Resolution stated that with regard to joint ventures involving foreign participation "the major interest in ownership and effective control should always be in Indian hands".[41] Such a control on foreign investment continued throughout the sixties and even during the Janata Party government at the centre in the late 1970s. In fact, during this time the pro-socialist Minister for Industry, George Fernandes tightened the control on foreign investment in India. Large American companies like Coca-Cola and IBM were forced out of India altogether, with highly publicized attempts being made to produce indigenous alternatives. The positions taken by India within transnational coalitions such as the Non-Aligned Movement (NAM) and the Group of 77 developing nations also manifested its reservations regarding free entry of foreign capital and goods.[42]

The socialist pattern of development was pursued under the mixed economy model which laid emphasis on centralised, planned and regulated development. This was institutionalised by important instruments such as the Industries Development and Regulation Act (IDRA) of 1951, the Monopolies and Restrictive Trade Practices Act (MRTP) of 1969, and the Foreign Exchange Regulation Act (FERA) of 1973. In theory, the model was designed to ensure that the economy would grow rapidly to reduce dependence on foreign capital and technology so as to achieve self-reliance. While this strategy established industrial and agricultural bases, it also led to certain negative features.

In practice, it resulted in slow rates of growth accompanied by massive corruption. There was also a problem of an economy of shortages.[43] Further, it was noted that the expanded public sector and heavy-industry sector under the 'commanding heights' of the economy could not draw sufficient population out of agriculture as had been envisaged.[44]

Attempts at Partial Economic Liberalization up to 1984

Some believe that economic liberalization in India was initiated as far back as the late 70s under the Janata Party government and subsequently carried on under the Congress government (1980-84) led by Indira Gandhi.[45]

The Janata Party government had taken some economic liberalization measures like import liberalization which was stimulated by the increasing foreign exchange reserves by the remittances from Indians working in the Gulf area. However, the basic features of the Nehruvian model of development remained almost intact, which was based on centralized planning, a mixed economy dominated by a public sector, and a private sector in which all basic management decisions involving investment, production, technology, location, prices, imports, exports, and foreign capital were controlled and regulated by the state.[46]

From early 1980, serious doubts regarding the efficacy of the Nehruvian development model began to surface. After coming back to power in 1980, Mrs Indira Gandhi herself was becoming conscious of the inefficiency of planning and state intervention strategy because the goals of rapid economic development were not achieved according, not merely to the anticipation of the public policy makers, but also to the expectations of the people.[47] She also realised that her populist programme of *Garibi Hatao* (Abolish Poverty) based on the notion of socialism had not born fruit."The support she was getting from the poor, therefore, was based not so much on concrete rewards, but primarily due to her ideological and rhetorical appeal".[48] Realising these factors Indira Gandhi had appointed a high powered committee under L.K. Jha for Economic and Administrative Reforms which went into all the different aspects of regulation. Towards the end of the period, she had appointed three committees; one under Abid Hussain to work out trade reforms, another under M. Narasimha to work out financial reforms and a third on public enterprises reforms. The purpose of these committees was to consider how to deregulate and liberalise the controlled markets.[49]

Economic liberalization programme of Mrs Gandhi was mainly concerned with deregulation of industrial licensing and softening of the restrictions on monopolies. One of the notable examples of these measures was that the government placed 20 important industries under "automatic licensing" following the recommendations of the Jha Commission on Economic and Administrative Reforms.[50] These kind of measures had the support of the domestic big business sector as they were not accompanied by any serious trade liberalisation measures which would have invited foreign competition. At the same time, Mrs. Gandhi encouraged the growth of small-scale industry by expanding the scope of reservations.[51] In this respect, it is said that decontrol by the government on expansion and new production was motivated by the desire to cultivate new bases of support, and that the business community was one such base. Thus, Atul Kohli argued that Mrs Indira Gandhi's economic liberalization is best understood as "an integral aspect of her overall political strategy".[52]

The economic liberalization under Mrs Gandhi in 1980s was also necessitated by the economic difficulties resulting from exogenous factors.[53] These were the second oil shock and another terrible drought in 1979-80. Agricultural output fell by 15.2 per cent and foodgrains production fell by 17.6 per cent. As a result, food prices rose by 8.4 per cent in 1979-80 and a further 11.3 per cent in 1980-81.[54] In addition to that, the second oil crisis was greater than the first in 1973-74. As a result, the oil import bill rose from $ 2 billion in 1978-79 to $ 6.6 billion in 1980-81. Worse, the Assam agitation of 1979-80 disrupted the oil supplies, shutting down the oil refineries causing an acute shortage of petroleum products. The current account moved from a surplus of Rs 5.8 billion in 1978-79 to a deficit of Rs. 2.02 billion in 1980-81. This current account deficit forced India to move into negotiations with the IMF for the short-to medium-term borrowing.[55]

The Government of India drew Rs 8.15 billion from the IMF Trust Fund and Compensatory Fund and in November 1981, entered into a fund programme with financing facilities of Special Drawing Rights (SDR) 5 billion, one of the largest that the IMF had negotiated with any developing country till then. Only SDR 3 billion out of an authorised sum of SDR 5 billion had been used when India terminated the arrangement in May 1984.[56] India used its reserves and resorted to commercial borrowing for the first time but at the end of 1984-85 the external debt to Gross Domestic Product (GDP) ratio was only 17 per cent, still a low figure compared with most developing countries.[57]

Soon after completing the loan agreement of SDR 5 billion

with the IMF, the Government of India further liberalised its economy. During 1981-82, steel and cement prices were decontrolled, manufactured imports were liberalised, and controls on both entry and expansion by national firms were relaxed. During 1981, the government sanctioned four times as many applications for expansion and new undertakings as in any of five preceding years.[58]

But, the restrictions imposed by the FERA of 1973 was still strong enough to limit the prospects of large private capital flows into India. Mrs Indira Gandhi did not change the 'commanding heights policy' of the economy. In her 1981 speech to Parliament, she talked about public enterprises still occupying the commanding heights of the economy. She said that "the public sector will maintain the commanding heights of the economy and I am sure that it will continue to expand. We should redouble our efforts to make it more efficient to produce higher returns and to serve our social purposes".[59] It is considered that Mrs Gandhi's approach to economic policy was still rooted in the spirit of the Nehruvian development model. Thus, Jagdish Bhagwati describes the economic liberalization under the Indira Gandhi government as "reform by stealth".[60]

Economic Liberalization under Rajiv Gandhi

However, it is generally believed, as Bimal Jalan pointed out, that the new era of India's approach to economic policy started from the beginning of 1985 with regard to taxation, industrial licensing, imports, technology, and investment priorities.[61]

Rajiv Gandhi who was of the post-independence generation, had a modern managerial style and clearly wanted to shed the ideological "baggage" of the past, which was forged on the anvil of India's struggle for independence from colonial rule.[62] The word "socialism" was not mentioned even once in the first budget speech of the Rajiv Gandhi government in 1985.[63] Rajiv Gandhi described his government's economic approach as involving a "judicious combination of deregulation, import liberalization and easier access to forcign technology".[64] It has also been pointed out that the liberalization policy of foreign technology was largely motivated by national security compulsions.[65]

Rajiv Gandhi declared in 1988: "Exports must become a major focus of Indian industry. A rapidly growing modernizing economy will need a growing volume of imports and an expanding flow of technology. We can only pay for the inflow if we can export more than we are doing now. This is the underpinning of real self-reliance. It is a major challenge to Indian industry. The international environment is far from ideal. But that only means we will have to try harder".[66] The emphasis on the export-oriented strategy was to redefine the central objective of self-reliance as not self-sufficiency but international competitiveness. This was a major change in Indian economic thinking, which was a fairly sharp break from the Nehruvian and Indira Gandhi's economic strategies.

The liberalising measures under the Rajiv Gandhi government were undertaken mostly in the early period of the regime. The main features of this economic liberalization programme could be summed up as follows:

- *Industrial deregulation.* There was some dilution of licensing requirements as regards entry and expansion of capacity. The list of industries open to large firms was extended. The asset threshold above which firms are subject to monopoly regulation was raised.
- *Import deregulation.* Restrictions on imports of capital goods were somewhat eased to encourage technological modernization. There was some replacement of quantitative import restrictions by tariffs, primarily in cases where there was no competing domestic production.
- *Export incentives.* These were substantially increased. Cash assistance and duty drawbacks went up. There was a widening of the coverage of products available to exporters against import replenishment licenses. Very substantial income tax concessions were given to business profits attributable to exports.
- *Exchange rate policy.* From 1986 there was a policy of active exchange rate depreciation.
- *Financial Liberalization.* The yield on long-term government securities was raised a little, in the direction

of market rates. There were some moves to develop the money market.

- *Taxation.* Rates of direct taxation were lowered to increase incentives and reduce evasion. The excise tax structure was modified to some extent in the direction of value added taxation in order to reduce inefficiencies resulting from the erstwhile cascading system that provided tax offsets for only a limited range of products. The import tariff structure was somewhat simplified (but the average tariff rate went up).[67]

It is significant to note that the immediate political background within which Rajiv Gandhi's economic liberalization programme was undertaken. In the 1984 general elections, he secured a massive victory, largely based on the sympathy factor accruing from the assassination of his mother Indira Gandhi. This provided him crucial political space and freedom of action both from the opposition groups and other interest-group pressures.[68] The initial economic liberalization programme of the Rajiv Gandhi government also got positive support from the middle classes. Such support was evidenced in popularity polls conducted by news magazines and in opinions expressed in English-language media catering primarily to those groups.[69]

However, from the middle of 1986, his economic liberalization programme began to face several challenges not only from within his Congress party but also from opposition parties who criticised the Rajiv government of neglecting the farmers and the poor.[70] Faced with manifold political problems and challenges to his authority, Rajiv Gandhi's push towards economic liberalization weakened. This became evident, especially after the Congress government lost a crucial mid-term election in Haryana in June 1987. Thus, a liberal model of economic development could not replace the socialist pattern of economic strategy with state controls and import substitution under the Rajiv Gandhi government. In this context, it is interesting to note that Jagdish Bhagwati called the economic liberalization initiated by Rajiv Gandhi as "reform with reluctance".[71]

Impact on Foreign Economic Policy

Thus, it is considered that the economic liberalization in India before 1990 was "a gradual and piecemeal liberalization of controls, but without any fundamental reform of the system".[72] Two features of this policy are significant. Firstly, since there was no fundamental change in the economic system, specially with regard to international competition, there was little change in India's foreign policy vis-a-vis greater emphasis on economic aspects, with the notable exception of the initial period of the Rajiv government. Secondly, the government under Rajiv Gandhi also tried to align its foreign policy to economic liberalization. In an unprecedented move, the Commerce and External Affairs Ministries were brought under one umbrella, with a view to 'bringing back political sense into trade policies'.[73]

Accordingly, Heads of missions were asked to ensure that political and economic diplomacy be synchronised. As the Commerce Minister, Mr Shiv Shankar put it: "In today's interdependent but fast changing world, India's political, economic and other objectives abroad must go hand in hand. Our foreign policy will surely be more effective if we adopt a multi-pronged, coordinated approach which can simultaneously promote our diplomatic and commercial interests in other countries. Indeed, our capacity to pursue our broader goals of peace, cooperation and justice in various regions will be greatly reinforced if our economic and trade interests are also strengthened".[74]

But, this kind of verbal effort was hardly followed by concrete economic policy changes. This was particularly due to the fact that the economic liberalization process had to slow down in order to build up political support in the face of growing opposition. It has been further pointed out that in the past, the conduct of Indian diplomacy tended to place too great an emphasis on the political aspects with economic side being often left to "the tender mercies" of the Commercial Attache who in turn confined himself to the grossly unimaginative routine set by the Commerce Ministry.[75] Worse, even the committed personnel for commercial work were not available in several Indian embassies in South-East Asia.[76]

In this regard, it is interesting to note what Natwar Singh

has revealed, "in my 31 years of service I never once spoke on economic issues. We thought it was infradig to do so and left it to our commercial officers".[77] The former Special Secretary (Economic Relations) in the Ministry of External Affairs untill early 1995, Mr P.M.S. Malik confirmed this past tendency in Indian diplomacy saying that "certainly till 1991 India's global profile hardly mirrored a Union agenda in which economic issues had come to increasingly occupy central place in the country's foreign policy. Both economic diplomacy and domestic thinking based on co-ordinated approaches and functioning were weak".[78]

Thus, it is seen that India's inward-looking import-substituting strategy under centralised economic planning continued till the 1970s and was partially liberalised during the 1980s. But, partial liberalization during the 1980s did not shift the emphasis from a socialist pattern of economic strategy, or direct it towards a liberal model of development which emphasised greater integration with the world economy. The pre-1990s' economic strategy of India was mainly centred on maintaining a level of independence and non-alignment, which focused on political aspects of foreign policy within the Cold War context. As a result, India's foreign economic policy was mainly guided by the political aspect of policies. However, the decade of the 1990s created a plethora of conditions which culminated in the programme of economic liberalization and globalization. At this juncture, when far reaching changes have taken place in India's economic and foreign policy, there is a vital need to understand the basic imperatives behind the country's economic liberalization programme and policies accruing from it.

NOTES AND REFERENCES

1. Jawaharlal Nehru quoted in Dewan C. Vohra, *Economic Relevance of Non-Alignment*, (Delhi: ABC Publishing House, 1983).
2. A Appadorai, *National Interest and India's Foreign Policy*, (Delhi: Kalinga Publications, 1992), p. 105.
3. World Bank, *World Development Report 1996: From Plan to Market*, (New York: Oxford University Press (hereafter referred to as OUP), 1996), p. 23.
4. Alex E. Fernandez Jilberto and Andre' Mommen (eds.), *Liberalisation*

in the Developing World: Institutional and Economic Change in Latin America, Africa and Asia, (London: Routledge, Kegan Paul, 1996), p. 6.

5. Ramesh K. Arora and Rajni Goyal, *Indian Public Administration: Institutions and Issues,* 2nd edition, (New Delhi: Wishwa Prakashan, 1996), p. 641.
6. Benjamin J. Cohen and Robert A. Pastor use the term "foreign economic policy". However, Stephen D. Conhen uses the term "international economic policy" as to mean the same. See Benjamin J. Conhen (ed.), *American Foreign Economic Policy,* (New York: Harper and Row Publishers, 1968), Robert A. Pastor, Congress and the Politics of U.S. *Foreign Economic Policy: 1929-1976,* (Berkeley: University of California Press, 1980), and Stephen D. Cohen, *The Making of Unities States International Economic Policy,* (New York: Preagen Publishers, 1977).
7. Benjamin J. Cohen, "American Foreign Economic Policy: Some General Principles of Analysis" in Benjamin J. Cohen (ed.), *op. cit.,* p. 10.
8. Stephen D. Cohen, *op. cit.,* p. 4.
9. Stephen D. Cohen and Ronald I. Meltzer, *United States International Economic Policy in Action: Diversity of Decision Making,* (New York: Preager, 1982), p. 4.
10. Sumitra Chishti, "India's Foreign Economic Policy" in Bimal Prasad (ed.), *India's Foreign Policy: Studies in Continuity and Change,* (New Delhi: Vikas Publisher, 1979), p. 35.
11. Jeffry A. Frieden and David A. Lake, *International Political Economy: Perspectives on Global Power and Wealth,* Third Edition, (New York: St. Martin's Press, 1995), p. 1.
12. Neera Chandhoke, "Marxian Political Economy as Method: How Political Is Political Economy?", *Economic and Political Weekly* (hereafter referred to as EPW), Vol. XXIX, No. 5, January 29, 1994., p. 15.
13. S. Rath, "Globalisation: A Realist Approach to International Political Economy", in Bijoyini Mohanty and S.C. Hazary, *Political Economy of India: Retrospects and Prospects,* (New Delhi: A.P.H. Publishing Corporation, 1997), p. 15.
14. Timothy M. Shaw and Olajide Aluko (eds.), *The Political Economy of African Foreign Policy: Comparative Analysis,* (Aldeshot: Gower Publishing Company, 1984), pp. 10-11.
15. More specifically, a public good is one that, in its purest form, is *nonrival in consumption and nonexcludable.* The first characteristic

means that consumption of the good by one person does not reduce the opportunities for others to consume the goods; for example, clean air can be breathed by one person without reducing its availability to others. The second characteristic means that nobody can be prevented from consuming the good: those who do not contribute to pollution control are still able to breathe clean air. Those who conditions are fully met only rarely, but goods that come close to them are generally considered public goods. Jeffry A. Frieden and David A. Lake, *op. cit.*, p. 16.

16. Stepehn D. Cohen and Ronald I. Meltzer, *op. cit.*, p. 10.
17. R.D. Mackinlay and R. Little, *Global Problems and World Order*, (London: Frances Pinter, 1986).
18. See Kenneth, J. Menkhaus and Charles W. Kegly, jr., "The Compliant Foreign Policy of the Dependent State Revisited: Empirical Linkages and Lessons from the Case of Somalia", *Comparative Political Studies*, Vol. 21, No. 3, October 1988, p. 317.
19. See, Milan Ri, *Comsky's Politics*, (Jaipur and New Delhi: Rawat Publications, 1997) and Noam Chomsky, *Profit Over People: Neoliberalism and Global Order*, (Delhi: Madhyam Books, 1999).
20. C.P. Bhambhri, *The Indian State: Fifty Years*, (New Delhi: Shipra Publications, 1997), p. 208.
21. Pranab Bardhan, *Political Economy of Development in India*, (Delhi: OUP, 1984).
22. Lloyd I. Rudolph and Susanne H. Rudolph, *In Pursuit of Lakshmi: The Political Economy of the Indian State*, (New Delhi: Orient Longman, 1987), p. 400.
23. The classical realist perspective on the nature of relations between political and economic factors is best reflected in Hans J. Morgenthau and Kenneth W. Thompson, *Politics Among Nations: The Struggle for Power and Peace*, 6th edn., (New York: McGraw, 1985).
24. John Gerald Ruggie, "Continuity and Transformation in the World Polity: Toward a Neo-Realist Synthesis", *World Politics*, (Baltimore), Vol. 35, January 1983, pp. 265-66.
25. Robert Gilpin, "The Politics of Transnational Economic Relations", in R. Keohane and J.S. Nye, eds., *Transnational Relations and World Politics*, (Cambridge: Harvard University Press, 1973), p. 53.
26. Jeffry A. Frieden and David A. Lake, *op. cit.*, p. 3.
27. R.J. Barry Jones (ed.), *The Worlds of Political Economy*, (London: Pinter Publishers, 1988), p. 8.
28. Harish Kapur, *India's Foreign Policy 1947-1992: Shadows and Substance*, (New Delhi: Sage Publication, 1994), pp. 53-57.

29. Rajni Kothari, *Politics in India,* (New Delhi: Orient Longman, 1970), p. 340.
30. For detailed studies of nonalignment, also see K.P. Karunakaran, *India in World Affairs 1950-53,* (Calcutta: OUP, 1958), K.P. Karunakaran, "Non-alignment", Seminar, March 18, 1961, A.P. Rana, *Imperatives of Non-Alignment,* (Delhi: Macmillan, 1976), and M.S. Rajan, *Nonalignment and Nonaligned Movement: Retrospect and Prospect,* (New Delhi: Vikas Publishing House, 1990).
31. Shanta Nedungadi Varma, *Foreign Policy Dynamics: Moscow and India,* (New Delhi: Deep and Deep Publications, 1999), p. 12.
32. D.N. Prasad, *Food for Peace: The Story of US Food Production to India,* (Bombay: Asia Publishing House, 1980).
33. Rama Shankar Singh, *Indo-Soviet Cooperation and India's Economic Development,* (New Delhi: Deep and Deep Publications, 1989), p. 10.
34. R. K. Sharma, *The Economics of Soviet Assistance to India,* (New Delhi: Allied Publishers, 1981), p. 2.
35. Harish Kapur, *op. cit.,* p. 84.
36. *Ibid.*
37. See, Ramesh Thakur, *The Politics and Economics of India's Foreign Policy,* (New Delhi: OUP, 1994), C. P. Bhambhri, "Foreign Economic Policy of India", in B.M. Jain (ed.), *Reflections on India's Foreign Policy,* (Jaipur: RBSA Publishers, 1989) and M. Agarwal, "India and the World Economy", *International Studies,* Vol. 24, No. 4, 1987.
38. See, A.K. Damodaran, "NAM: The Road Ahead", in Foreign Service Institute, *Indian Foreign Policy: Agenda for the 21st Century,* Vol. 1, (New Delhi: Konark Publishers, 1997).
39. Jawaharlal Nehru, *op. cit.*
40. Arjun Asrani, "India-Japan Relations" in Foreign Service Institute, *Indian Foreign Policy: Agenda for the 21st Century,* Vol. 2, (New Delhi: Konark Publishers, 1998), p. 345.
41. Quoted in K. V. Iyer and L.R. Kumar, *Foreign Collaboration in Industry-Policies and Procedures,* Vol. 1, (New Delhi: Indu Publications, 1985), p. 2.
42. Stephen D. Mcdowell, "India, the LDCs and GATT Negotiations on Trade and Investment in Services" in Richard Stubbs and Geoffrey R.D. Underhill (eds.), *Political Economy and the Changing Global Order,* (London: Macmillan, 1994), p. 499.
43. Prem Shankar Jha, *India: A Political Economy of Stagnation,* (Bombay: OUP, 1980).
44. V. M. Dandekar, *The Indian Economy: 1949-92,* Vol. 1, Agriculture,

(New Delhi: Sage Publications, 1994).

45. Atul Kohli, "Politics of Economic Liberalization in India", *World Development*, Vol. 17, No. 3, 1989 and Vijay Joshi and I.M.D. Little, *India: Macroeconomics and Political Economy 1964-91*, (Delhi: OUP, 1994).
46. Robert L. Hardgrave, Jr., and Stanley Kochanek, *India: Government and Politics in a Developing Nation*, 4th edition, (New York: Harcourt Brace Jovanovich, 1986), pp. 308-335.
47. C.P. Bhambhri, *The Indian State: Fifty Years, op. cit.*, p. 239.
48. Atul Kohli, *op. cit.*, p.308.
49. Arjun Sengupta, "Indira Gandhi's Economic Reforms", *Mainstream*, December 9, 1995, p. 29.
50. *The Economic Times*, September 1, 1984.
51. Vijay Joshi and I.M.D. Little, *op. cit.*
52. Atul Kohli, *op. cit.*, p. 310.
53. Arjun Sengupta, *op. cit.*
54. Vijay Joshi and I.M.D. Little, "Indian Macro Economic Policies", *EPW*, Vol. XXII, No. 9, February 28, 1987, p. 374.
55. M.S. Ahluwalia, "Balance of Payments Adjustment in India 1970-71 to 1983-84", *World Development*, Vol. 14, No. 8, 1986, p. 946.
56. Vijay Joshi and I.M.D. Little (1987), *op. cit.*, p. 374.
57. *Ibid.*
58. P.S. Jha, "The End of the Tunnel: Return to Sanity in Economic Policy", *Times of India*, August 13, 1982.
59. Quoted in Arjun Sengupta, *op. cit.*, p. 31.
60. Jagdish Bhagwati, *India's Transition: Freeing the Economy*, (Delhi: OUP, 1994), p. 3.
61. See Bimal Jalan, *India's Economic Crisis: The Way Ahead*, 2nd impression, (Delhi: OUP, 1993).
62. T.V. Sathyamurthy, "India's International Role: Economic Dependence" in T.V. Sathyamurthy (ed.), *Social Change and Political Discourse in India*, Vol.1, State and Nation in the Context of Social Change, (Delhi: OUP, 1994), p. 161.
63. For a summary and a discussion of the 1985-86 budget, see *Times of India*, March 21, 1985. For the critical views of the budget, see Bhabatosh Datta, "The Central Budget and the New Economic Policy", EPW, April 20, 1985, pp. 693-8.
64. Quoted in *Times of India*, January 6, 1986.
65. For a detailed arguments, see E. Sridharan, "Liberalization and Technology Policy: Redefining Self-Reliance" in T.V. Sathyamurthy (ed.), *Social Change and Political Discourse in India*,

Vol. 2, Industry and Agriculture in India since Independence, (Delhi: OUP, 1995).

66. Quoted in Harish Kapur, *op. cit.*, p. 70.
67. Vijay Joshi and I.M.D. Little (1994), *op. cit.*, pp. 62-63.
68. Atul Kohli, *op. cit.*
69. See, for example, the various popularity polls in *India Today* throughout 1985 and 1986.
70. For a detailed study, see Atul Kohli, *op. cit.*
71. Jagdish Bhagwati, *op. cit.*
72. Vijay Joshi and I.M.D. Little (1994), *op. cit.*, p. 67.
73. B.M., "Aligning Foreign Policy to Economic Liberalization", *EPW*, Vol. XXI, No. 30, July 26, 1986, pp. 1299-1300.
74. *Times of India*, July 1986.
75. P.M.S. Malik, "The Changing Face of India's Economic Diplomacy: The Role of Ministry of External Affairs" in Foreign Service Institute, Vol. 1, *op. cit.*, p. 234.
76. It was noted by the trade delegation sponsored by the Associated Chambers of Commerce and Industry (ASSOCHAM). See, N.M. Khilnani, *New Dimensions of Indian Foreign Policy*, (New Delhi: Westvill Publishing House, 1995), p. 61.
77. Quoted in *The Sunday Times of India*, Special Report: From talking shop to talking business, February 7, 1993.
78. P. M. S. Malik, *op. cit.*, p. 235.

Two

Domestic and Global Imperatives

Economic liberalization has become a global phenomenon in the 1990's. Most of the countries have opened their previously closed economies to the forces of global economic competition. States have increasingly made reforms in a new complex and competitive global environment for survival in an age of economic gloom. This does not mean that it is economic depression alone that has shaped the way in which the economies have liberalized in the 1990's. Like any change, there have been not only significant domestic socio-political elements but also factors of global power equation at work. The explanation for India's economic liberalization in 1990's is no exception.

As India entered the decade of 1990's, her economy and foreign policy witnessed various perplexing developments within the country as well as in the international political and economic scene. During 1990 and 1991, political turmoil deepened with the Ram Janma Bhoomi - Babri Masjd issue, the row over the Mandal Commission Report, fall of two governments and the assassination of a leader. During this period, the country faced a full-scale macro economic crisis. The balance of payments position was adversely affected by the loss of confidence in India's short - term viability of debt repayment because of these political instabilities. Fiscal and current account deficits remained high. Both internal and foreign debts were accumulating at an accelerating rate. And the rate of inflation was above 10 per cent. In the international scene, the Uruguay Round of negotiations on multilateral trade saw a period of deadlock in the early 1990's, but dramatically concluded with the birth of World Trade Organization (WTO). Global political transformations were momentous. While the Gulf War was subsiding, the Cold War ended, Communist regimes in

Eastern Europe and in the Soviet Union collapsed, culminating in the dramatic disintegration of the erstwhile Soviet Union. The economic agenda began to dominate international relations. This trend encouraged most of the nations to seek economic regionalism and liberalization.

Such developments made it imperative for India to adjust her economic and foreign policies. The development strategies which became dysfunctional had to be changed and the ground prepared for stabilization and structural adjustment measures, so that the country was not left behind in the global race for integration with the world economy.

This chapter addresses important questions such as why did the Indian policy makers and planners have to think of a dramatic change in the direction of economic policies which had been consistently pursued for over forty years and more particularly during the decade of 1980s? What were the compulsions which actually forced the Government of India to drastically change the course of its earlier economic policies? How did the government react to the economic crisis? This chapter discusses the major domestic and global imperatives that influenced the nature, scope, direction and objectives of India's economic liberalization and foreign policy during 1990-1995.

DOMESTIC IMPERATIVES

There were three main sources of compulsions at the domestic level. These consisted of the political, socio-economic and the purely economic factors. Within each of these categories, there were a number of influencing factors.

Political Factors

There are many political factors within democratic systems that can decide the process of economic liberalization. It seems that greater political freedom, a strong political leadership, a new ideology of the ruling elite, electoral support, etc are required for managing the transition of the economy in a democratic country. If a democratic government has these factors, there is little support for one common understanding that unpopular economic reforms are more successfully introduced and implemented under authoritarian regimes than democracies.[1] Then what were the political factors which helped the Rao regime to introduce stabilization and structural adjustment packages? Two main components of political developments contributed to this. One was the existence of considerable freedom of political manoeuvre and the other was the consolidation of the Prime Minister's position.

Freedom of Political Manoeuvre

How could the Congress minority government headed by Narasimha Rao in the 1991 launch the fairly sudden economic liberalization programme described as "reform by storm" by Jagdish Bhagwati[2] within months of assuming power, although the Congress' electoral manifesto of 1991 reaffirmed "its commitment to the path of planning for development, the seeds of which were sown during the freedom struggle".[3]

The Rao government appears to have enjoyed considerable freedom of political manoeuvre with regard to challenges from the opposition parties. This was particularly noticeable during "the honeymoon period". "The honeymoon period" refers to the period when "economic reforms are likely to enjoy greater freedom of political manoeuvre immediately after they take office, when difficult decisions can be blamed as the legacy of the out going government".[4]

If one looks at the Prime Minister's statement in his address to the nation that was addressed soon after he took office, apparently the Congress government justified its liberalization measure while blaming the previous governments. The statement said that "for the last 18 months there had been paralysis on the economic front. The last two governments postponed taking vital decisions. The fiscal position was allowed to deteriorate. The balance of payments crisis became unmanageable. Non-resident Indians and foreign lenders became more and more reluctant to lend money to India."[5] It is true that the non-Congress governments could not manage the economy properly because the political situations were very disturbed and preoccupied the attention of most of the governments. During the government of the Janata Dal, headed by V.P. Singh, regional and ethnic tensions worsened in Punjab, Assam and Kashmir. In all these states, elected government was suspended and replaced by President's rule. Progress was difficult because the coalition could not last long in view of the emerging conflict among the leaders. India's Deputy Prime Minister was ousted from the cabinet in July 1990. This was followed by certain other domestic developments, particularly the announcement regarding implementation of the Mandal Commission Report. In response, the BJP bid for support from all Hindus by raising the Ram Janma Bhoomi - Babri Masjid issue that brought the fall of the V.P. Singh regime on 7th November 1990.

To make the political situation worse, a minority government headed by Chandra Shekhar was formed at the centre. The ruling party had only seventy members of Parliament, and the government could function in parliament only with the support of the Congress(I). The government could, therefore, not initiate any measures for correction of the fiscal and the balance of payments crisis. With the withdrawal of support by the Congress party, the government collapsed in March 1991. Then a fresh general election was called. On May 21, a day after polling started, Rajiv Gandhi was assassinated.

This political turmoil shook the international confidence in India. The foreign exchange reserves dipped to a record low; it became difficult for India to borrow in the international financial markets. There was also adverse impact on the inflow of funds from non-resident Indians after the Gulf War. During this period, the economy in India was drifting along, with uncertain political winds.

Therefore, while condemning the short-lived non - Congress governments, the new Congress government headed by P.V. Narasimha Rao could justify its economic liberalization as measures to restore India's credibility in the world and generate economic growth.

The Congress government also used the reforms to portray its own dynamic, when the outside world had a poor opinion of India, especially after the demolition of the Mosque at Ayodhya by the frenzied Hindu communal forces on 6th December 1992.[6] The government had to ensure foreign governments and foreign direct investors that India was a safe place for their investments. Soon, several new reform policies were started. The government presented another radical budget in 1993, while included the unification of the exchange rate and floating of the Rupee, to show that India would continue its reforms, and that the liberalization programmes would not be affected by communal violence.

This is only one part of the story. It is widely believed that in a democracy, a government may carry out unpopular reform packages, when the ruling party has majority seats in parliament. Then how was it that the minority Congress government had to face little challenge on its economic liberalization policies in parliament? This was due to the fact that the opposition parties in India during the period of the Rao government were divided and fragmented on many national issues including the economic reforms on the basis of their ideologies and political interests. The main opposition party, the Bharatiya Janata Party (BJP), in fact, supported economic liberalization measures like deregulation of bureaucratic control over industrial expansion and privatization of the public sectors if they did not make profits. Therefore, they welcomed the Rao government's economic reforms initially. They even helped the government in the controversial vote on 9th March 1992 in the Lok Sabha on the IMF - World Bank agenda.[7] On the other hand, the National Front and Left Front criticised the reform policies. They often raised voices that India's economic sovereignty had been surrendered and the interests of the poor marginalized under Rao's economic policies. This difference between the BJP and the National Front - Left Front helped the ruling party to carry out its liberalization policies.

Secondly, the newly elected members of Parliament and political parties did not see any advantages in dissolving the Lok Sabha in the middle and to have yet another elections. Therefore, the reforms could go smoothly without any major challenge from the opposition parties, though initially the Congress did not have even a simple majority in the Lok Sabha. This does not mean that due to these factors the government carried out the reforms 'speedily'. It is argued that if the Congress had the clear two third majority in the Lok Sabha, perhaps they might have pursued the unpopular measures more 'speedily' than it had.[8]

The Consolidation of the Prime Minister's Position

The consolidation of the Prime Minister's position in the government and in the party made it possible for him to push the liberalization that otherwise would have been politically risky.

After the assassination of Rajiv Gandhi, Mr. Rao emerged as the consensus leader for the Prime Minister's post and the president of the Congress party, both as a result of Mrs. Sonia Gandhi's rejection of the offer of the post and Mr. Rao's political management as a neutral person within the party. Mrs Gandhi's decision to avoid electoral politics strengthened the Prime Minister's position. Some of the members from Rajiv Gandhi's 'coterie' shifted their loyalties to the Prime Minister.

He was given unlimited powers not only to select candidates for elections, but also to nominate the Pradesh Congress(I) Committee(PCC-I) chiefs. Within the government, Rao had kept several portfolios with himself, including the key defence and industry ministries for over two years. In the era of the liberalization, all major investment proposals from abroad were cleared by his principal secretary A.N. Varma who headed the Foreign Investment promotion Board in the PMO. As one minister observed "Rao's PMO wielded more power than even Indira Gandhi's".

Even after the inner party elections in held after 20 years at Tirupati, Mr. Rao remained as the most credible leader in the party. Further, the All India Congress Committee(AICC) at Surajkund in 1993 made Rao's position stronger both within the government and in the party, saying that "One - Man - One - Post principle shall not apply to the Congress President and Prime Minister".[9] This indicated that even though there were some challenges to Rao's leadership from the rank and file of the Congress like Arjun Singh and N.D. Tiwari, most of the members showed their loyalties to Mr Rao and supported the economic liberalization programme which was the prime policy of the Prime Minister.

Mr Arjun Singh and N.D. Tiwari condemned Rao's

liberalization policies as a radical departure from the Nehruvian model of economic planing and self-reliance. They, however, could not marginalize Rao's robust position. If one goes through the economic resolutions of the Congress of 1992, 1993 and 1994, it becomes clear that the AICC fully supported the reforms in the economy. They further refined the concept of self-reliance saying that "our policies of trade liberalization, easier entry to foreign investment, reduction of exchange controls and rupee convertibility etc. are motivated by the compulsions to earn foreign exchange surpluses and make India truly self-reliant."[10]

Here, clearly under the leadership of Mr Rao, the Congress ideology regarding the economy changed to an export-oriented and market-oriented policy that drifted from the inward-looking trade policy of the Nehruvian model. Rao's economic ministers like Dr. Manmohan Singh and P. Chidambaram who were pro-market and part of a foreign educated elite reconfirmed the ruling party's ideology on economic issues. In addition to this, most of the key positions in the economic policy establishment under the Congress government passed into the hands of ex-World Bank officials. This list included the then Finance Secretary, Mr Montek Singh Ahluwalia; Economic Advisor in the Finance Ministry, Mr Percy Mistry; Chief Economic Advisory Council to the Prime Minister; Economic Advisor in Ministry of Industry, Mr Rakesh Mohan; and Economic Advisor in Ministry of Commerce, Mr Jayanto Roy.[11]

However, the liberalization in the multilayered and multilevel federal economy of India could not be carried on without support from the socio-economic forces.

Socio-Economic Forces

It is significant that at the time of their introduction, there was neither much public debate on the desirability of reforms in India nor any social consensus in favour of the economic reforms. In other words, the economic liberalization of the Rao government did not depend on public opinion polls. There were, however, certain socio-economic groups supporting a market-oriented strategy. As explained by Pranab Bardhan,[12] these were the industrial bourgeoisie, the rich farmers and the middle classes. Of course the interaction between state and socio-economic forces is a complex process and cannot be captured by any simple unidimensional description, but it is clear that the powerful socio-economic forces always respond to national policies on the basis of their sectional interests. They are important not only because of their considerable political influence which enables a change in the directions of national policies, but also because of their lobbying capability and significant role in mobilizing electoral support.

The Middle Class

Since independence, the middle class, who work mainly in the professions and in the services or are self-employed, have continuously increased in terms of its number as well as its influence on national politics. By and large they have favoured the globalization of India's economy to enjoy the benefits of free competition in commodities, imported goods and technology. The middle classes gave positive support to the economic policies of the Rao government just as they had favoured the economic reforms of Rajiv Gandhi regime in the mid-80's.[13] As consumerists, the middle classes have supported the liberalization of economy because the new programme has provided abundance of consumer goods for them. The liberalization for the middle classes meant not only higher incomes in the domestic and foreign private companies but also more intimate and wide-ranging interaction and communication with foreign countries.

From the political point of view, " the political class reconciled itself to the limited task of satisfying the needs and desires of the middle classes. In the process, it sought to redefine political morals and manners to suit the ultimate requirement of the Narasimha Rao period: the single-minded pursuit of political stability so that the process of economic reform(s) should continue apace. More importantly, it was concluded that the middle classes - the presumed beneficiaries of the economic reforms - were large enough to provide the necessary support and political constituency"[14]

The Industrial Class

Since industrial class in a contemporary society has a

relatively high capacity to influence associations quickly, it can exhibit a high organizational response to government's economic decisions. Indian business organizations have often been involved in formal and informal consultations with government departments at various levels and have been an accepted voice in terms of government's economic decisions.[15]

Structural adjustment was enthusiastically welcomed by the business groups, who suffered from state intervention and anti-business sentiments during the early years. Generally the industrialist class embraced technological collaboration with foreign companies to enhance their competitiveness in the world markets. On the other hand, just as opinion was divided within the business circles during the Rajiv Gandhi government on the issue of opening up consumer goods imports, so was industry divided on this crucial question under the P.V. Narasimha Rao government. While large segments of business class were keen on the removal of restrictions on imports of consumer goods, an equally vocal section was set against the move. Leading the pro-import lobby was the rising Confederation of Indian Industry (CII) and arraigned against imports were the older Federation of Indian Chambers of Commerce and Industry (FICCI)[16] and the Associated Chambers of Commerce and Industry of India(ASSOCHAM).

The Rich Farmers

The rich farmers are organized very effectively as a class.[17] Their power has increased over four decades as a result of conventional electoral politics and various rural development programmes including the government sponsored Green Revolution. They generally supported the reforms of the Rao government though subsidies were cut on agriculture in part. This was because they "now started diversifying their investments and branching out outside agriculture into private trade and commerce, real estate, transport and into small and medium-sized industry."[18] These intrests were represented by leaders like Sharad Joshi and activists such as Gail Omvedt of the Shetkari Sanghatana (a powerful farmer group). Sharad Joshi took a strong stand in support of liberalization of the economy and even the controversial

Dunkel Draft.[19] Gail Omvedt argues that free trade has not ruined agriculture in the Third World. The real reason is lack of remunerative prices and subsidised agriculture exports. It is better to open trade and halt subsidies that actually constrain production and block exports.[20]

The NRI Factor

There is the non-resident Indians (NRI) factor which also influenced the dominant classes' attitudes towards India's economic strategy. Many industrial and middle classes in particular but also some rich farmer and trader families, have close or distant relatives among the NRIs.[21] Recently, Jayati Ghosh, while analysing various factors which have influenced a change in the economic strategy, pointed out "the growing globalization of Indian society" as an important factor. She stated that "the 'NRI phenomenon', by means of which a qualitatively significant number of people from the Indian elites and middle classes actually became residents abroad, contributed in no small measure to the consumerist demands which fuelled the drive for import liberalization and other forms of opening up of the economy. The political and economic importance of Non Resident Indians stems not only from the fact that they are viewed as potentially important sources of capital inflow, but also because of their close links with (and in some instances, the fact that they are virtually indistinguishable from) politically dominant groups within the domestic society".[22]

The Low Income Classes

Unlike the above classes, the low income classes fared poorly in the stabilization and structural adjustment packages. They, however, could not block the reforms. Whether the low income classes resisted and blocked the economic liberalization depended in part on their degree of organization and how they were represented in the political system as a whole. They have been subjected to an unprecedented degree of intensive and far-reaching differentiation, polarization, marginalization, and in urban and rural India they were imperfectly mobilized and far from homogeneous in political outlook and behaviour.[23]

According to one study, most of the working people are engaged in the rural sector without proper records and a very small portion is in regular employment and even smaller in organised sector and not more than 3 per cent of the working people can be called industrial workers, private and public sector combined. Only 2 per cent of the working people are unionised.[24] This is only on paper, the picture on the ground is more dismal. Even this small portion of the organized working class were only marginaly conscious about a working class indentity, but rather identified themselves on the basis of their religion, caste, region. As a result, the left parties, which were supposed to protect the working class' interests against the economic liberalization and privatization policies, were tardy in their seriousness about self-reliance. They were equally interested in obtaining foreign investment and inviting MNCs. In this regard, one may say that it is a total misconception to think that in the state elections, the people rejected the new policy of liberalization and globalization. Rather the clear message was that the people were disgusted with the prevailing corruption and inefficiency of the men in power. They voted for change, and that is why in the states where the Congress party was in power, they returned non-Congress candidates, and in the states where a non-Congress party was in power they returned the Congress party.[25]

Economic Conditions

Economic liberalization programme in India was also conceived as a response to the unprecedented macroeconomic crisis in 1990-1991. Recently John Williamson and Stephan Haggard have drawn attention to the economic crisis, while analysing the causes of economic reforms in various countries. They concluded that "crisis is clearly neither a necessary nor a sufficient condition to initiate reform. It has nevertheless often played a critical role in stimulating reform".[26] This perspective appears to be relevant to India's economic reforms in 1991. The economic crisis in 1990-91 played a crucial role in enabling the new Congress government led by the Prime Minister Mr P. V. Narasimha Rao, to gather enough political courage to reverse the major policies pursued during the last forty years, and to implement economic reforms. This is all the more remarkable since such radical reforms had been effected by a minority government. The economic crisis can be directly attributed to the large and persistent macro-economic imbalances for a long time, specially during the 80s.[27] Explaining the crisis of 1990-91, therefore, requires close examination of macroeconomic policies and performance earlier in the decade.

Balance of Payments Crisis

In mid-1991, the Government of India faced an immediate balance of payments crisis. Bimal Jalan used the following two criteria as a rough measure of the balance of payments problem in a particular year: (i) the current account deficit was more than one per cent of GDP and (ii) the foreign exchange reserve were less than necessary to cover three months' imports.[28] Judging by these criteria, if one looks at India's balance of payments situations in the late 80s and early 90s, India had very critical balance of payments problems. The Economic Survey for 1992-93 had noted that the balance of payments was under great pressure by 1988-89 when the current account deficit as a proportion of GDP peaked at 2.9 per cent (compared to around 1.3 per cent level in the early 1980s). Foreign exchange reserves of India had declined to $ 1.1 billion, which was almost a fortnight's import requirement in June 1991. This situation had arisen as a result of a large - and steadily growing - deficit in the balance of payments during the Seventh Plan (1985-90) which was not sustainable.

In fact, during the first four years of the Sixth plan (1980-81 to 1983-84), the deficit in balance of trade was around Rs 6,000 crores per annum. In the last year of the Plan 1984-85, this shot upto Rs 6,721 crores. The trade deficit in the first three years of the Seventh Plan (1985-86 to 1987-88) exceeded Rs 9,000 crores per annum and in the fourth and fifth years (1988-89 and 1989-90) exceeded Rs 12, 000 crores per year. In 1990-91 the deficit touched the astronomical figure of Rs 16,934 crores. This shows the difficult position that India faced on the balance of payments front.

The Gulf Crisis during the year (1990-91) further worsened

the balance of payments problem. In addition to a massive trade deficit of Rs 16,934 crores, there was a deterioration in the invisible account as well, due to lower remittances and higher interest payments. Earnings from invisible were substantial throughout the Sixth Plan period. They touched the highest level ever in the planning period during 1980-81. In that year they stood at Rs 4,311 crores. In subsequent years of the plan, earnings from invisible declined somewhat but in each year they were Rs 3,500 crores or more. However, during the Seventh Plan period private remittances from Middle East countries showed tendencies of flattening out . As a result, earnings from invisible declined consistently and fell to Rs 1,025 crores in 1989-90. Whereas, net invisible financed, on an average more than 60 per cent of trade deficit during the Sixth Plan, they financed only 24 per cent of trade deficit during the Seventh Plan. In fact, during the last year of the Seventh Plan, invisible financed only 8.3 per cent of the trade deficit.[29]

The economic crisis was also due to a sharp downgrading of India's credit rating. The international banking community lost confidence in India's ability to honour its debt servicing obligations by October 1990. Moody's, the US credit rating agency, downgraded India's credit rating by two grades from A2 to BAA1. External commercial borrowing dried up and there was an outflow of the NRI deposits thereafter.

As Deepak Nayyar pointed out that the vulnerability of the balance of payments was accentuated by two other factors. First, it became exceedingly difficult to roll over the existing short-term debt in the range of $ 6 billion because of adverse international perceptions of the situation and the overnight borrowing in international capital markets was as much as $ 2 billion. Second, non-resident deposits, where the outstanding amount then was more than $ 10 billion, levelled off in September 1990 with a modest net outflow of $ 0.3 billion in the period October 1990 to March 1991 to September 1991.[30]

The Economic Survey 1991-92 revealed that in order to prevent a default on external payments, the Government of India allowed the RBI to ship 47 tonnes of gold to the Bank of England as collateral for loan in addition to the 20 tonnes of gold leased to the State Bank of India by the Government out of its stocks to sell it abroad. This economic situation was certainly unprecedented as Dr Manmohan Singh, the then Finance Minister said in his speech on the Union Budget for 1991-92 that "we have not experienced anything similar in the history of Independent India".[31] Under such an economic condition, the government had to resort to massive support from the IMF and the World Bank and introduce wide-ranging changes in industrial and trade policies.

Inflation

Generally rates of inflation in India had always been influenced by exogenous shocks such as oil price increase or endogenous shocks such as bad weather while real disproportionalities have always been an important underlying factor. In the crisis year of 1990-91, however, overall rate of inflation accelerated to more than 10 per cent and prices of food items rose more than 12 per cent, in spite of three good monsoons in a row. The inflation of 1990-91 was more worrying than India's periodic inflationary bubbles because it was not triggered by endogenous shocks like a drought.

The inflationary spiral had intensified since November 1990 before its downward journey began. The annual rate of inflation as measured by the point-to-point movements in the Wholesale Price Index (WPI) which had already touched 8.9 per cent level in October 1990 clearly crossed the much dreaded double digit level in November 1990 (having then reached 10.5 per cent level) and climbed to 13.5 per cent rate in February 1991. Then the inflationary spiral continued with the rate of inflation peaking at 16.3 per cent level in September 1991 before its downward journey began in October with 14.7 per cent level of inflation.[32] The Economic Survey 1992-93 stated that primary goods led the inflationary surge with an inflation rate of 21.6 per cent in the middle of November 1991; the pressure on foodgrain prices was even higher. The prices of manufactured goods and fuels also firmed up. The spurt in foodgrain prices pushed up consumer prices both in rural and urban areas.

Part of the reason for the inflationary spiral was the lagged effect of the increase in monetary growth in 1989-90. That was an election year and a large rise in the fiscal imbalance and budgetary deficit spilled over into money supply growth. In addition, a large increase in import prices and in many domestically administered prices, including food prices in 1990-91 was attributable to the build-up of inflationary pressures.

High Fiscal Deficit

The root of both the balance of payments crisis and the inflation problem could be traced to the unsustainable high fiscal deficit, in particular the revenue deficit, and the monetised deficit. Table-1 shows that using the IMF definition of overall fiscal deficit (which excludes all types of borrowing by the Government) as a proportion of GDP, the average fiscal deficit ratio had increased from 6.3 per cent level for the Sixth Five-Year Plan period (1985-81 to 1984-85) to 8.2 per cent level for the Seventh Five-Year Plan period (1985-86 to 1989-90). Fiscal deficit of 1990-91 was at the level of 8.4 per cent. It peaked at an uncomfortably high level from 4.1 per cent level in 1975-76.

Table 1 shows the change in the central government deficit as a percentage of GDP in various years, specially during the Sixth and Seventh Plan periods.

The root cause of the fiscal crisis was to be found in the areas of the growth of the revenue deficit and of the monetised deficit. For the central government, the revenue deficit as a proportion of GDP which averaged 1.1 per cent level in the period 1980-81 to 1984-85 had increased to 2.6 per cent level in the period 1985-1986 to 1989-1990. The revenue deficit peaked at the uncomfortably high level of 3.5 per cent in 1990-91. Most of the centre's net tax revenue was expended on subsidies, defence and interest payments, which put an unsustainable burden on India's finances. In this regard, one government report stated that in the fiscal year 1988-89 the "three components of non-plan expenditure, viz., defence, interest payments and major subsidies alone pre-emptied about 105 per cent of the Centre's net tax revenue".[33] The monetised deficit which has the maximum inflationary potential had increased from 2.0

per cent level in 1981-82 to a peak of 3.0 per cent level in 1989-90 and was still at the high enough level of 2.8 per cent level in 1990-91.

TABLE 1
CENTRAL GOVERNMENT DEFICIT
(per cent of GDP at current market prices)

	Budget Deficit	*Revenue Deficit*	*Monetised Deficit*	*Fiscal Deficit*	*Primary Deficit*
1975-76	0.5	1.1	0.0	4.1	2.5
1980-81	1.8	1.5	2.6	6.2	4.3
1981-82	0.9	0.2	2.0	5.4	3.4
1982-83	0.9	0.7	1.9	6.0	3.8
1983-84	0.7	1.2	1.9	6.3	4.0
1984-85	1.6	1.8	2.6	7.5	5.0
Average 6th Plan	1.2	1.1	2.2	6.3	4.1
1985-86	2.0	2.2	2.4	8.3	5.5
1986-87	2.8	2.7	2.4	9.0	5.8
1987-88	1.7	2.7	2.0	8.1	4.7
1988-89	1.4	2.7	1.6	7.8	4.2
1989-90	2.3	2.6	3.0	7.8	3.9
Average 7th Plan	2.1	2.6	2.3	8.2	4.8
1990-91	2.1	3.5	2.8	8.4	4.4

Source: Economic Survey 1992-93, Government of India, Table 2.1.

Add to it the fiscal deficit of the all the State governments in the Indian Union which hovered between 2.0 to 3.0 per cent of GDP, the combined overall fiscal deficit of the Central and State governments as a proportion of GDP had nearly crossed the dangerously high level of 11.4 per cent level in 1990-91.[34] There is no doubt that this fiscal imbalance created the inflationary spiral in 1990-91 affecting both growth and equity. This fiscal deficit had also spilled over on to the balance of payments. Naturally the balance of payments was under severe pressure and significant loss of foreign exchange reserves was experienced.

The widening gap between income and expenditure of the Government of India led to mounting fiscal deficits, which had to be met by borrowing at home. In fact, "there were no constraints on the domestic borrowing by the government. In effect, the automatic borrowing from the central bank at low interest rates and the preemptive borrowing from the commercial banking system (based on the high statutory liquidity ratio) at modest interest rates were not subject to any stipulated limits".[35] As a result, India was virtually on the way to entering the internal debt trap as more than two-thirds of additional domestic borrowing was going into servicing the outstanding debt.[36] India's internal liabilities registered a sharp increase from 35.6 per cent of GDP in 1980-81 to 53.3 per cent in 1990-91.[37]

The steady increase in the difference between the income and the expenditure of the economy as a whole led to persistent current account deficit in the balance of payments in the 1980s, which had to be financed by borrowing from abroad.[38] For instance, the share of external commercial borrowing and NRI deposits in external assistance rose from 16.1 per cent in 1980 to 29.4 per cent in 1986 and further to 39.9 per cent in 1991. This increasing share of external commercial borrowing and the NRI deposits has raised the cost of external debt considerably over time. According to Economic Survey 1992-93, India's external debt steadily increased in the 1980s, from Rs. 13,479 crores in 1980-81 to Rs. 54,100 crores in 1989-90 and further to Rs. 66,314 crores in 1990-91. In terms of percentage of GDP level, the external liabilities of the Central government rapidly rose from 9.9 per cent at the end of 1980-81 to 11.9 per cent at the end of 1989-90 and further to 12.5 per cent at the end of 1990-91.[39]

In the late 1980s there was a strong agricultural recovery, helped by good weather. Exports and manufacturing output registered buoyancy. But, all the while the underlying macroeconomic condition was getting worse. It was clear by the late 1980s that India was in an internal debt trap which would soon engulf her in an external debt trap. Rather than mobilization of its internal resources through structural reforms and introduction of strict discipline within the economic and political system in general, and take corrective action on the fiscal front in particular,[40] India was merrily borrowing more and more at home and on shorter terms abroad. It seems that for India's political representatives and leading classes, internal and external borrowing represented a soft option than internal reforms in the economy.

It was usual in India, specially in the late 1980s and the beginning of 1990s that political considerations took precedence over economic rationale for ensuring macro-economic efficiency. The V.P. Singh government took office at the end of 1989, and added to the macroeconomic problem by the controversial reservation policy and implementing its pre-election promise of loan waivers from small farmers. It was then obvious that the fiscal problem was in a precarious state. Even so, no determined attempt to resolve the problem was continued. In the latter half of 1990-91, political instability at the Centre made major economic policy changes very difficult as seen in the political factors above. As a result, even a temporary shock of the Gulf War was enough to trigger a full-scale economic crisis in India in 1990-91.

Global Imperatives

India's economic liberalization programme was also subjected to various global imperatives and changes that took place in the 1990s. With the unleashing of the Gulf War, collapse of the Socialist regimes in the Eastern European countries and the disintegration of the Soviet Union as well as the end of the Cold War, a new global order came into being. While India's participation in the global economy had been marginal, global economic environment changed with a new tendency towards liberalization and privatization in many countries and a new trend towards globalisation of world economy as well as economic regionalism. This section attempts to understand how India proceeded with its economic liberalization in view of such complex and varied global imperatives.

The Gulf War

India's persistent fiscal imbalances were accentuated by the Gulf War which intensified strains on an economy that was already in the throes of a severe balance of payments crisis. The consequences of the Gulf crisis was disastrous for India in terms of higher prices of oil, lost export markets, sudden stop in remittances and cost of repatriation and rehabilitation. According to Economic Survey 1990-91, the War imposed directly additional burden of $ 2,887 million equivalent to Rs. 5,180 crores on the current account of India's balance of payments for the fiscal year 1990-91.

Oil Prices

The Gulf area of desert sands contain around two-thirds of the world's oil reserves which has thereby become a significant strategic area for all its energy users. In India, even with an extremely low level of per capita energy consumption the dependence on oil, as an energy source is very high.[41] It is thus very heavily dependent upon the Gulf region for its needs. Kuwait and Iraq were supplying nearly 40 per cent of India's import requirements before the war. Here a question arises as to why India depended so heavily on Iraq and Kuwait for its oil resources, though there were other oil rich states like Iran and Saudi Arabia. According to Sandy Gordon, India has preferred more secular states of Iraq and Kuwait rather than more theocratic Gulf states like Iran and Saudi Arabia because the latter might be subjected to pressure from Pakistan.[42]

The Gulf crisis thus caused a serious impact on India's petroleum, oil and lubricants(POL) supply. The rise in India's oil import bill in 1990-91 was as much due to higher volumes of oil and petroleum products imported as to a rise in (average) prices for these imports over 1989-90. The average crude oil price was $ 17 per barrel in 1989-90. A week after Iraqi troops entered Kuwait, spot price of crude from the Gulf jumped from around $ 17 a barrel to $ 23, then shot up to $ 30 per barrel during August-November 1990.[43] The spurt in price of crude oil and petroleum products resulted in severe strains on India's foreign exchange position and

POL bill.

It was estimated that the POL bill during the 1990-91 was around Rs. 10,820 crores ($ 6.0 billion) as against Rs. 6,273 crores ($ 3.8 billion) for 1989-90. It meant that the POL bill jumped about 72 per cent in rupee terms and 58 per cent in dollar terms. After adjusting for exports of petroleum products, the net POL burden was figured at Rs. 3,625 crores ($ around 2.0 billion). Due to mainly the POL bill's burden, India's trade deficit during 1990-91 was at Rs. 10,644 crores which was 38 per cent higher than in 1989-90.[44] As a result, India's foreign exchange reserves during 1990-91 had sharply gone down.

Remittances

Even as the import bill was soaring, remittances which was one key source of foreign exchange declined. The Government of India calculated the loss in private remittances from Kuwait and Iraq was at Rs. 490 crores($ 273 million) during the period (see table-2). Besides this, due to a negative perception of Indian banks on the fate of the Kuwait currency, India lost a sizeable amount of foreign currency(between $ 5-7 billion) to the Western banks which accepted the Kuwait currency without hesitations.[45]

Exports

India's exports to the Gulf states too were affected. India exported to the Middle East about 7.2 per cent of its total exports. Kuwait and Iraq accounted 0.7 and 0.5 per cent respectively in 1989-90. During the period of 1990-91, the loss in exports to the region was significant due to trade embargo on Iraq and dislocation of trade to other countries in the Gulf area. India lost a total export of 500 corers from the region including Rs. 270 crores from Kuwait and Iraq alone. Added to this India could not realise other export dues from Iraq such as of $ 114 million during the Gulf War period which deterred payments arrangement.

Evacuation

Evacuation of about 180,000 Indians working in Kuwait and Iraq was estimated to have cost $200 million or Rs. 360 crores. The following table shows the direct impact of the Gulf crisis during 1990-91 on India's balance of payments.

TABLE 2
DIRECT BOP IMPACT OF THE GULF CRISIS DURING 1990-1991

	Item	*Rs. Crores*	*$ Million*
1.	Additional POL import bill (net of POL exports)	3625	2020
2.	Export loss to West Asia	500	280
	(of which Iraq and Kuwait)	(270)	(150)
3.	Non-realisation of other export dues from Iraq	205	144
4.	Loss in remittances from Iraq and Kuwait	490	273
5.	Foreign exchange costs of emergency repatriation	360	200
	TOTAL	5180	2887

Source: Economic Survey 1990-1991, Government of India, p. 156.

Collapse of the European Socialist Regimes, Disintegration of the USSR and The End of the Cold War

In the light of the collapse of the European socialist regimes, particularly the disintegration of the Soviet Union besides the end of the Cold War, India's overall development strategy and foreign policy needed to be reformulated for its future developments. Drastic events in the Communist European bloc countries had far-reaching consequences for every country in the world, but they had special meaning for India's foreign economic policy.

Economic Relationship With the Soviet Union and the European Socialist Countries During The Cold War Era.

India had robust economic relations with the socialist countries and this was a very important factor for India's bargaining diplomacy with the Western countries. Until 1990 the socialist bloc constituted an important trading region for India. The region was known as the Rupee Trade Area because India's trade with the former Soviet Union and the Eastern countries had been in rupees since the mid-1950s, bypassing hard currency transactions. For a large number of traditional and manufactured goods, the socialist bloc was a major market for India: its share in total exports by commodity in 1990-91 ranged from 12-13 per cent for leather and manufactures to over 50 per cent for tea and coffee.[46]

India was the former Soviet Union's largest trading partner among the developing countries. The economic relationship between the two countries was dynamic and multifaceted due to geo-political reasons during the Cold War era. The Soviet Union had a consistent trade deficit with India since 1975 despite supplying large quantities of essential materials such as crude oil and fertilizers on a rupee payment basis. The managed rupee-rouble exchange rate and bilateral clearings in these transactions were indefensible in terms of economical calculation, but they were sustained and justified by geo-political defence imperatives.

Even though the complexion of international political economy had been changing quite rapidly since the advent of Mikhail Gorbachev to power in Kremlin during 1985, there seemed to be no change in the thinking of India's leadership on its close economic relationship with the Soviet Union. India's leadership also continued to maintain close relations with the Eastern European Socialist countries.

During the Rajiv Gandhi government, the Indian Prime Minister and the President of the Soviet Union exchanged official visits twice and assessed the dynamic development of mutually advantageous economic, commercial, scientific and technological cooperation on a planned and long term basis. Even after the change of leadership in Eastern European states in late 1989 and the virtual demise of the Warsaw Pact, India and the Soviet Union reaffirmed the status quo of their trade relations during V.P. Singh's visit to Moscow in 1990.

There were compulsions for India to maintain continuity in

the framework of trade relations, which had advantages like the rupee trade and bilateral balancing of trade amongst others, because India faced several economic difficulties. These included a trade deficit on foreign trade account, budgetary deficit, inflation, unemployment and other problems. Furthermore, there was a demand within the Soviet Union that trade with India should be converted into hard currency and India should repay Soviet debt in hard currency. The rouble-rupee arrangements had enabled India to purchase Soviet arms without expending hard currency. Thus, these kinds of compulsions operated for India to hold the rupee-rouble arrangements.

Impact on India's Economic and Political-Security Concerns

India's trade turnover with the socialist bloc countries declined significantly, by a margin of between 30 and 60 per cent with individual countries in 1990 and 1991. The share of India's exports to the former Soviet Union had been steadily growing during the 1980s. In 1980s the Soviet Union accounted for 16-18 per cent of India's exports. However, it drastically came down to 9.2 per cent in 1991-92 and further to 3.2 per cent in 1992-93.[47] This decline of export market was a major shock to India's export effort in the post-Cold War era. As a result, the first year of the economic reforms under the Rao government required an additional structural adjustment.[48]

At the beginning of 1992, trade with the Commonwealth of Independent States (CIS) virtually came to halt: according to Indian press reports hundreds of units were faced with an abrupt loss of orders, while many others failed to receive payments for the earlier sales. Several units in the Kandla Free Trade Zone set up exclusively to cater to the former Soviet Union market had to be closed. In other words, exports which depended substantially on the Soviet market were the worst affected.

On the foreign aid front, India was severely affected by the collapse of the Soviet Union. The share of the Soviet Union in total aid utilised by India during the period of 1985-90 averaged around 11 per cent. However, after the demise of the Soviet Union, the amount of aid from the USSR was dramatically reduced from $

164 million in 1990-91 to $ 55 million in 1991-92.[49]

In view of all these, with the disintegration of the Soviet Union and the transition of the Eastern European countries, there were more disadvantages for India than advantages. Moreover, newly independent Russia was keen to reformulate its foreign policy in keeping with its own perceived interest. During the first few months of 1992, being euphoric about its new relations with the West, Russia was almost obsessively inclined towards the West.[50] Hence, developing countries like India were not considered significant for Russia's immediate interest. As a result, Russia shifted its relations with India from political-security to economic-commercial concerns.[51] During his visit, Yeltsin gave a clear indication of this policy shift. He said that while in the past relations between India and the former Soviet Union had formed a counterweight against China and the US, the new ties with India would not be directed against any third countries.[52]

This also affected India's bargaining diplomacy with the Western countries, particularly the US. The episode of the cancellation of the Russian rocket technology deal was a good instance of this. In January 1991, India agreed to purchase Russian rocket technology and equipment for its space programme. But due to the US pressure Russia finally announced that the Indo-Russian rocket deal with reference to transfer of technology would be cancelled in May 1993. Russia attached higher priority to relations with the US so as to have access to Western capital, technology, etc. A report noted that if Russia disregarded the US warning, it risked the loss of $ 4 billion worth of aid.[53] Thus, it may be said that the absence of a countervailing power against the US posed a new challenge for the foreign economic policy of India.

Impact on Ideologies of India's Ruling Elites

The Cold War was replaced by trade war among super economic powers[54] like the US, Japan and Germany. Military alliances came to have lesser relevance in international society that they did during the Cold War years. There has been a growing emphasis on economic competition among the economic super powers. Developing countries have been wooed to have trade agreements instead of military alliances with them.

The post-Cold War and post-Soviet situations significantly influenced the minds of the ruling elites in India on the economic agenda. The Prime Minister said that "now Cold War is over. there is an element of cooperation instead of confrontation. It is a new situation. And we have to respond to that also. So certain policy reorientation will take place to ensure that our national interest does not suffer".[55] Dr Manmohan Singh, the principal architect of economic liberalization under the Rao government, said that "the economic reforms and the compulsions of economic management were also an important input" in the event of the collapse of the socialist countries and the end of the Cold War.[56] Thus, it can be said that the new global system in the post-Cold War era, without a socialist bloc, influenced Indian leadership to accept a more market oriented economy.

The transformations of the socialist countries in Eastern Europe had been hailed by many in the West as an ideological victory of the capitalist model of democracy. This line of argument is relevant in the Indian context because planing in India was given a particular boost by the influence of the Soviet experience and ideology. The Mahalanobis model in India during the 1950s is clear evidence of this. This model of strategy continued to be accepted as the basic development strategy, even though significant shifts in approach took place from one plan to the next. Several other features of the Soviet system also indirectly influenced the Indian system and process of decision making.

The unprecedented demise of Socialist regimes in Eastern Europe did confirm the fundamental weakness of the economy of the Soviet type. Under Gorbachev's leadership Perestroika and Glasnost in the former Soviet Union, and the corresponding upsurge of the revolutionary tide in Eastern Europe in late 1989 had produced the image of the socialist planned economy as a crisis-ridden mechanism. In the early 1990, Hungary, Poland, Czechoslovakia and Yugoslavia had undertaken some liberalization, marketization and privatization in their economies. As a result, the sheltered market condition that prevailed for a large variety of Indian goods, was no more in existence due to opening of Eastern European economies and their ongoing transition to market-oriented system. These events had, as Isher Judge Ahluwalia pointed out, "a powerful effect in breaking the psychological resistance to change"[57] from India's past economic strategy.

It is clear that far-reaching changes in the field of economies of Eastern Europe including that of the Soviet Union had been traumatic for the leadership of India. Soon after he took the office, the Prime Minister, P.V. Narasimha Rao stated to the nation that "we believe that India has much to learn from what is happening elsewhere in the world. Many countries are bringing in far-reaching changes. We find major economic transformation sweeping large countries like the Soviet Union and China, as well as small countries in Eastern Europe. There is a change in outlook, a change in mindset everywhere. India too cannot lag behind if she has to survive, as she must in the new environment".[58]

Further, the change of the economic strategy in the Soviet Union gave a justification for the Rao government to liberalize its economy. In a reply to the Rajya Sabha on the debate of the new liberalized industrial policy, the Prime Minister said that "the Soviet Union, which was following communism for decades, had to give way to liberalization. What is wrong if India is liberalising its policies?"[59]

Thus, it is clear that liberalization of its economy and integration with the world capitalist system in 1990s had become imperative for India because of the collapse of the European Socialist countries, the disintegration of the Soviet Union and the end of the Cold War,[60] which have changed the international economic environment in general and stimulated economic regionalism. It has also made international economic institutions more powerful.

India in the World Economy and the Global Economic Environment

For four decades India followed its broad inward looking development strategy through extensive bureaucratic direct controls over production, investment and trade. In contrast, many developing countries, specially East Asian countries, have shifted their development strategies to export-oriented models for their economic development, which put their economies on the world's economic map as a significant player by the end of the 1980s. As a result, India lagged behind many developing countries by the end of the 1980s in terms of economic development.

India's participation in the world economy has been very marginal. India's share in the world output had fallen from 2.1 per cent in 1951 to 1.1 per cent in 1989. At the same time its per capita income which was one-eighth of the world average had deteriorated to one-twelveth.[61] Growth in trade had also regressed as India's share in world exports which used to be about 2 per cent in early 1950s declined to 0.5 per cent by 1990.

Many say that it is difficult to make comparisons between India and other developing countries, specially the newly industrialising countries like the city states of Hong Kong and Singapore because the former is certainly bigger in geographical size and population. However, today, the economic size of a nation matters as much as its physical size. In any case, China and Brazil, both have much bigger physical area and China has a much higher population than India. Indonesia has a fair size in terms of both area and population. It might, therefore, be imprudent to believe that India is unique and its economic performance cannot be compared with other developing countries.[62]

South Korea's per capita income was lower than India's in 1951 and in 1990 it was more than 10 times than India's. In terms of the rates of growth with the 12 selected developing countries, India was in the 9th position in 1980-91 among the 12 developing countries. In terms of dollar value of per capita GDP at official exchange rate, India was at the bottom of the league of 12 countries with a per capita GDP of a mere $ 330 in 1990.[63] India's international competitiveness has been also quite low among the 15 selected developing countries. According to the World Competitiveness Report 1993, India was 11th in both quantitative and qualitative in macro- and micro-managements among the selected nations in 1992.[64] In terms of industrialisation, India was a leading country in 1960s. But soon after it also lagged behind several developing countries in this respect.

Global Economic Environment

A country decides its economic policy in relation to the broader aspects of the international economic climate. In this respect, the enthusiasm of Indian planners for the market-oriented approach must be understood against the background of shift and changes in the global economic environment.

The 1980s witnessed the ascendancy of the market model of economic management with a reduced role for the state in a national economy in both its domestic and external dimensions. The thrust to liberalization and privatization picked up momentum in many developing countries in the second half of the eighties, when a number of countries in Latin America and Africa adopted liberalization and privatization as a means of solving the resource problems of debt-ridden and loss-making enterprises.

In the 80s and 90s, the policies of privatization and liberalization have also been sustained by the international economic institutions which will be analysed in detail in the context of India in Chapter-IV. The World Bank and the International Monetary Fund (IMF) have supported the policies as part of their structural adjustment programmes in developing countries.

Whether under external pressure or not, there is little doubt that the government of India under P.V. Narasimha Rao followed the typical IMF-World Bank stabilization and structural adjustment packages. These included devaluation of the rupee, reduction in the budget deficit, liberalising foreign trade regime, greater freedom to foreign investment and practical privatization of the public sector.

In the post-Cold War years, there has been rapid strides in the globalization of the world economy. Globalization refers to the growing economic interdependence between nations in production, trade and finance. With the primary objective of trade globalisation, the Uruguay Round of the General Agreement on Tariffs and Trade (GATT) was conceived in 1985, launched in September 1986 at Punta Dei Este, in Uruguay, and was concluded at Marrakesh in April 1994. Once the negotiations started, it became evident that real intention was to use the GATT commitment to the liberalization of trade to 'persuade' member countries to provide unrestricted freedom to the transnational corporations, not only in manufacturing and trade but also in sectors like banking, insurance, transport and telecommunications.[65]

The transnational corporations have occasionally forced many developing countries to rethink their domestic economic policies. As Sumitra Chishti pointed out that as a developing country, "India has also had to change the objectives of its economic policy or to respond otherwise to the developments arising out of the operations of the transnational corporations".[66]

Since the late 1980s, a wave of economic regionalism has been underway by a new phenomenon, i.e.,economic agenda that has begun to dominate international society. This trend has encouraged many nations to seek economic regionalism.

One of the major reasons for the emergence of economic regionalism in the post-Cold War era has been the successful evolution of the regional grouping in Europe. It is the Community's initiative, started in 1985, to create a single European Market by 1992 and the subsequent move, codified in the Maastricht Treaty of 1991, to transform the European Community (EC) into a 'European Union', with the Economic and Monetary Union— to be realized by the end of the century— a major milestone. As one of reactions to the Single European Market and growing regionalism in Europe, the US also took a regional approach. As a part of the US initiative, the Canada-US Free Trade Agreement (CUSTA) was concluded in 1988, and on December 17, 1992 the North American Free Trade Agreement (NAFTA) was signed by the US, Mexico and Canada. Beside these economic groupings, there have been the Association of South-East Asian Nations (ASEAN) and the Asia-Pacific Economic Cooperation (APEC), which India has wanted to join.

But India's own regional grouping-the South Asian Association for Regional Cooperation (SAARC)- could not function as successfully, as an economic grouping in the manner of the EC and the NAFTA. In this situation, Jagdish Bhagwati and T.N. Srinivasan suggested in their report to the Ministry of Finance that "exploring seriously the possibilities of joining one or more of the existing and emerging trade blocs is now a "must" for India. For, access to one of these blocs is a powerful incentive for multinationals to come in: this in fact is a main reason why President Salinas had been pushing for NAFTA, the free trade agreement with the US and Canada".[67] With this challenge India had positively examined an Indian Ocean Economic Grouping (IOEC) which was proposed by South Africa. Now the IOEC has been formally launched.

It seems that with the advent of globalization, liberalization and regionalism in the world economy, it became imperative for India to launch a special effort and programme to globalize and liberalize its economy. While defending the new economic initiatives, Prime Minister, P.V. Narasimha Rao argued that "these had become imperative in the fast-changing world economic scene...The Indian economy would have to integrate itself into the world economy and the new initiative marked a facilitating step in this direction".[68]

Thus it may be wrong to say that the response of economic liberalization in India in the early 1990s was only 'crisis-driven' as Amit Bhaduri and Deepak Nayyar[69] argued. It was a combination of socio-political economic realities in the national context and the changing political and economic environments in the international context which provided the impetus for sudden change in India's economic direction.

REFERENCES

1. In this connection, see Joan Nelson, (ed.), *Economic Crisis and Policy Choice*, (Princepton: Princepton University Press, 1990), Adam Przeworski and Fernando Limongi, "Political Regimes and Economic Growth", *Journal of Economic Perspectives*, No. 3, Summer, 1993, pp. 51-69., and Robert H. Bates and Anne O. Krueger, *Political Economic Interaction in Economic Policy Reforms*, (Oxford: Basil Backwell, 1993).
2. Jagdish Bhagwati, *India In Transition: Freeing The Economy*, (Delhi: OUP, 1995), p. 3.
3. All India Congress (I) Committee (AICC), 1991 General Election Manifesto of INC(I), New Delhi, 1991, p. 21.
4. John Williamson and Stephen Haggard, "The Political Condition for Economic Reform" in John Williamson, (ed.), *The Political Economy of Policy Reform*, (Institute for International Economics,

1994), p. 571.

5. National Herald, July 10, 1991. See also AICC(I), Tirupati Session of INC(I), Economic Resolution, New Delhi, 1992.
6. This proposition was agreed by the former Minister of Finance, Dr. Manmohan Singh and the former Secretary of External Affairs, Prof. Muchkund Dubey. Interview with Manmohan Singh, March 6, 1997 and Muchkund Dubey, January 18, 1997. See also, Ashutosh Varshney, "Battling the Past, Forging a Future? Ayodhya and Beyond" in Philip Oldenburg, (ed.), *India Briefing*, (Boulder coll: Westview, 1993).
7. See Michel Chossudovsky, " India under IMF Rule", *EPW*, March 6, 1993, p. 387.
8. The former Minister of Commerce and External Affairs, Mr. Pranab Mukherjee agreed with this view. Interview with Pranab Mukherjee, January 24, 1997.
9. AICC(I), Surajkund Session of the INC(I), One-Man-One-Post Resolution, New Delhi, 1993, p. 1.
10. AICC(I), Economic Policy Resolution, *op. cit.*, p. 5.
11. Public Interest Research Group, *The World Bank and India*, Delhi, 1995, p. 20.
12. See Pranab Bardhan, *The Political Economy of Development in India*, (Delhi: OUP, 1984). Dr, Manmohan Singh, the then Finance Minister under Rao regime, revealed in an interview that in the short term, these dominant classes will get benefits from the liberalization programmes, while the poor are inevitably hurt more. Interview with Manmohan Singh, March 6, 1997.
13. In this regard, see Atul Kohli, *Democracy and Discontent: India's Growing Crisis of Governability*, (Cambridge: Cambridge University Press, 1991).
14. Harish Khare, "India Means Business", *Seminar*, 425 Annual, January 1995, p. 34.
15. Interview with Assistant Secretary of FICCI, Ashok Amurm, New Delhi, November 22, 1996. See also J. N. Dixit, *My South Block Years*, (New Delhi: UBSPD, 1996), p. 392.
16. The FICCI has changed its stand on the consumer goods imports. They have supported the imports since 1996. Interview with Assistant Secretary of FICCI, ibid.
17. T.J. Byres, "A Chicago View of the Indian State: An Oriental Grin without an Oriental Cat and Political Economy without Classes", *Journal of Commonwealth and Comparative Politics*, November 1988.
18. Pranab Bardhan, "A Political Economy Perspective on Development" in Bimal Jalan (ed.), *The Indian Economy: Problems and Prospects*, (New Delhi: Penguin Books, 1993), p. 333.
19. See G.O., *EPW*, December 11, 1993, pp. 2708-2710.

20. See Gail Omvedt, "Three Sides of Every Story", *Down to Earth*, July 31, 1993.
21. See in this regard, Pranab Bardhan, *The Political Economy of Development in India*, Expanded Edition, (Delhi: OUP, 1998).
22. Jayati Ghosh, "Development Strategy in India: A Political Economy Perspective", in Sugata Bose and Ayesha Jalan (eds.), *Nationalism, Democracy and Development: State and Politics in India*, (Delhi: OUP, 1997), pp. 179-80.
23. See Atul Kohli (ed.), *India's Democracy: An Analysis of Changing State-Society Relations*, (New Delhi: Orient Longman, 1991), and Lloyd I. Rudolph and Susanne Rudolph, *In Pursuit of Lakshmi: The Political Economy of The Indian State*, (Bombay: Orient Longman, 1987).
24. A.K. Roy, "Elections and the Working Class: Puzzling Political Response", *EPW*, Vol. XXXII, No. 14, April 5, 1997, p. 696.
25. N.A. Palkhivala, "The Union Budget 1995-96: An Election-Oriented Approach", *The Times of India*, March 21, 1995, p. 21.
26. John Williamson and Stephan Haggard, op. cit., p. 565. See also Allan Drazen and Vittorio Grilli, "The Benefits of Crisis for Economic Reforms", *American Economic Review*, Vol. 83, No. 3, June 1993, pp. 598-607. They said that economic crisis can prove to be a blessing in disguise in leading governments in some cases (even without change of the ruling party or a dictator) to reverse the earlier policies. They illustrated this with reference to the adoption of radical economic reforms in some of the Latin American countries to control ongoing hyper-inflation which had threatened the survival of the political and social systems.
27. Deepak Nayyar, *Economic Liberalization in India: Analytics, Experience and Lessons*, (Calcutta: Orient Longman, 1996) and Vijay Joshi and I.M.D. Littlc, *India: Macroeconomics and political Economy 1964-1991*, (Delhi: OUP, 1994).
28. Bimal Jalan, "Balance of Payments, 1956 to 1991", in Bimal Jalan (ed.), *op. cit.*, pp. 163-194.
29. Calculated from the various years of *Economic Survey*, Government of India. See also Arun Ghosh, "Eighth Plan: Challenges and possibilities", EPW, February 9, 1991, and Jayati Ghosh, "Statistical Quibbles", *The Economic Times*, October 10, 1990.
30. Deepark Nayyar, *op. cit.*, p. 7.
31. Quoted in Charan D. Wadhva, *Economic Reforms in India and the Market Economy*, (New Delhi: Allied Publishers, 1994), p. 3.
32. See Government of India, Ministry of Finance, *Economic Survey 1992-93*, (New Delhi: Government of India Press, 1993), Table-4.2.
33. Reserve Bank of India, *Annual Report 1988-89*, Bombay, 1989.

34. Charan D. Wadhva, *op. cit.*, p. 6.
35. Deepak Nayyar, *op. cit.*, p. 9
36. See A. Sheshan, "The Burden of Domestic Debt in India", Reserve Bank of India, *Occasional Papers*, Vol. 8, No.1, 1987.
37. *Economic Survey 1992-93, op. cit.* p. 22.
38. "In the first half of the decade the current account deficit was financed by medium- and long-term borrowing, and loans from the IMF. In the second half of the decade IMF borrowing was replaced by IMF repayments. Concessional long term borrowing from IDA fell, but there was a big increase in non-concessional borrowing from the IBRD and private commercial sources (including non-resident deposits)." Vijay Joshi and I.M.D. Little, *op. cit.*, p. 186.
39. This figure is converted at current end-of the year exchange rates. It is end-March rates. For 1980-81, the rates prevailing at the end of March, 1981; for 1990-91, the rates prevailing at the end of March, 1991.
40. One of the senior civil servants in India stated that "Since 1985 three successive governments have acknowledged the severity of the economic crisis... Successive finance ministers have, in their budget speeches, mouthed commitments to control budgetary deficits... In reality, however, budgetary deficits have continued to grow." Bimal Jalan, *India's Economic Crisis: The Way Ahead*, (Delhi: OUP, 1991), pp. 6-7.
41. Of all the sources of commercial energy in 1990-91, oil was the highest import content, at about 40 per cent of India's requirement. See *Economic Survey 1990-1991, op. cit.*, p. 59.
42. Gordon Sandy, *India's Rise to Power in the Twentieth Century and Beyond*, (New York: Martin's Press, 1995), p. 251.
43. See *The Economic Times*, August to November 1990.
44. See Government of India, Ministry of Finance, *Economic Survey 1990-91.*
45. See Prabhat Patnaik and C.P. Chandrasekhar, "Indian Economy under 'Structural Adjustment'", *EPW*, Vol. XXX, No. 47, November 25, 1995, p. 3001.
46. Reserve Bank of India, *Report on Currency and Finance 1991-92*, Vol.-II, Bombay, 1992, pp. 174-6.
47. See *Economic Survey 1993-94, op. cit.*, Table 5.6
48. Isher Judge Ahluwalia, "New Economic Policies, Enterprises, and Privatization in India" in Robert Cassen and Vijay Joshi (eds.), *India: The Future of Economic Reform*, (New Delhi: OUP, 1995), p. 256.
49. *Economic Survey 1994-95, op. cit.*, p. S-109.
50. For a detailed study, see Shanta Nedungadi Varma, Foreign Policy

Dynamics: Moscow and India, (New Delhi: Deep and Deep Publications, 1999).

51. See Ramesh Thakur, *The Politics and Economics of India's Foreign Policy*, (New Delhi: OUP, 1994).
52. *Ibid.*, p. 146.
53. Quoted in Ramesh Thakur, *op. cit.*
54. I.K. Gujral, "Dilemmas of the Third World", *The Hindu*, August 1993.
55. *Sunday*, New Delhi, September 29, 1991.
56. Interview with Manmohan Singh, March 6, 1997.
57. Isher Judge Ahluwalia, *op. cit.*, p. 246. One eminent scholar of neo-Marxist, Pranab Bardhan also expressed a similar view that 'the ideological props for pervasiveness of State control and regulations that the left intellectual community used to provide have been crumbling with the precipitous decline of State socialism in different parts of the world.' Pranab Bardhan (1998), *op. cit.*, p. 132.
58. *National Herald*, July 10, 1991.
59. *The Economic Times*, August 8, 1991.
60. In this regard, see C.P. Bhambhri, *The Indian State: Fifty Years*, (New Delhi: Shipra Publications, 1997), p. 193.
61. Kamla Suri, *India's Economy and The World*, (New Delhi: Vikas Publishing, 1992), pp. 82-4.
62. Charan D. Wadhva, *op. cit.*, p. 21.
63. The 12 countries are Brazil, China, Hong Kong, India, Indonesia, Korea, Malaysia, Mexico, Pakistan, Singapore, Sri Lanka, and Thailand. See World Bank, *World Development Report 1993*, (New York: OUP, 1993).
64. World Economic Forum (International Management Development Institute), *World Competitiveness Report 1993*, Geneva, 1993. The 15 selected countries are Singapore, Hong Kong, Taiwan, Malaysia, Chile, South Korea, Thailand, Mexico, Venezuela, Indonesia, South Africa, Hungary, India, Brazil, and Pakistan.
65. C.T. Kurien, *Global Capitalism and The Indian Economy*, (New Delhi: Orient Longman, 1994), p. 70.
66. Sumitra Chishti, "India's Foreign Economic Policy", in Bimal Prasad (ed.) *India's Foreign Policy: Studies in Continuity and Change*, (New Delhi: Vikas Publisher, 1979), p. 40.
67. Jagdish Bhagwati and T.N. Srinivasan, *India's Economic Reforms*, (New Delhi: Government of India, Ministry of Finance, 1993), p. iv.
68. *The Hindustan Times*, October 8, 1991.
69. Amit Bhaduri and Deepak Nayyar, *The Intelligent Person's Guide to Liberalization*, (New Delhi: Penguin Books, 1996).

Three

Nature of Economic Liberalization

Since the middle of 1991, liberalization of economic policies dominated the principal agenda of the P.V. Narasimha Rao government. Policy initiatives of July 1991 had the two-pronged strategy of stabilisation-cum-structural reforms. The stabilisation phase was begun with reducing balance of payments gap and the internal budget deficits. Simultaneously structural reform was undertaken in the fields of the industrial and trade policy framework. Since one of the major objectives of the liberalization measures was to increase the degree of openness of the Indian economy to integrate with the rest of the world through trade, investment and technology flows, this chapter mainly focuses on the structural adjustment programmes which were designed to improve the efficiency, productivity and international competitiveness of Indian industry. In the process of economic globalization, the private sector was given a larger role to play for industrial development. The state, in turn, would focus its attention more on social sector development and institutional changes. During the Congress government under the leadership of PV Narasimha Rao, while the results of privatisation of the existing public sector enterprises (PSEs) were less than satisfactory, India's foreign trade and foreign investment showed distinct signs of improvement compared to the past. However, the record on social sector development and institutional changes was very poor, which posed considerable challenges to the country's economic development.

INTERNAL LIBERALIZATION: PUBLIC SECTOR

In the internal economic liberalization programme of India during the first half of the 1990s, the public sector constituted an important area. The public sector for a long time had been a symbol of India's inefficient economic policy. Many of the public sector undertakings (PSUs) could not generate adequate return on past investments which put the burden on the fiscal front of both the central and states governments. Naturally the public sector became one of the main targets of the economic reforms of the Narasimha Rao government. In this context, this section will discuss how the public sector enterprises performed over the last forty years and how India liberalized these enterprises in view of socio-political difficulties.

The Performance of the Public Sector

With a socialist oriented economic ideology of the ruling elite, the two Industrial Policy Resolutions of 1948 and 1956 had placed a number of key industries in India in the exclusive domain of the public sector. Thereafter, the public sector in India expanded at a very rapid pace in terms of the area of activities and the share in GDP. The area of activities of the public sector was not limited only to the defence-related industries, but it also covered a large number of infrastructural areas such as heavy machinery, coal, railways and airlines, atomic energy, iron and steel, telecommunications, and the generation and distribution of electricity. In terms of its share in GDP, the public sector expanded rapidly from 8 per cent in 1960's to 14 per cent in 1970's. It further rose to 20 per cent in 1980's, and by 1992-93 it stood at 25 per cent of GDP.

There were only 5 central public sector enterprises at the commencement of the First Five Year Plan with investment amounting to only Rs 29 crores. As on March 31, 1991, the number had risen to 246 central public enterprises owned by the Government of India. Of these, the number of operating enterprises was 236 with total capital employed in them touching the huge amount of Rs. 102,083 crores. However, many of these mega-industries in the public sector could not be operated efficiently in terms of ratio of gross margins and gross profits to capital employed. For instance, the ratio of gross margins to capital employed declined from 18.29 per cent in 1981-82 to 17.94 per cent in 1990-91 while gross profit as a proportion of capital employed declined from 12.10 per cent to 10.88 per cent over the same period. The losses of loss-making enterprises, which had to be covered by a high cost of fresh loans from the market or the government banks, also increased from Rs. 848 crores to 3064 crores over the same period.[1] The most important criticism levied against the public sector has been that, in relation to the capital employed, the level of profits has been too low. As is pointed out by Jagdish Bhagwati, this low profitability of the public sector contributed to the fiscal and foreign exchange crises during the early 1990s,[2] which was one of the main reasons for the Rao government's launching of vigorous macroeconomic and microeconomic reforms.

The question of profitability of the public sector remained a disturbing affair during the liberalization drive of the Congress government. It means that the government had been accumulating additional public debt in order to meet both capital and revenue requirements of enterprises. The consistent failure of the public sector on profitability front was reflected by the fact that of the total internal public debt of Rs. 500,000 crores of the Central government in 1994-95, nearly one-third of it was accounted for by assets held in the public sector. The interest payment on public sector stood at around Rs 50,000 crores, which constituted around 90 per cent of the Centre's fiscal deficit.[3] Thus, Bimal Jalan points out in his latest book, India's Economic Policy: Preparing For The Twenty-First Century that " to a large extent, the fiscal crisis of the Central government is a reflection of the financial crisis of the public sector. If investment in the public sector were more remunerative, or if the government had not borrowed to invest in public enterprises, the fiscal and the debt situation would have been much more manageable."[4]

Then how about the performance of State Level Public Enterprises (SLPEs)? Turning to the SLPEs, I.J. Ahluwalia in her analysis of the performance of the public sector, concludes that "by all accounts, the financial performance of the State public sector undertakings was much worse that of the central public sector enterprises".[5] According to Eighth Five Year Plan: 1992-97, in 1991 there were in all about 1100 SLPEs with an estimated investment of about Rs. 50,000 crores, and a large proportion of these SLPEs had not been performing satisfactorily. Thus, it is natural that the states received very little in return for their investments. For example, the total investment by states in electricity boards and power undertakings was estimated to be in excess of Rs. 45,000 crores at the end of 1994-95. Far from getting any return on this huge investment, they were incurring further debt to cover losses of Rs. 6,000 crores in that year.[6] In this regard, it is interesting to note the criticism of the government document that "it is anomalous that while the state governments are raising power rates to meet the losses of State Electricity Boards (SEBs), they are also offering power subsidy to new units. Similarly, most state governments have announced deferment exemption of sales tax for new units, capital subsidy and subsidy for purchase of generating sets. As most states are announcing similar incentives, it is a zero sum game, with the state governments giving up revenue."[7] The revenue deficit of the States has trebled over the 1990s so far. In some cases 'devlopment grants' for capital projects authorized by the Planning Commission are being used by the States largely to pay salaries to public officials. An increasingly larger share of the Central loan to the States is utilized to repay earlier loans.Circumventing the constitutional ceiling on market borrowings by State governments, the State-owned enterprises are issuing bonds with State government guarantees (generating large contingent liabilities) whose outstanding level nearly quadrupled over the first half of the 1990s.[8]

This was not the sole reason why the public sector could not make profit, there were other reasons behind this. One of the them was, as one expert has opined,"since most of public sector enterprises operated as monopolies, without internal or external competition, there was no financial accountability or pressure to generate profits".[9] A similar but more critical comment on the commercial and economic aspects of the public sector has been made by an another scholar. It was argued that far from providing technological leadership, the Indian public sector often became the victim of an over-regulated and over-centralized policy regime where the choice of technology for a public sector enterprise was not left to the enterprise to decide based on commercial economic cosiderations, but was seriously influenced by politico-economic factors. The public sector also failed to provide leadership in the field of research and development in industry because of bureaucratic ways of approaching research issues.[10]

For all these and other reasons, the public sector which was supposed to generate resources to supplement the growth of the economy, gradually became a net drain on the society as a whole. Even the government has criticised the public sector enterprises on this count. For instance, the Eighth Five Year Plan notes that the public sector has been unable to generate adequate resources for sustaining growth process.[11]

About half of the enterprises made losses, which had to be covered by fresh loans from the government or government banks. This had the disastrous consequence that the central government and the states not only received very little in return for their investments, in fact they were borrowing substantial amounts at high interest rates to cover the deficits of these public enterprises. A typical example is the financial position of irrigation schemes of the states. In all states, the expenditure on running these schemes far exceeded their return. With a couple of exceptions, all states in India had debts that they could not repay, and revenue deficits that they could not finance.

As is pointed out by some that "this has serious consequences because the resource-generation capacity of the SLPEs has a direct bearing on their capacity to invest and contribute to the crucial infrastructure needs of the economy."[12] A slowdown in the investment in infrastructure contributed to the infrastructure bottlenecks that in turn bestowed to the low productivity of investment in many user-industries including the private sector. An adverse fallout of non-performance of the PSEs had been to reduce the expenditure on education and health. The government subsidies to centrally owned public enterprises were about five times the Central government's budget for education.[13] In a situation where budgetary resources are scarce, and there are heavy unmet demands for expenditure in critical sectors such as education and health, where larger expenditures are necessary for the well-being of the poor, it can't be expected of the Budget to bear the burden of maintaining sick public sector units. Nor should the budget be expected to bear the burden of providing resources for expansion of inefficient public sector units. Thus, the failure of public sector enterprises to generate adequate return on past investments can be considered as an important reason for the state of 'fiscal incapacity'. Therefore, it is suggested that there is no option for the government except to reduce substantially its debt by liquidating the debt financed assets in the public sector. Or take stringent action to enhance the profitability of the PSEs.

Liberalization of Public Sector and Privatisation

To pursue a market-oriented economic strategy and initiate a move toward privatisation, it seemed that one of the primary objectives of the Government of India was to reduce the activities of the public sector, to facilitate the closure of loss-making units in the public sector, and to ease the burden on the exchequer on account of the public sector. It emphasized that the public sector focuses only on those sectors which are strategic and demand high-technology inputs or constitute an integral part of the essential infrastructure. With regard to the past performance of the public enterprises, the Government of India took some positive steps based on economic viability of the PSUs to generate adequate resources for sustaining the growth process. During the period of 1991-95 there had been four major policy changes with regard to the liberalization of the public sector in India.

1. Restructuring of the Loss Making Public Enterprises

To enable restructuring or liquidation of chronically loss making public enterprises, the Sick Industrial Companies Act of 1985 was amended in December 1991 to bring these enterprises under the purview of the Board of Industrial and Financial Restructuring (BIFR). It has been stated that public sector enterprises which are chronically sick will be referred to the Board of Industrial and Financial Reconstruction, which would decide whether these units can be effectively reconstituted or they should simply be closed down.[14] This objective could not be achieved. By the end of

1995, 138 PSU were referred to the BIFR. Winding up notices were issued to 14 sick public enterprises, but by the end of 1995, none of these enterprises was liquidated (see table-1). The following is a table showing status of the PSU cases referred to the BIFR as on December 31, 1995.

TABLE - 1
STATUS OF PSU CASES REFERRED TO BIFR AS ON 31.12.1995

	Central	*State*	*Total*
Reference registered	59	79	138
Dismissed as not maintainable	3	23	26
Revival scheme sanctioned	13	16	29
Winding up recommended to the concerned High Court	5	9	—
Stayed by Courts	5	—	5

Source: Government of India, *Economic Survey 1995-96*, Table 7.13

The BIFR has only power to order a closedown. Then, this has to be implemented by the respective high courts after the state governments' clearances of winding up, retrenchment and sale of land. However, fearing the social and political implications of such a step, the state governments did not grant clearances. Also such a step has an inherent weakness in that concerned parties can challenge the BIFR order in the high courts. As a quasi-judicial body, however, BIFR cannot appear in court to argue its case.

Questions have been raised as to why haven't the public enterprises which have been recommended for winding up by the BIFR, been wound up so far? There seem to be two main reasons. First, the BIFR process was biased against winding up and was very slow. Second reason was the socio-political compulsions for the state. Such a case can be seen in the changing budgetary support to PSU. When the economic liberalization picked up high momentum, PSU were subjected to a hard budget constraint. Loans to PSU declined from 0.7 per cent of GDP in 1990-1991 to 0.4 per cent in 1992-1993, but jumped to 0.6 per cent in 1993-1994. In addition, in the 1994-1995 Budget, loans to a number of sick PSU were significantly increased. When the full liberalization program was put in place, then India's macroeconomic situation improved and the external pressure for liberalization weakened, the government again restored to non-commercial objectives.

2. The Memoranda of Understanding (MOU) System

The MOU system, which has been given strong emphasis by the Government, was designed in 1988-89, to remove frequent interference by the Government so as to make its institutional relationship with commercial enterprises more formal and contractual. During 1990-91, 23 public enterprises signed MOUs with their administrative ministries. Out of 23 enterprises, 14 were rated as excellent, eight as very good and a meagre one as poor. The MOU system has been greatly strengthened. In 1994-95, 99 PSEs had signed MOUs, while 104 enterprises had signed for 1995-96, of which 51 were evaluated as excellent, 31 very good and two rated as poor. In this regard, it was pointed out that these quantitative indicators, however, do not address the real problem of lack of autonomy and accountability for public sector enterprises. It is not surprising then that while more and more MOUs were being entered into, the financial performance of public enterprises actually took a turn for the worse at the turn of the decade.[15]

3. Fresh Equity

Earlier public enterprises were constrained by the government regulation. A new lease of freedom has been granted to them to issue fresh equities. Public enterprises have been encouraged to issue fresh equity directly from the public than from the government in order to finance their expansion. This was an endeavour to impart a commercial orientation to the public sector. This could also become a mechanism for forming joint ventures of strategic alliances between existing public sector units and major multinational companies interested in investing in these areas.

The willingness of the government to form strategic alliances has been demonstrated in the case of Maruti Udyog Ltd. (MUL), an automobile joint venture with Suzuki Motor Corporation (SMC) of Japan. Until mid-1992 MUL used to be a public enterprise, with the government of India holding 60 per cent of its equity and SMC holding the remaining 40 per cent. As part of the policy of encouraging foreign investors to increase their shareholding, SMC was allowed to increase its shareholding to 50 per cent by purchase of fresh equity and also to acquire greater management control. The government holding decreased to 49.74 per cent and the remaining 0.26 per cent was left with the MUL employees.[16] However, this diluting of government's equity holding has not deterred it from interfering in the managerial decisions of the MUL. The irony is that all this is being allowed to happen despite the promise that the government has made in recent years about getting out of non-core sectors.

4. Disinvestment of Public Sector

In order to raise resources and create conditions for greater commercial orientation and accountability of the public sector in the market economy, the new industry policy in July 1991 began with the partial divestment of the equity. In the five years, 1991-92 to 1995-96 around Rs 10, 500 crores were realized from these sales.[17] Most of the equity that had been held so far, however, had been sold only to public entities in the financial sector, with the Unit Trust of India alone, for example, accounting for 67.4 per cent of the total sales in 1991-92.[18] It was because, as the Finance Minister stated in the Rajya Sabha, "it was the government's intention to ensure that the benefits accrued to public sector institutions rather than private entities in the event of the sales taking place at an under-priced level".[19]

The Economic Survey 1995-96 provides details of the equity sale of the PSUs on the annual basis during the period July 1, 1991 to December 31, 1995. It reveals that of the 246 non-departmental central public enterprises (CPEs), only 40 CPEs' equity was sold during this period. Of the 40 CPEs, about two-third of the CPEs' equity sales added up to less than 20 percentage points. The highest promotion of equity sold was 48.20 per cent. This means that the government did not intend to sell its CPEs' equity beyond 49 per cent. In other words, it did not intend to privatize its CPEs. If the government owns more than half the equity, the controlling ownership and management of all the firms remains with it. The controlling ownership and management of all the 40 CPEs continued to remain with the Government of India. Criticizing the disinvestment policy, I.J. Ahluwalia points out that "the whole disinvestment approach is so incremental and so thinly spread that it fails to address the basic issue of how to improve the very low returns on the capital invested in the public sector. Not much has been done to bring about effective change in the functioning of these enterprises".[20]

Political Economy of Privatisation in India

The move towards privatisation[21] gained public notice with the emergence of conservative governments in the West like UK, USA during the early 1980s. The policy was supported by the international financial institutions such as the World Bank and the IMF. The movement towards privatisation across the globe reached significant momentum with the dramatic collapse of communism beginning in 1989 which led to a widespread interest in privatising state assets throughout the former socialist countries. The Government of India also tried to pursue a privatisation of its public sector influenced by the above external factors as well as its own economic liberalization. Yet privatisation did not make much headway in India due to many reasons. One of the important reasons was political compulsion that came in the way of implementing the liberalization of the PSUs. Indian politicians' and policy-makers' commitment to privatisation can be highlighted with the examples given below.

In 1994, the government of West Bengal decided to privatise Great Eastern Hotel, a government of West Bengal enterprise and transfer the control and management to Accor Asia Pacific. But four labour unions, including those affiliated to the Centre for Indian Trade Union (CITU) and the Indian National Trade Union Conference (INTUC), rejected the state government's decision. Jyoti Basu, Chief Minister of the state announced that the hotel would have to be closed if it was not privatised, given that the government did not have the funds to subsidise it. But the CITU leaders were reported to have impressed upon the Chief Minster that the privatisation of the hotel just before the Lok Sabha and the West Bengal Assembly elections would not be politically wise. According to them, the Congress Party could use this as a weapon against the CPI(M), especially when the CPI(M) had opposed the privatisation of Bailadila mines.[22] This example shows that the liberalization of PSUs in India is technically and politically difficult to implement. Often, well-designed programmes have fallen short in implementation. In the other words, this is essentially a question of sustainability of liberalization.

It is observed that India's privatisation is neither based on any presumed inherent superiority of private enterprises over public enterprises nor based on any ideological grounds. It is pursued because of the two reasons. First, "it is to enable the government (as the owner) to reduce its liabilities to the public...A second reason is the inability of the Central and state governments to find an effective alternative solution to problems of the public sector".[23]

As a recent study reveals that Indian politicians' and policy-makers' opposition to privatisation has been influenced much less by ideological considerations than by considerations of self-interest. For example, the BJP leaders, including the present Chief Minister of UP Mr. Kalyan Singh, opposed the privatisation of the Auto Tractors Limited (ATL) in Uttar Pradesh during Mulayam Singh Yadav's regime. They supported the workers' agitation and openly announced during the election campaign that if the BJP was voted to power, they would scrap the moves to privatise ATL. But after the installation of the BJP government in UP, the same leaders did a volte-face and drifted away from their initial commitment to the workers of ATL.[24]

The political economy of privatisation of PSUs can be summed up by the observation that there were some hesitant steps, in terms of legislative amendments and administrative arrangements, that may make it possible to close units in public sector and retrench workers with suitable compensation. Much of this, however, remained in the sphere of intentions, for the political constituencies for such changes were not yet created. As a result, the aims of the public sector reforms could not be achieved to promote competitive efficiency, reduce political interference, produce higher quality products, provide better services to consumers, optimise resources, generate employment opportunities and reduce budgetary deficit.

FOREIGN TRADE

After independence, India followed an inward-looking strategy of development, which was supposed to fulfill the objectives of self-reliance and encourage industrialisation. This development strategy supported protectionist trade policies, which discouraged the expansion of exports. By late 1970s, however, it became clear that this inward-oriented policy could not reduce external dependence. Moreover, India could not export enough by the policy to pay even for her import requirements. Consequently, deficit in the balance of payments and external debt kept on growing. Thus, new industrial and trade policies were to be considered. Following the Report of the Alexander Committee (1978), the Government of India emphasised on export promotion and import liberalization. For instance, what was not specified on the restricted list of imports could be imported automatically on Open General Licence (OGL). Further liberalization of foreign trade policy was carried forward in the eighties by two more official committees - the Tandon Committee (1982) and the Hussain Committee (1985). As one points out, however, "exports were still regarded as something 'exceptional' and not as an integral part of domestic industrial policy. The basic framework of industrial and trade policies remained virtually unchanged. A fundamental transformation of the trade regime was not effected until after the economic crisis of 1990-91."[25]

Liberalization of Foreign Trade Policy

Trade between two or more countries is called foreign trade which has been one of the oldest and most visible forms of international relations and is central to how states pursue wealth and power. Some economists call foreign trade as an engine of growth because of its effects in raising the level of capital accumulation, specialization of labour, technological improvement and market expansion. All the nations engaged in trade benefit from it through ultimate increase in the quantity and quality of production.

Foreign trade plays an important role in a developing country by raising the general standard of productivity, induction of new techniques and innovations, increasing specialization of labour and factors of production, enlarging the size of domestic and international markets, increasing the mobility of the factors, promoting international markets, increasing capital accumulation and social overhead capital and above all increasing the level of socio-economic awareness in the country.[26] Foreign trade policy is defined as "the sum total of actions by the state intended to affect the extent, composition and direction of its imports and exports of goods and services."[27]

In general terms, trade liberalization means that a country's trade system is less regulated by direct government intervention and market forces play a large role in its trade movements. Thus, the trade policies of India during the first half of the 1990s can be said as heralding an era of liberalization. The new trade policies liberalized India's foreign exchange rate and import procedures, decanalised several import and export products, abolished several licensing categories, and reduced custom tariffs. Let us look more closely at the major changes that took place during the years.

Liberalization of Foreign Exchange Rate: A beginning in the area of trade liberalization policies was made by devaluing the rupee by about 22 per cent in two stages in early July 1991. In the Budget for 1992-93, the Government of India announced the Liberalized Exchange Rate Mechanism System (LERMS),[28] which introduced partial convertibility of the rupee on trade and current accounts. Under this system a dual exchange rate was fixed under which 40 per cent of foreign exchange earnings had to be surrendered at the official exchange rate, which was to be used for essential imports like petroleum products, fertilisers, etc. The rest of 60 per cent was to be converted at a determined market exchange rate, which was to be used to pay for private sector imports. This implied that, as Jagdish Bhagwati asserts, "governmental subsidization of essential imports was at the expense of exporters and on private transactions, there was a bias against exports".[29]

By March 1993 the dual exchange rate was unified and the rupee became fully convertible on trade account. The foreign exchange market was widened and deepened in August 1994 when the rupee was fully convertible on current account transactions, earning India Article VIII status with the IMF.[30] The adjustment of exchange rate of the rupee was intended to improve India's export competitiveness in the world markets and correct the imbalances in trade and current accounts.

Reduction of Import Tariff: It seems that the new trade policy in India paid relatively more attention on tariff reforms. One of the reasons may be because India's import duties were at very high levels compared to the levels prevailing in most other developing countries.[31] The high levels of tariffs provided, as the Economic Survey for 1991-92 referred, the "extra-ordinarily high protection given to indigenous industries", which led to inefficiencies in resources use. The tariffs also created a significant bias against exports.[32] It was felt that decreasing the tariff rates substantially was essential to reduce the degree of protection earlier provided to indigenous industries in India. It would help Indian industries to be more competitive in exporting their products in the global markets.

Beginning with the Budget for 1991-92, India launched a phased reduction of import tariff, bringing down the maximum from 300 per cent in 1990-91 to 50 per cent at the beginning of 1995-96. These changes brought the import-weighted average tariff down to 27 per cent in March 1995 from 87 per cent in 1990-91. This reduction of import tariff had been loosely guided by the Tax Reforms Committee (TRC) under the chairmanship of Dr R. J. Chelliah. The TRC was constituted in August 1991, whose interim report[33] was published in December 1991.

In the interim report, a 50 per cent reduction in the general level of protective tariff by 1995-96 was recommended and a further substantial reduction in tariff rates by 1998-99 was proposed so as to bring down the average rate of tariff to about 25 per cent (from 87 per cent in 1989-90). It was positively regarded by the Ministry of Finance. The Finance Minister brought down the peak tariff level from 150 per cent in 1991-92 to 110 per cent in 1992-93. The general rate of customs duty for capital equipment was lowered from 85 per cent to 55 per cent. A significant reduction to a uniform 30 per cent rate was made applicable for the capital goods for projects of coal mining and petroleum refining as well as for power projects.

In its Final Report (Part II)[34] of January 1993, the Committee recommended drastic reductions in import duties. The Report said the rupee had depreciated largely in the 80s and the early 90s pushing up the degree of protection to Indian industries considerably.[35] In this regard, the Committee suggested the structure of ad valorem duties should be 5, 10, 15, 20, 25, 30 and 50 per cent by 1997-98.

The 5 per cent of duty rate is to apply to inputs for essential items like fertilizer and newsprint. Basic inputs such as metals would be taxed at 10 and 15 per cent rates. The 20 and 25 per cent rates are to apply for capital goods and chemical intermediates. The 30 per cent would be attracted by other final products. The highest rate of 50 per cent will be applied to non-essential consumer goods when their imports are allowed. Guided by this Report, the tariff rates were significantly reduced in the Budget for 1993-94 and 1994-95.

The 1993-94 Budget reduced the peak rate of duty to 85 per cent from 110 per cent in 1992-93. The general rate of customs duty for capital goods was lowered from 55 per cent in 1992-93 to 35 per cent. The process of lowering of the general rate for capital goods was continued in the Budget for 1994-95 from 35 per cent to 25 per cent. The corresponding year of the Budget further brought down the maximum rate of duty from 85 per cent to 65 per cent. This highest import duty was again cut by the 1995-96 Budget from 65 to 50 per cent. Tariff rates on general machinery, machine tools, instruments and projects were also unified at 25 per cent. But if we compare these achievements against the recommendations of the TRC's Final Report, there was still scope for further reduction in import duties on several products. Also, if we look at import weighted tariffs in countries like Mexico with 10 per cent tariff in 1990, Brazil with 14 per cent in 1993, Indonesia with 10 per cent in 1989-91, and Korea with 9 per cent in 1985-92,[36] Indian tariff rates were still very high. Nevertheless, compared to its own past, the progress in tariff reductions had been reasonably impressive, except in consumer goods.

The 1992-97 Exim Policy: With a view to reinforcing the trade policy reforms and complementing the fiscal, industrial and investment measures, the new five-year Export-Import Policy (1992-97) was introduced with effect from April 1, 1992. This major departure from the earlier three-year policy regime was to impart stability in the policy framework. The new policy was made co-terminus with the Eighth Plan. Besides, changes or amendments, if any, in the policy were to be made once in a quarter. Earlier, frequent changes were announced in the policy through notifications which tended to defeat the purpose of stability with the consequent disadvantage to the industry and trade.

In the restructuring trade policy, India gave a major trust towards exports. Earlier the policy was known as Import-Export Policy; the new policy was titled Export-Import Policy. The document itself was reduced to 85 pages and its contents were made simple, albeit easy, to comprehend. The hallmark of the new policy was substantial elimination of licensing, quantitative restrictions, regulatory measures and discretionary controls. Except for two small negative lists - one for imports and another for exports - all goods were allowed to be imported and exported freely.[37]

The vision of globalisation underlying the formulation of the 1992-97 Exim policy was based on raising the combined contribution of exports and imports to GDP from the existing level of 15 per cent to 20 per cent by the end of the Eight Five Year Plan period (March 1997).

The 1992-97 Exim Policy was modified in April 1993 in the light of the developments in the macroeconomic performance of the economy in 1992-93 and in response to the ongoing structural economic reforms in several areas. The modified policy emphasised exports of agro-based (and "allied") products and of "services" broadly defined. The allied sectors to agriculture include aquaculture, animal husbandry, floriculture, pisciculture, poultry and sericulture. These sectors were allowed to import capital goods at the new concessional duty rates (of 15 per cent). Exporting units in these sectors located anywhere had been extended the benefits of the Export-Oriented Units (EOUs) and Export Processing Zones (EPZ) scheme for the service sector. This put a wide variety of services "at par" with the manufacturing sector. These include consultancy, architecture, education, medical advice, etc.

The modified policy had further deregulated exports by removing 144 items from the negative list of exports. It had also further simplified the procedures relating to imports and exports.

Further annual modifications in the Export-Import Policy for 1994-95 were announced by the Ministry of Commerce on March 30, 1994. These modifications carried this policy another step forward in the direction of liberalisation of trade and trade-related investment with special emphasis on accelerating growth of India's exports and facilitated coordination with the changes in the other macro-economic policies.[38]

The Exim Policy (April 1, 1995) further liberalized imports of consumer goods.[39] The Special Import Licence (SIL), which enabled importers of consumer goods to purchase the import license from exporters to whom it was granted in proportion of their exports, had been increased from 42 to 75. The new items included computer systems, TV tubes, commercial refrigeration equipment, battery and electrically-operated vehicles, refrigerated trucks, cash registers, and sewing machines. Several consumer items were also removed from the negative list and added to the Open General Licence (OGL) freely importable list. Among them were personal computers, CD ROM, diskettes, coffee, fish, paper and paper products, cameras, sports goods, and some baby products.

The Exim Policy in 1995 also took several steps to enhance export incentives. They included extending the Export Promotion Capital Goods (EPCG) scheme. The scheme allowed exporters to import capital goods at a concessional tariff of 15 per cent, subject to an export obligation of four times the c.i.f. value of imports to be fulfilled within a period of five years from the date of issue of the import licence. The extension allowed duty-free imports of capital goods against export obligation in cases where the Cost, Insurance and freight (C.I.F.) value is over Rs. 200 million (about $6 million). The export obligation was six times the c.i.f. value of imports in eight years. Unlike earlier, this scheme was extended on the same conditions to both merchant exporters as well as the service sector.[40]

Performance of Foreign Trade

As we have seen the liberalization of India's trade policy, initiated in the early 1990s, reduced the policy constraints vis-a-vis exports and contributed to a considerable increase in trade volume. This is certainly a major departure from the relatively protectionist trade policies till late 1970s. The trade policy in the first half of the 1990s seemed to have been guided mainly by the concerns regarding globalisation of Indian economy, improving competitiveness of its industry, and adverse balance of payments situation. This policy enabled India to attain an accelerated trade growth rate in spite of weakening of world economic activity and fall in the growth rate of world trade volume (goods and services). To examine the issue of trade growth in greater depth, let's look at India's trade performance during the period of 1990-91 to 1995-96.

The data available for the first five years of 1990s shows that India's trade had increased significantly during the post-liberalization period reflecting a sustained expansion in the domestic economic activity and continued liberalization of trade. To be precise, the share of India's trade in GDP had risen from the level of around 15 per cent during the 1980s to more than 24 per cent in 1995-96. The period 1990-91 to 1995-96 recorded a higher growth in India's exports (11.95 per cent per annum) than in imports (9.75 per cent per annum), despite a significant percentage of decline in exports to the former Soviet bloc. This export growth contributed to the decline of trade deficit from around US $ 5-6 billion per annum in 1980s to around 2 billion during 1991-95. Viewed differently, the average reduction in the trade deficit since 1991-92 has resulted in considerable foreign exchange savings. During 1995-96, India's exports increased to $ 31.8 billion from $ 26.3 billion in 1994-95, registering a growth of 21 per cent. On the other hand, imports too increased during 1995-96 from $ 28.2 billion in 1994-95 to $ 36.4 billion in 1995-96 as shown in table 2.

Further more, domestic industry experienced a broad-based recovery with industrial growth of more than 10 per cent in 1995-96 (as against 0.5 per cent in 1991-92). The capital goods sector, despite import liberalization, grew by nearly 25 per cent in 1994-95.[41] The steady improvement in both net terms of trade and income terms of trade was not seen in 1970s and 1980s, and is thus a reflection of the impact of trade liberalization. Thus, as Bimal Jalan argues, it is clear that trade liberalization is good for the development of Indian industry and the popular belief of the export pessimism during fifties and sixties could be dismissed.[42] The following is the table showing India's exports and imports during the period of 1990-91 to 1995-96.

TABLE-2
INDIA'S EXPORTS AND IMPORTS, 1990-91 TO 1995-96

($ Million)

	Exports	*Imports*	*Trade Balance*
1990-91	18,143	24,075	-5,932
1991-92	17,865	19,411	-1,546
1992-93	18,536	21,880	-3,344
1993-94	22,234	23,303	-1,069
1994-95	26,231	28,259	-1,069
1995-96	31,831	36,370	-4,539

Source: Rajesh Mehta, "Trade Policy Reforms, 1991-92 to 1995-96: Their Impact on External Trade", EPW, Vol. XXXII No. 15, April 12-18, 1997, p. 779.

India's Exports

It is well known that the share of India's exports in world trade had consistently fallen from 2 per cent in 1950s to around 0.6 per cent in 1970s. The share had remained more or less close to 0.5 per cent from 1973 onwards reflecting that India's exports had increased at more or less the same rate as in the world trade. The rapid increase in India's exports during the first half of the 1990s led to increase in its share of world trade to around 0.8 per cent in 1995-96. The value of India's exports, during 1990-91 to 1995-96 increased at annual rate of 12 per cent which was significantly higher than the value of world trade which increased at an annual average rate of 7.5 per cent during 1990-95.[43]

Direction of Exports

As shown table-3, there was significant changes during the first half of the 1990s in India's export markets to different countries (it will be discussed in detail in Chapter-V). Most of the directional changes were in favour of Asian market and they registered higher growth in the value of their trade. The share of this region in total India's exports had risen from 13.1 per cent in 1980-81 to 22.9 per cent in 1995-96. On the other hand, the share of Eastern Europe, which was one of the principal markets for India's exports in total India's exports, declined from 22.1 per cent in 1980-81 to 4.2 per cent in 1995-96.[44] Although the Western countries remained the major destination for India's exports, their share in India's exports had declined.

TABLE-3
DIRECTION OF INDIA'S EXPORTS BY COUNTRIES
1990-91 TO 1995-96

Countries	*Per Cent of Total Share*			*Growth of India's Exports* (Per Cent Per Annum)*
	1990-91	*1994-95*	*1995-96*	
US	14.74	19.13	17.34	15.76
Japan	9.30	7.74	6.96	6.47
Germany	7.79	6.62	6.23	7.29
UK	6.53	6.44	6.31	11.56
Hong Kong	3.30	5.78	5.71	26.33
UAE	2.40	4.78	4.47	28.69
Belgium	3.86	3.77	3.51	10.34
Italy	3.08	3.27	3.19	13.74
Singapore	2.09	2.91	2.82	20.30
Bangladesh	1.68	2.43	3.26	29.25

Netherlands	2.00	2.22	2.39	16.30
France	2.35	2.22	2.34	12.25
Saudi Arabia	1.29	1.65	1.51	17.44
Thailand	1.36	1.55	1.49	15.91
Sri Lanka	0.72	1.40	1.25	25.60
Australia	0.99	1.32	1.18	16.63
South Korea	1.01	1.21	1.38	22.31
Malaysia	0.82	1.09	1.23	22.43
Indonesia	0.60	1.04	2.08	50.73
Spain	0.86	1.02	1.23	21.59
Switzerland	1.23	0.94	0.89	5.13
Total	100.00	100.00	100.00	11.95

*Based on value in US $ for the period 1990-91 to 1995-96.
Source: Ibid, p. 783.

Composition of India's Exports

Unlike the direction of India's exports, the composition of India's exports during the first half of the 1990s had not shown any dramatic change. But, certain items such as rice and software constituted high growth rates and showed clear international competitiveness. The share of manufactured exports in total exports increased almost steadily form 71.6 per cent in 1990-91 to 77.4 per cent in 1994-95, except for a slight dip in 1993-94. The share of primary products, on the other hand, declined from 23.8 per cent to 19.8 per cent during the same period. However, primary exports with a rise of 39.3 per cent in 1995-96 eclipsing a small growth rate of 6.1 per cent recorded during the previous year, resulted in a compositional change. The share of manufactured goods in total exports declined from 77.5 per cent to 74.4 per cent between 1994-95 and 1995-96 while that of primary exports went up from 19.8 per cent to 22.8 per cent. In terms of incremental exports, while the share of manufactured goods contracted from 91.5 per cent during 1994-95 to 59.5 per cent in 1995-96, that of primary exports expanded from 7.3 per cent to 37.3 per cent, reflecting a structural change in exports.[45]

This indicates a departure in the growth trend of India's exports by commodities from the trend recorded in the earlier period. During 1995-96 the agricultural and allied sector contributed significantly to India's exports. Responding to the special incentives given to foster primary exports in the post-reform period, the agricultural and allied sector under this category registered high growth rates during 1995-96. Among the primary commodities, the highest growth was registered by sugar and molasses (660.1 per cent) followed by rice (254.5 per cent), processed fruits, juices and miscellaneous processed items (131.7 per cent). The rice export which has been identified by the Minister of Commerce as an "extreme focus item" for export promotion, registered an impressive rise of 254.5 per cent and thereby contributed nearly half of the incremental exports of primary products. An increase of about 1,000 times in the exports of non-basmati rice during 1995-96 under review over the previous year was largely in response to the removal of the stipulation of minimum export price on these items in 1994-95.[46]

If one looks at three successful export industries- diamond cutting and polishing, garments and software, it will be more clear that the reforms have contributed not only to an increase in export volume but also to the international competitiveness of Indian industries. The dollar volume of India's exports of cut and polished diamonds grew at a compound annual growth rate of 12 per cent between 1990-91 and 1995-96, and the ratio of domestic value addition to export revenues increased from 23 per cent in 1990-91 to 30 per cent by 1995-96. Garment exports grew at an average rate of 27 per cent in rupee terms between 1989-90 and 1995-96. India's software exports increased from $ 128 million in 1990-91 to $ 1.1 billion in 1996-97, with a compound annual growth rate of 43 per cent.[47]

According to one study, trade policy liberalization in 1990s has enhanced India's competitiveness in labour- and skill-intensive industries; reduced the dependence of competitive industries on inefficient domestic suppliers and infrastructure; and enhanced domestic competitive conditions.[48]

India's Imports

The first half of the 1990s with buoyancy in domestic demand for imports reflected accelerated growth of industrial production and rise in overall domestic output. Thus, imports at US $ 36,370 million registered a growth rate of 26.9 per cent in 1995-96 reflecting a rise of significant percentage points over 1991-92 with the growth of negative points of 19.4 per cent. Consequently, trade deficit had increased by US $ 4,539 million from US $ 1,546 million.[49]

Composition of India's Imports

The varying rates of growth of various imported products over the years had resulted in a change in the composition of imports. The bulk items with a share of 44.8 per cent in total imports in 1991-92, accounted for much lower portion at 39.1 per cent in 1995-96 whereas the share of non-bulk items rose from 55.2 per cent in 1991-92 to 60.9 per cent in 1995-96. Among the bulk imports, the important commodities that had marked high growth rates in 1995-96 were petroleum products, fertilizers and edible vegetable oil. In the category of non-bulk imports, capital goods in terms of share, had gained a substantial rise of 28.0 per cent from 21.8 per cent over the period of 1991-92 to 1995-96. This may be regarded as mainly reflective of the ongoing process of expansion and modernisation of Indian industries.

Direction of India's Imports

Like direction of India's exports, India's import direction had also changed over the first half of the 1990s. Over the period the share of the Organisation for Economic Co-operation and Development countries (OECD) shrank from 57.2 per cent to in 1990-91 to 52.3 per cent in 1995-96. On the other hand, the developing countries had assumed increasing importance as sources of India's imports in terms of the value as well as the volume over the period. Consequently, their share had gone up from 18.7 per cent in 1990-91 to 24.3 per cent in 1995-96.

FOREIGN DIRECT INVESTMENT

Foreign Direct Investment (FDI) is generally defined as a form of long-term international capital movement, which takes place to facilitate productive activity and accompanied by the intention of managerial control or participation in the management of a foreign firm. It is different from indirect (portfolio or securities) long-term investment where the investor is concerned only with the yields on securities or other claims acquired.[50] The essence of FDI is the transmission to the host country of a package of capital, managerial skill and technical knowledge.[51] Thus, FDI is viewed as an important source of non-debt inflows and is widely welcomed to receive technology, assimilate overseas management techniques, expand export market shares, utilize industrial property rights, and garner the benefits rendered by the government.

One of the main objectives of economic liberalization under the Rao Government was to increase the degree of openness of Indian economy in order to integrate with the international economy in a fast changing global economic environment. The effort was, therefore, not limited to foreign trade only, it was extended to foreign capital and foreign technology flows. The New Industrial Policy of 1991 says "the relationship between domestic and foreign industry needs to be much more dynamic than it has been in the past in terms of both technology and investment. Foreign investment would bring attendant advantages of technology transfer, marketing expertise, introduction of modern managerial techniques and new possibilities for promotion of exports. This is particularly necessary in the changing global scenario of industrial and economic cooperation marked by mobility of capital."[52] Consequently, the Rao Government liberalized the industrial policy with a range of spheres. Let us see the salient features of the Government's policy and the changing approach toward FDI.

The Government Policy Towards FDI

Automatic approval for projects with foreign equity participation up to 51 per cent was permissible in specified industries producing intermediate and capital goods if certain norms were satisfied. FDI proposals did not necessarily have to be accompanied by technology transfer agreements. No permission was required for hiring foreign technicians. Income derived by foreign companies such as dividend, interest, royalty or technical fee was taxed at a rate lower than applicable to domestic companies. Trading companies engaged primarily in export activities were also allowed up to 51 per cent foreign equity. To attract MNCs in the energy sector, 100 per cent foreign equity was permitted in the power generation. Non-Resident Indians (NRIs) and overseas corporate bodies were permitted to invest 100 per cent foreign equity in high priority industries with facilities for full repatriation. International companies were allowed to explore non-associated natural gas and develop gas fields including laying down pipelines and setting up liquefied petroleum gas projects.

A new package for 100 per cent export-oriented projects and Companies in export processing zones was announced. A Foreign investment Promotion Board (FIPB) authorised to provide a single window clearance was set up in the Prime Minister's Office (PMO) to invite and felicitate investment in India by international companies. The existing companies were also allowed to raise foreign equity levels to 51 per cent for proposed expansion in priority industries. The use of foreign brand names for goods manufactured by domestic industry which was restricted was also liberalised. The Foreign Exchange Regulation Act (FERA)of 1973 was amended and restrictions placed on foreign companies by the FERA were lifted. Companies with more than 40 per cent of foreign equity were treated on par with fully Indian-owned companies. New sectors such as mining, banking, telecommunications, highways construction and management had been thrown open to private, including foreign owned, companies.

Additionally India became a signatory to the convention of the Multilateral Investment Guarantee Agency (MIGA) of the World Bank, which ensures protection to foreign investors from political and non-commercial risks. Bilateral investment promotion and protection agreements had been signed with a large number of countries.

Another major step towards attracting FDI was the reduction of bureaucratic interference in foreign technology agreements. The policy statement says that "in the fast changing world of technology the relationship between the suppliers and users of technology must be a continuous one. Such a relationship becomes difficult to achieve when the approval process includes unnecessary governmental interference on a case to case basis involving endemic delays and fostering uncertainty. The Indian entrepreneur has now come of age so that he no longer needs such bureaucratic clearances of his commercial technology relationships with foreign technology suppliers."[53] It has been considered as a very positive feature of the policy. The discretionary case by case system of approval in the past sent negative signals to foreign investors.[54]

FDI Flows

FDI comes under three categories: those subject to automatic approval by RBI; those approved by the Secretariat for Industrial approvals (SIA); and those that are approved by the Foreign Investment Promotion Board (FIPB), the difference between each being dependent on the size and extent of foreign equity. The automatic approval route of RBI was introduced to facilatate FDI inflows. During the post-liberalization period in 1991to1995, the actual investment flows through the automatic route of the RBI against total amount of FDI flows was quite insignificant. This was partly due to the fact that crucial areas like electronics, services and minerals were left out of the automatic approval route. Another limitation was the ceiling of 51 per cent on foreign equity holding. An increasing number of proposals were cleared through the FIPB route while the automatic approval route had been declining in relative importance since 1994.

As a result of the liberalization of the foreign investment policy, the FDI picture in India had undergone a significant change as reflected in the higher value of approvals and the rising trend in the actual inflows. The total stock of FDI as at the end of March 1990 barely valued at Rs. 27 billion. During the period 1991 to 1995 the total value of FDI approvals, however, went up substantially from Rs. 534 crore in 1991 to 3888 crore in 1992 and rose further to Rs. 8859 crore in 1993. The total FDI approvals recorded at Rs. 30881 crore at the end of 1995 (Table-4). The actual inflows of FDI grew at a slower pace from Rs. 3.5 billion in 1991 to Rs. 63.7 billion in 1995. These constitute about 20 per cent of the approved investment in the post-liberalization period. The following table is showing the total FDI approvals and investment inflows in India.

TABLE-4
TOTAL FOREIGN DIRECT INVESTMENT APPROVALS AND INVESTMENT INFLOWS

Year	*Number of Approvals*	*Amount (Rs Crore)*	*Actual Inflow (Rs Crore)*
1991	289	534	351
1992	692	3888	675
1993	785	8859	1786
1994	1040	8960(*)	2982
1995	1351	30881(#)	6370
Total	4157	53122	12164

* Excludes 22 approvals of GDRs involving Rs. 5230 crores.
# Excludes 4 approvals of GDRs involving Rs. 1190 crores.[55]
Source: Government of India, Handbook of Industrial Policy and Statistics 1996.

It is interesting to note that the majority of FDI approvals during the 1991-95 were in high priority sectors such as power generation, oil refinery, electrical equipment, chemicals and food processing sectors. According to Handbook of Industrial Policy and Statistics 1996, more than 80 per cent of these approvals was in core sectors. But while the pattern of industry-wise inflows of approved FDI indicated the importance of core sectors, the figures for industry-wise inflows of actual FDI reveal a different picture. From table-5, it can be seen that the actual FDI into domestic appliances, finance, services, electronics and electrical equipment and food and dairy products combined together accounted for 29.3 per cent of the total actual FDI in 1992-93, 44.9 per cent in 1993-94, 47.7 per cent in 1994-95 and 41.2 per cent in 1995-96.[56]

TABLE - 5
ACTUAL FOREIGN DIRECT INVESTMENT INFLOWS: INDUSTRY-WISE
(US $ Million)

Industry	*1992-93*	*1993-94*	*1994-95*	*1995-96*

Chemicals and Allied Products	47.0	(16.8)	37.5	(10.2)	141.2	(16.2)	126.7	(8.9)
Engineering	69.8	(24.9)	32.9	(8.9)	131.6	(15.1)	251.9	(17.8)
Domestic Appliances	15.8	(5.6)	2.4	(0.7)	108.3	(12.4)	0.5	(0.0)
Finance	3.7	(1.3)	42.2	(11.4)	97.7	(11.2)	270.0	(19.0)
Services	2.4	(0.8)	20.2	(5.5)	93.4	(10.7)	100.5	(7.1)
Electronics and Electrical Equipment	32.8	(11.7)	57.1	(15.5)	56.4	(6.5)	129.6	(9.1)
Food and Dairy Products	27.9	(9.9)	43.5	(11.8)	60.9	(6.9)	85.0	(6.0)
Computers	8.3	(2.9)	7.6	(2.1)	10.2	(1.2)	52.1	(3.7)
Pharmaceuticals	3.1	(1.1)	49.5	(13.4)	10.1	(1.2)	54.8	(3.9)
Others	69.2	(24.7)	76.1	(20.6)	162.2	(18.6)	346.9	(24.5)
Total	280	(100)	369	(100)	872	(100)	1418	(100)

*Bracketed figures are percentages of column totals.
Source: Government of India, *RBI Annual Report, 1995.*

Thus, as one study reveals a major motivating factor behind FDI was to explore India's sizeable and expanding domestic market.[57] It is also clear that export markets were not major attraction despite low costs of the Indian operations. For China, export markets have been major attraction for FDI. This explains why FDI in China has been concentrated mainly in the coastal areas, and particularly in the two southern ones, Guangdong and Fujian.[58]

Liberalization and Changing Sources of FDI in India

The foreign investment markets in the world have been huge. In 1992 total FDI in the world amounted roughly to $ 170 billion. Only a meager 0.001 per cent of $ 261 million came to India. It increased, however, to 0.28 per cent in 1993 and 0.42 per cent in 1994.[59] Therefore, it may be said that the liberalization of policy regime by India during the first half of the 1990s had not yet led to a significant improvement in India's relative attractiveness as a host of FDI amongst major Western countries, specially European countries.

Liberalization had, however, helped India diversify her sources of FDI. For instance, the newly industrialising Asian countries had recently emerged as important sources of FDI for India during the first half of the 1990s.

Country wise approvals show that European countries', which were major sources of FDI inflows to India until 1990, exhibited declining relative importance during the period of 1991-1995. Major European countries (which include the UK, Germany, France, Switzerland, Sweden, Italy and Netherlands) accounted for 69 and 66 per cent of FDI stock in 1980 and 1990 respectively. The UK alone recorded 54 and 49 per cent in the same years respectively.[60] The UK, however, constituted for only 7 per cent share of FDI inflows approved between 1991-1995. As table-6 shows, liberalization on the front of foreign direct investment in India did not seem to have attracted a greater response of European investing countries like UK and Germany. If one looks at Japan from the point of its economic size as the second richest country in the world, it also did not show much interest in the liberalization of FDI in India. On the other hand, it is noticed that the US companies had shown the best response to the liberalization. The US had become as the single most important source of FDI during the same period with a share of 29 per cent.

During the period of 1991-95, the importance of intra-regional and inter-regional FDI inflows was on the increase. This was evident from the fact that of the top 13 FDI source countries in India, six were from the Asian-sub region. They were South Korea, Malaysia, Thailand, Japan, Singapore and China. These countries had emerged as significant sources of FDI to India in this period. One major development in the directional pattern was the emergence of Israel as the second in ranking among the major contributors of FDI in 1995 with 13 per cent. Significant contributions had also come from Mauritius and Australia with 5.8 and 4.8 per cent respectively. This was an important trend of rising importance of non-conventional sources of FDI over the period. Therefore, it seems that the policy of liberalization of FDI during period the 1991-1995 period impelled India to diversify its sources of FDI.

During the same period NRIs also started looking back at home market. Their share which used to be nominal in 1980s started increasing gradually till 1993. The share of NRIs investment approval (in rupees) in the grand total investment approvals which was only 3.7 per cent in 1991 increased to 11 per cent in 1992 and 11.7 per cent in 1993. But their share declined drastically to 2.2 per cent in the grand total of foreign investment in 1995. Hence, it is said that the increase and the amount of investment approvals of NRIs were still no match to Non Resident Chinese (NRCs) flow back to China.[61]

TABLE - 6
COUNTRY-WISE BREAKUP OF FDI APPROVED DURING 1991 TO 1995

	1991	*1992*	*1993*	*1994*	*1995*
U.S.A.	186	1232	3462	3488	7054
Israel	0	1	2	9	4137
S. Korea	62	394	293	1069	3142
Malaysia	0	74	9	25	2386
Thailand	0	3	368	10	1968
Mauritius	0	0	124	535	1809
U.K.	32	118	623	1299	1725
Japan	53	610	257	401	1514
Australia	3	78	30	388	1504
Germany	42	86	176	569	1339
Singapore	1	60	67	266	991
Netherlands	56	97	322	207	966
N.R.I.*	20	439	1043	491	709
China	1	0	62	27	581
Others	78	696	2021	173	1057
TOTAL	534	3888	8859	8957	30882

*Excludes the NRI Direct Investment approved by RBI.

Source: Based on data provided by RBI, *Report on Currency and Finance 1995-96.*

The efficiency-seeking FDI had yet to start flowing to the country in a considerable manner. In an era of stiff competition among developing countries to attract export-oriented FDIs, liberalization of policies alone may not be enough to win the race. Policy makers need to send clear signals to foreign investors that the measures adopted can be expected to be sustained. That anticipated policy changes contribute to the increased interest of private investors have been shown in many case studies.

Questions of Policy Credibility and Continuity on FDI

When there was a peak momentum in FDI in 1995, there was also ironically questions of policy credibility and continuity of the liberalization, specially on FDI which created a confusion among foreign investors. Contradictory statements by Central ministers, Chief Ministers, important politicians and some top businessmen in 1995 caused considerable confusion among prospective foreign investors. The Indian government under P.V. Narasimha Rao had a fairly welcoming attitude to foreign investment till 1994. But specially from 1995 some ministers sent negative signals to foreign investors. In December 1994, the Government of India opened up the air transportation sector to foreign investment with an equity participation in the newly created scheduled airlines, on a case-by-case basis, subject to a cap of 40 per cent.[62] But in early 1995, the very concerned civil aviation minister, Mr Azad, questioned the need for a foreign airline joint venture.

The main opposition party, the BJP also gave confused signals to foreign investors. While the BJP's official stand was to allow foreign investment into hi-tech and export-oriented industries, an important functionary of the party, Mr Pramod Mahajan, questioned the need for foreign investment in airlines. Also causing confusion were contradictory statements made by some chief ministers. The then Chief Minister, Mr Manohar Joshi in Maharashtra, where the BJP was part of the government, said that Indian industrialists will be given preference over foreign companies for projects in his state and only those will be given to foreign companies which do not solicit interest from local companies.[63] While Mr Rama Rao, the then Chief Minister of Andhra Pradesh, told a gathering of the Confederation of Indian Industry (CII) that he would welcome foreign investment in "microchips as well as potato chips", his National Front colleague, Mr Laloo Prasad Yadav, the then chief minister of Bihar, said to the same gathering that " we cannot allow multinationals to prosper at the cost of our own industry. They are welcome in infrastructure but certainly not in consumer goods."[64]

If liberalization was launched with good vigour and spirit, why were there many changes and different stances on economic liberalization in 1995? One of the possible answers was that the economic environment in 1995 was different as compared to 1991-92 which had made it possible for the government to create a broad political consensus on the economic liberalization. Mr. Pramod Mahajan, all-India general secretary of the BJP and the one in-charge of the party's 1996 general election campaigning, said in an interview that " unlike the Congress, we do not think only foreign companies can help India. Such an attitude may have been valid in 1991 when India had a serious balance of payments problem, but no longer".[65]

Another possible answer would be the electoral compulsion. After the Congress lost its elections in the States in December 1994 and as Lok Sabha elections ahead in 1996, political compulsions began to cast a long shadow over FDI. The Enron affair in 1995, where a contract signed with this corporation was reopened with a change in the state government and became the warning signal to the foreign investors. According to S.C. Chung, commercial counsellor in the South Korean Embassy, Korean involvement in India's power sector had been "weakened with the Enron cancellation. Even machinery and petrochemical companies were very concerned about this".[66] The BJP believed that the scrapping of the Enron deal boosted its electoral prospects. The Congress government at the Centre sent mixed signals on FDI. In 1995, foreign companies like Wrigleys, Reebok and Quaker Oats had their proposals for 100 per cent equity ventures turned down by the Foreign Investment Promotion Board (FIPB). From July 1991 to 1994, in fact the FIPB had rarely turned down any FDI proposals. Companies such as Cadbury Schweppes, Procter & Gamble, Pepsi and Kelloggs, among others, had been allowed to set up fully-owned subsidiaries.[67] This created an impression that only the early foreign birds got a place in the Indian markets.

Thus, the key question for policy makers was how to undertake and encourage the necessary investment in an economic and political environment that was and contiues to be delicate.

Overseas Investment

India gradually assumed a certain degree of responsibility to share its industrial and technological development experience and expertise with other countries, especially with developing world to promote South-South cooperation. It was recognised that joint ventures were one of the significant means of this end. Keeping this in mind the major Indian enterprises ventured into overseas investment in a number of developing countries. But their efforts in this area did not become especially significant. Since the liberalization of 1991, economic realities have changed dramatically causing Indian firms to advance into overseas markets in a serious manner in order to maintain international competitiveness. The guidelines for setting up of joint ventures abroad by Indian corporates had been liberalized in 1992. The commerce ministry in 1995 further liberalized its guidelines for investment by Indian companies in joint ventures abroad, making it easier for them to acquire companies overseas. The liberalization of overseas investment had progressively increased Indian joint ventures abroad. At the end of December 1991, there were only 245 joint ventures, out of which 161 joint ventures were in operation and 84 were at different stages of implementation.[68] As table-7 indicates, however, at the end of November 1995, there were 592 outward joint ventures, out of which 185 were in production/ operation and 407 were under stages of implementation. Thus, 58.6 per cent of 592 ventures had been completed between 1992-1995. It is clear that the liberal policy measures also made dramatic changes to the overseas investment.

Equity participation by Indian firms which were in operation was Rs. 221.86 crores as at end-November 1995 as against Rs. 120.92 crores at end-December 1991. The approved Indian participation in the equity of the joint ventures under implementation stood at Rs. 1,620 crores at the end of November 1995 against Rs. 454.67 crores at the end of December 1991. Of the 185 operating joint ventures, 56 per cent were in manufacturing and 44 per cent in non-manufacturing sectors.[69]

Region-wise, European countries (including Central Europe) accounted for a big chunk (27.7 per cent) of Indian joint ventures abroad at the end of November 1995. One of the major contributors to this was the emergence of East Europe as host countries. East Asia (including South East Asia) hosted 141 ventures with a 23.8 per cent share. Bulk of it, however, was in Malaysia, Singapore, Thailand, Indonesia and Hong Kong. India's neighbours in South Asia attracted 82 ventures with a 13.8 per cent of total investments. Indian joint ventures in this region had been mainly restricted to Nepal and Sri Lanka. Till the end of November 1995, there was no any single Indian joint venture in Pakistan. West accounted 13 per cent of Indian joint ventures followed by 58 joint ventures (9.8 per cent) in America region, 55 (9.3 per cent) in Africa and Oceania for 14 (2.3 per cent).

TABLE - 7

INDIAN JOINT VENTURES ABROAD AS ON NOVEMBER 1995

Regions	*In Operation*	*Under Implementation*	*Total*
East Asia	61	80	141
South Asia	26	56	82
Oceania	4	10	14
America	15	43	58
Europe	31	133	164
Africa	28	27	55
West Asia	20	58	78
All Countries	185	407	592

Source: Based on data compiled from Ministry of Commerce, Annual Report 1995-96, New Delhi.

According to the RBI Report on Currency and Finance 1991-92, the number of approved Wholly Owned Subsidiary (WOS) abroad, wholly owned by one or more Indian corporate bodies were 66 as at end-December 1991, of which 44 were in operation and the remaining 22 were under various stages of implementation. These figures increased greatly by the end of November 1995 with the grand total of 421 wholly owned subsidiaries of Indian companies, of which 81 were in operation and the 340 under various stages of implementation. Therefore, about 84 per cent of the WOS was approved between 1992 to the end of November 1995. The value of the total equity held in these subsidiaries merely amounted to Rs. 74.84 crores as at the end of December 1991. This shot up to Rs. 1,618.9 crores by the end of November 1995.[70] Hence, in the Indian joint ventures abroad case too, the policy of liberalization greatly promoted to integrate the Indian economy with the global economy.

As we have seen above, India's foreign trade and foreign investment had improved a lot during the Rao government. These successes, notwithstanding, there were also problems and challenges which limited the effectiveness of the liberalization. Now we turn to these issues.

PROBLEMS AND CHALLENGES

Economic liberalization faced several problems and challenges.These were related to poverty alleviation, agricultural reform, infrastructural development, administrative and institutional barriers, social sector developments amongst others. This part will, however, only deal with administrative and institutional barriers and social sector development, as the performance of an economy is dependent generally on supporting administrative and institutional reforms. Most of Indian and outside cooperations complained about the administrative and institutional barriers in India for availing the benefits of liberalization. And social sector developments such as education and health play a crucial role for growth in market economies. Thus, as one argued that "the main economic task of the government, under structural adjustment programme, is to promote 'human capital formation'. Universalisation of literacy, priority extension of technical education and access to safe drinking water and health facilities by all, are major areas of governmental activity".[71] The Narasimha Rao government neglected, however, this very task of the government, which was criticized by many.

The Administrative and Institutional Barriers to Liberalization

It is generally known that changes in economic policies are not enough for the success of reforms. A country also needs supportive administrative and institutional systems for these to succeed. It is commonly accepted that the administrative and institutional (including legal) systems constitute the backbone for speedy implementation of economic reforms in letter and spirit for maximising the productivity of these reforms. International experiences on the implementation of economic reforms conclusively show that efficient implementation greatly facilitates the successful completion of reforms (as has happened in the case of East Asian and southeast Asian countries). Thus, economic reforms will yield the desired results only when administrative and institutional norms also change and can be effectively enforced. In practice, this can be difficult as has been demonstrated in a wide swathe of reforming countries from India to Russia. In India the Rao government could achieve very little with regard to removing the administrative and institutional barriers. This part attempts to analyse how the administrative and institutional barriers in India created problems and challenges for successfull implementation of economic reforms.

Indian entrepreneurs and the Chambers of Industry and Commerce generally welcomed the post-1991 economic reforms especially the deregulatory aspects of these reforms. However, their common complaint frequently voiced in the media and their meetings with the government officials has been regarding the hurdles in accessing these reforms at the lower rungs of the bureaucracy at the Central, the State and the grass root levels. The Confederation of Indian Industry (CII) background paper clearly mentions that "much of the procedures and administrative hassles continue to remain at the Centre and State levels. The industry and even the general public continue to be faced with enormous red tape."[72] The former Minister of Commerce and External Affairs under the Prime Minister, P.V. Narasimha Rao, Pranab Mukherjee admitted in an interview that one of the challenges of the liberalization was the bureaucratic approach of the status quoism. He said that "in fact our delivery system could not satisfy the people because of the bureaucratic lethargies and status quoism."[73]

The situation was compounded by the fact that bureaucrats, like all other individuals, care most about the size of their departments and to maximise the size of their budgets. As bureaucrats accumulate monopoly control or political power, they tend to delay innovation and reallocation of resources needed for rapid growth.[74]

There was another concern from the multinational corporations about this problem. A survey of the investment perceptions of 16 leading multinational corporations, cited an array of difficulties in operating in India. The complex web of regulatory controls and bureaucratic interventions were of particular concern.[75] Despite the Central Government's efforts to nearly abolish licensing, as many as 18 agencies had to be approached by the industry for obtaining clearances under the Industrial Development and Regulation Act and had to face 51 inspectors for statutory inspection under as many statues relating to industrial laws. Due to the absence of single window clearance, it generally took more than one month to obtain clearances. In Singapore, the Government grants clearance in less than two weeks.[76]

While Bhagwati and Srinivasan recognized "the sweeping nature of the reforms to date", they also payed attention to "several problem areas where reforms are necessary to cement what happened so far". One of them is "state-level restrictions".[77] Delicensing had to be done at state levels as numerous restrictions continue at the states level. But it was hardly carried out. This again poses the question: since virtually any industrial plant must be physically located in a state, how can effective delicensing be achieved if state-level restrictions continue in place?

State governments and their bureaucracies were also not fully aware of the very fundamental changes which the Central Government was bringing about in the Indian economy and in the management of the Indian economic activities. This was manifested when a Korean business delegation visited the State Electricity Boards (SEBs) of Delhi, Maharashtra, Andhra Pradesh and West Bengal to explore investment opportunity in the power sector in 1995. There was confusion among the state officials on the liberalization policy of the power sector.[78] One official pointed out in an interview that "only the policy-makers know the economic liberalization policy. Rest of the people do not know about the policy. So, bureaucrats' reaction to the new economic policy are very very limited and individual".[79] According to J. N. Dixit, this was one of the major difficulties and a significant hurdle encountered while trying to project India's economic policies and programmes through India's foreign policy statements and through the operations of its missions.[80] He further stated that "more importantly, this state of affairs adversely affected the image of our efficiency and our credibility in the eyes of the world at large".[81] The New York Times reported that "a year after the new policies were announced by Prime Minister P.V. Narasimha Rao, far less has been accomplished than promised, bureaucratic red tape still hamstrings new investment, both foreign and domestic, and not a single one of India's huge, bankrupt state controlled industries has been shut".[82]

Due to bureaucratic hurdles, crores of rupees have been lost. According to a research by FICCI in 1988, a year's delay in clearing private sector projects taken up during the seventh plan (1985-90) cost over Rs. 17,160 crore in lost production. That's over Rs. 20 crore a day.[83] Worse, in some cases delay means death for projects. For example, Mr Suneel Sardana, a Dubai-based NRI, was one of the many NRIs who responded to the call of the government to invest in their motherland. After waiting for almost three years to get the requisite clearances for his project, he became disillusioned and was all set to shelve his Rs. 150 crores denim project in Gujarat, under the name of Densons Denim Ltd. He said in an interview that "now I have decided to sell off my project site. I have already spent Rs 20 crores on the project, which was scheduled to start production in January 1993, but due to bureaucratic hurdles the project is yet to take off."[84]

Lack of co-ordination at the administrative level between the government at the levels of Centre and the States in many way continued to haunt the process of implementation of the economic reforms during the first half of the 1990s. This led to several anomalies in the design of various measures constituting economic reforms. One study reveals that the coordination between the Centre and the State governments in the implementation of the economic reforms was nearly non-existent.[85] The State governments were mostly bypassed in active communication and their involvement in the design and implementation of the economic reforms especially on the issues concerning Centre-State coordination.

Success in sustaining and consolidating reform requires building bases of support. In the absence of such bases of support, reforms become politically isolated and programmes become vulnerable to reversal. Bhagwati and Srinivasan recommended in their report submitted to the Ministry of Finance in 1993 that the Government continually needs to explain to the public about the rationale and importance of the reforms at every opportunity by the political leadership, and remove the misunderstandings of the reforms from the public. They warned that "if this is not done, the reforms are likely to lose support as misunderstanding multiply and acquire cogency simply because no coherent rationale and defence of the reforms is available".[86] This was not done, specially to the vast majority of the poor.

According to James Manor, the lack of any concerted effort to cultivate support was not due to absent-mindness on the part of the Prime Minister, P.V. Narasimha Rao.[87] India's economic liberalization, as we have seen in Chapter-II, received the support of the three dominant proprietary classes' - the industrial bourgeoisie, the rich farmers and the professionals.[88] The reformers' solicitous attitude towards these groups is not surprising. It helps to explain why the liberalization was moved ahead without many challenges till the Congress Party lost in the State elections of December 1994.

In addition to this, there was a problem regarding the size of the government. One study pointed out that the civilian staff of the Central government including departmental undertakings numbers around 4 million and of this 1 million were added during the

1980's. It is also to be noted that between 1984-91, the number of posts of Secretary to the Government of India increased from 61 to 131 and those of additional and joint secretaries from 258 to 758.[89] Although no comparative figures are available at State level, states are unlikely to have lagged behind in this respect. In this overstaffed bureaucracy, productivity and efficiency aspects have never been effectively pursued as worthy objectives for attainment by the governmental functionaries; a concept of work culture has been lacking, and no efforts ever made to enforce accountability. Thus, it is held that "there is a slow, and at times grudging, acceptance within the bureaucracy that the Indian State has overextended itself in the economy, far beyond the limits of its administrative capacity".[90]

A general absence of work ethos has got further compounded by scant attention being paid to office timings, punctuality, and by a surfeit of holidays and leave concessions. If one takes the problem of holidays, he/ she will be surprised by that taking into account the gazetted and other types of closed days observed in the government offices, a government servant normally enjoys 166 holidays (other than the sick leave of 30 days which he is entitled to).[91] This means that the government servants work at most for only about half the days in a year. Besides this, most employees are callous about duty timings. During office hours too, the work performance comprises more of multiplying paper work than effecting real disposal of cases. There is inherent lethargy prompted largely by an attitude of avoidance of responsibility.

Social Sectors

In the 1980s, a large number of countries in Latin America and sub-Saharan Africa initiated stabilisation-cum-structural adjustment programmes with the active support of the international financial institutions. There is a large body of literature that reveals the consequences of these programmes on the economies and peoples of developing countries, and proves that they could often lead to a deterioration in social sector development, particularly in the short run, unless specific measures are taken to avoid such an occurrence.[92] International experience with these programmes shows that the vulnerable sections of the societies,[93] who lack the savings to pay for their health, education and other services, suffer in the process of the economic reforms. The negative impact of these measures on social sectors, especially on education and health of the people, of these countries have led to a call for 'adjustment with a human face'.[94] Adjustment with a human face calls for required adjustment to be implemented with the minimum harm to the most vulnerable groups. It was one of the major challenges faced by these governments in implementing stabilisation and structural adjustment programmes.

Since mid-1991 India has also launched economic liberalization helped by the IMF and the World Bank. The Government of India under Narasimha Rao's leadership had been repeatedly assuring the nation that adjustment in India would be with a 'human face'. Moreover, during the liberalization under the Rao government, there had been much talk about the importance of human development and the need to give it a high priority. Many official pronouncements in this direction had been made and many new schemes had been launched. For example, the Eighth Plan (1992-97) gave a high priority to human development. It stated that "human development will be the ultimate goal of the Eighth Plan. It is towards this that employment generation, population control, literacy, education, health, drinking water and basic infrastructure are listed as the priorities. The provision of the basic elements, which help development of human capital remain the primary responsibility of the Government of India."[95]

Even though for the first time in the history of planning in India, human development had been made ' the ultimate goal', it was ironical that the share of these very sectors in the total plan outlay had suffered a decline. It is commonly known that expenditure reduction, which is a part of an orthodox stabilisation package, usually results in reduced spending on education, health, social welfare programmes that directly benefit low-income groups in the economy. It was not an exceptional case in this regard. For instance, allocations to education and health in 1992-93 and 1993-94 had been lower than the plan target.[96]

It has been observed that the estimates for 1991-92 and 1992-93 show a decline in the health and education expenditures compared to the earlier period. Between 1990 and 1992, education expenditures by all the states taken together fell from Rs. 7,161.35 crores to Rs. 6,886.5 crores, a decline of 4 per cent. Similarly, health expenditures decreased from Rs. 3,055.53 crores to Rs. 2,918.87 crores (a decline of 4 per cent). Per capita expenditures on health and education by the individual states also declined between 1990 and 1992. Health expenditures per capita declined by 7.4 per cent (from Rs. 36.88 in 1990 to Rs. 33.93 in 1992) while education expenditure declined by 8 per cent (from Rs 84.52 in 1990 to Rs. 80.05 in 1992).[97]

Public expenditure on social sectors such as education and health in India is undertaken largely by the states. In 1992-93, for example, the Centre accounted for 11 per cent of total expenditure respectively on education and health.[98] Hence the respective state governments' financial position and their commitment to these sectors' development were very important in pursuing the economic reform with a human face.

S.P. Gupta and A.K. Sarkar examine expenditures under the broad head of "human resource development" for all states combined. They show that the share of this expenditure going to "education, sport, art and culture" has declined on both capital and revenue accounts in the early 1990s.

For India as a whole, the per capita expenditure for the enrolled population increased from Rs 398 in 1986-87 to Rs. 798 in 1993-94 with an annual growth of 9.9 per cent during the period.[99] A closer look, however, reveals that there is no change in real terms because, as Srinivasan and Shariff point out, "the expenditure figures are at nominal, or current prices any growth rate below 10 per cent which has been the approximate average rate to inflation".[100] Thus, Jean Dreze and Amartya Sen write that since the stabilization-cum-structural adjustment programme in mid-1991, "education expenditure has declined in real terms in many states".[101]

TABLE-8

PERCENTAGE SHARE OF HUMAN RESOURCE DEVELOPMENT EXPENDITURE ALLOCATED TO EDUCATION, SPORT, ART AND CULTURE, ALL STATES 1989-90 TO 1992-93

	Plan Expenditure		*Non-Plan Expenditure*		*Total*
	Revenue Account	*Capital Account*	*Revenue Account*	*Capital Account*	
1989-90	14	2.2	24.6	0.10	1.6
1990-91	9	2.1	24.7	0.03	1.5
1991-92	10	1.9	22.9	0.08	1.4
1992-93	11.9	2.0	22.4	0.07	1.5

Source: S.P. Gupta and A.K. Sarkar, 'Fiscal Correction and Human Resource Development: Expenditure at Central and State Levels', EPW, March 26, 1994, Table 5.

Expenditure on education remained grossly inadequate and was also very low (both in absolute terms and as a proportion of GDP) as compared to other developed and developing countries. Data in the Human Development Report 1994 shows that India ranked 82nd out of 116 countries in terms of the proportion of public expenditure on education to GDP. And, in terms of the share of education in public expenditure, India ranked 68th out of 89 countries.[102]

There was also a decline in absolute number of teachers in elementary schools between 1991-92 and 1992-93, when nearly 14,000 female teaching jobs alone were lost.[103] A study reveals that for India as a whole the Teacher-Student Ratio (TSR) increased from 38 in 1981-82 to 48 in 1994-95. This negative growth in TSRs in some years would mean that "new teachers were not appointed".[104] The condition of education has been generally pathetic in the already backward states like Uttar Pradesh which also has a high incidence of poverty.

In rural Uttar Pradesh, Dreze and Gazdar found that while most of the sample schools had dilapidated buildings, not a single school made full use of their building. In fact, they note, "the most commonly-used part of the building was the veranda, where children of all grades were huddled together".[105] Dreze and Gazdar's study describes the problem of chronic teacher absenteeism in Uttar Pradesh. They found in their sample of schools that the teachers were present only 30 per cent of the time they were required to. In several instances they found that the school had been closed without prior notice " because the teacher(s) had decided to engage in some other activity".[106]

In the field of health care, too, there was little sign of any determination to address the limitations of liberalization policy. Health care facilities in many parts of rural India had been extensively diverted to forceful programmes of family planning (mainly based on female sterilization), compounding the problem of persistently high levels of morbidity and mortality. Similarly, a recent survey of family health in India reveals that 30 per cent of all children aged 12-23 months had never received any vaccination, that only half of all pregnant women go through some kind of antenatal check-up, and that only a tiny minority of married women had convenient access to non-terminal methods of modern contraception (with much worse figures in rural areas, among disadvantaged social groups, and in states where health policy had been particularly neglected).[107] These failures in a crucially important field of government action received very little attention in current debates. Even J. Bhagwati and T.N. Srinivasan's report, which was submitted to the Ministry of Finance, is silent on the matter, while they discuss the challenge of the economic reforms.[108]

The central expenditure (plan and non-plan) on health had been raised from Rs 844 crore in 1993-94 (revised estimate) to Rs. 915 crore in 1994-95, an increase of just about 8.4 per cent and the budget allocation for family planning has been raised from Rs. 1,285 crore to Rs 1,442 crore (or by 12.3 per cent). This means that in real terms resources available for health in the budget remained the same as the previous year, health accounted for a minuscule 0.58 per cent of the budget.[109]

There had been some efforts by the Rao government to improve human development indications. The National Programme of Nutritional Support to Primary Education (Mid-Day Meal Programme) launched from 15th August 1995, intended to give a boost to universalization of education, increasing enrolment, retention and attendance simultaneously, and improving on nutrition of students in primary classes (I-IV). It must be noted, however, that this programme was launched first prior to the Lok Sabha elections was ahead. In Andhra Pradesh, the subsidised rice scheme was also carried out by N.T. Rama Rao's Telugu Desam Party with elections round the corner.

In this connection, it is interesting to note that most of the initiatives observed in the more active states had been taken in the context of electoral politics. They were even at the forefront of electoral debates. In the large North Indian States, by contrast, social security and related issues had found little place in party programmes and electoral debates; their electoral policies seemed to give more room to tactical factionalism, with alliances being made and broken depending on personalities and power bases, and little time being "wasted" on real issues such as undernutrition, illiteracy, or ill health. Politicians did not bother since education and health did not bring them votes.

If one looks at the United Nations' study, this appears as a serious problem for India's economic development. According to the study, an increased calorie intake can lead to gains in labour productivity of up to 47 per cent—for farmers in Sierra Leone, sugar cane workers in Guatemala and road construction workers in Kenya. Most of the studies show that when workers get more calories or macronutrients, such as vitamins or minerals, their productivity improves almost immediately.[110] There are also many examples about education vis-a-vis economic growth. Research suggests that increasing the labour force's average education by one year raises GDP by 9 per cent. But this holds only for the first three years of extra education. After that, the returns to each additional year diminish to around 4 per cent of GDP. This spotlights a major opportunity. Countries with low initial schooling stand to gain enormously by investing in primary education.[111]

These empirical studies indicate that a healthier and better educated population is capable of being economically more productive. It suggests that massive investment in human development, particularly education and health, can enhance countries' abilities for the sustainable growth. This need has become even more compelling as the global economy becomes more integrated and countries face stiff competition in the global market. Thus, it is considered, as S.P. Gupta argues,[112] that the process of economic liberalization could be more easy and quick if it was supported by high human development activity in India. But this does not mean that the only purpose of investments in health and education is to improve productivity -or that one should not make investments that do not improve productivity. Kerala's poor growth performance is a good example for this, despite high educational and social achievements.

Since the bulk of expenditure on social sectors is incurred by the state governments, there was a limitation for the Central Government to promote education levels and health care. Furthermore, during the stabilisation and structural adjustment programmes, spending on education and health programmes had been reduced in real terms.[113] Therefore, the Central Government could not ensure that the ongoing reforms did not lead to any adverse effect on vulnerable sections, who are generally illiterate and in poor health. This was, as the former Finance Minister Manmohan Singh admitted in the interview, one of the greatest challenges and problems for the government which was carrying on economic liberalization.[114]

To sum up the foregoing discussion on internal and external economic liberalization, and problems and challenges besetting the task in the form of institutional rigidities and the lagging performance of the social sector, one may conclude their the reform measures during the period of 1991-1995 largely avoided the more difficult task of restructuring PSUs. There was no effective privatisation of any PSUs. On the other hand, the external sectors such as foreign trade and foreign investment policies were liberalized greatly by Indian standards. The removal of several licensing categories, decanalising several import and export products, etc., and several measures to promote foreign direct investment could form a helpful part of economic liberalization and lead to a more widely shared growth. However, it achieved relatively little in the absence of more active public policy aimed at removing the administrative and institutional barriers, and the other social problems that shackle the Indian economy reducing the wellbeing of the population. The absence of real reform in the field of basic education and health care were a telling illustration of the negative aspects of economic liberalization, which was supported by the international economic institutions.

REFERENCES

1. Government of India, Ministry of Finance, *Economic Survey 1992-93,* (New Delhi: Government of India Press, 1993), Table-6.16, p. 146.
2. Jagdish Bhagwati, *India in Transition: Freeing The Economy,* (Delhi: OUP, 1995).
3. Bimal Jalan, *India's Economic Policy: Preparing for the Twenty-First Century,* (New Delhi: Viking, 1996), p. 20.
4. *Ibid,* p. 21.
5. Isher Judge Ahluwalia, "New Economic Policies, Enterprises, and Privatization in India" in Robert Cassen and Vijay Joshi (eds.), *India: The Future of Economic Reform,* (New Delhi: OUP, 1995), p. 242.
6. Bimal Jalan, *op. cit.,* p. 22.
7. Government of India, *Eighth Five Year Plan Year: 1992-97,* Vol II (New Delhi: Planning Commission, 1992), p. 107. In 1994-95 the gross electricity subsidy of all states for the agricultural sector alone exceeded Rs. 100 billion. See Pranab Bardhan, *The Political Economy of Development in India,* Expanded Edition with an Epilogue on the Political Economy of Reform in India, (New Delhi: OUP, 1998), pp. 129-30.
8. *Ibid.,* p. 129.
9. Biaml Jalan, *op. cit.,* p. 24
10. I.J. Ahluwalia, *op. cit.,* p. 240.
11. *Eighth Five Year Plan 1992-1997,* Vol. II. *op. cit.,* p.108.
12. I. J. Ahluwalia, *op. cit.,* p. 242.
13. World Bank, *Bureaucrats in Business,* Washington, D.C., 1995.
14. Amit Bhaduri and Deepak Nayyar, *The Intelligent Person's Guide to Liberalization,* (New Delhi: Penguin Books, 1996), p. 41.
15. I.J. Ahluwalia, *op. cit.,* p. 252.

16. Ibid., p. 255, and Anand P. Gupta, "Political Economy of Privatisation in India", *EPW*, Vol. XXXI, September 28, 1996, p. 2691.
17. *Economic Survey 1995-96, op. cit.*, p. 120.
18. Anand P. Gupta, *op. cit.*, p. 2689.
19. *Times of India*, August 7, 1993.
20. I.J. Ahluwalia, *op. cit.*, p. 254. In fact, according to one of World Bank studies, public enterprise reform turns out to be the most difficult of all reforms incorporated in structural adjustment. See Development Committee, 47th Meeting, (Washington D.C.: World Bank, 1993).
21. Privatisation means the transfer of ownership and control of an existing public enterprise, activity or service to the private sector. (Privatisation may be full or partial. It may be selective, i.e., some functions are transferred to the private sector, while others are retained in the public sector.) V.V. Bhanoji Rao, *India's Economic Future: Government, People and Attitudes*, (New Delhi: Tata MacGraw-Hill, 1993), p. 106.
22. *Times of India*, August 22, 1995.
23. Bimal Jalan, *op. cit.*, p. 33.
24. Mukul, "Uttar Pradesh: Workers Challenge Privatisation", *EPW*, Vol. XXVI, January 4-11, 1992, p. 25.
25. Bimal Jalan, *op. cit.*, p. 95.
26. Bora Dalip Kumar S., *India's Foreign Trade With the European Economic Community*, (Almora: Shri Almora Book Depot, 1994), p. 9.
27. Benjamin J. Cohen, ed., *American Foreign Economic Policy: Essays and Comments*, (New York: Harper and Row, 1968), p. 20.
28. According to *Economic Survey for 1992-93*, the LERMS "has been introduced as a transitional arrangement towards a unified exchange rate with current account convertibility. Meanwhile, it has simplified the trade policy regime by eliminating detailed exchange control". *Economic Survey 1992-93, op. cit.*, p. 103.
29. Jagdish Bhagwati, *op. cit.*, p. 88.
30. *Economic Developments in India: Achievements and Challenges*, (Washington, D.C., World Bank, 1995), p. 31.
31. See B. Goldar, A. V. L. Narayana and H. N. Saleem, "Structure of Nominal Tariff Rates in India, Studies in Industrial Development", Ministry of Industry, Government of India, July 1992.
32. See M. A. Aksoy and F. M. Ettori, "Protection and Industrial Structure in India", Policy Research Working Paper, No. 990, World Bank, October 1992.

33. Government of India, Ministry of Finance, *Interim Report of the Tax Reforms Committee*, December 1991.
34. For a quick review of the major features and critical appreciation of the Final Report (Part II) on customs duties, see Vijay Joshi and I.M.D. Little, *India's Economic Reforms 1991-2001*, (New Delhi: OUP, 1996), pp. 66-77.
35. In the case of Dimethyl Trephthlate (DMT), the Committee says that "the degree of protection has increased by 48 per cent in 1992-93 as compared to 1986-87, if only the depreciation in the external value of the rupee and the change in the import duty rate are taken account. Thus although the duty has been reduced from 190 per cent to 110 per cent, it is as though the duty is now 330.5 per cent with unchanged exchange rate. Hence even a duty reduction by 50 percentage points would still leave the commodity well "protected", since the international price of the commodity has not fallen in relation to the price level in 1986-87." See Government of India, *Tax Reforms Committee - Final Report Part II*, 1993, p. 4.
36. I. J. Ahluwalia, "India's Opening up to Trade and Investment" in I. J. Ahluwalia *et al.*, *Policy Reform in India*, (Paris: Development Centre Seminars, OECD, 1996).
37. M.L. Varma, *International Trade*, (New Delhi: Vikas Publishing House, 1995), p. 120.
38. Charan D. Wadhva, *Economic Reforms in India and the Market Economy*, (New Delhi: Allied Publishers, 1994), p. 68.
39. According to one study, The virtual ban on the import of consumer goods was a major policy defect. Yet there were strong fiscal and monetary reasons why imports of consumption goods should had been allowed in the past three years. See, Vijay Joshi and I.M.D. Little, *op. cit.*, p. 67.
40. *Economic Developments In India: Achievements and Challenges*, *op. cit.*, p. 31.
41. Bimal Jalan, *op. cit.*, p. 96.
42. *Ibid.* The former Finance Minister, Manmohan Singh argued, in his D. Phil. thesis at Oxford under Ian Little in 1961, that India's export pessimism was unjustified. See Singh M., India Export Trends, (London: OUP, 1964).
43. Rajesh Mehta, "Trade Policy Reforms, 1991-92 to 1995-96: Their Impact on External Trade", *EPW*, Vol. XXXII, No. 15, April 12-18, 1997, p. 782.
44. Government of India, *Report on Currency and Finance 1995-96*,

(Bombay: Reserve Bank of India, 1996), p. ix-4.

45. *Report on Currency and Finance 1994-95 and 1995-96, op. cit.*
46. *Report on Currency and Finance 1995-96, op. cit.*, pp. ix2 -ix3.
47. Pankaj Ghemawat and Murali Patibandla, "India's exports since the reforms", *EPW*, Vol. XXXIII, May 16-22, 1998.
48. *Ibid.*
49. *Report on Currency and Finance 1995-96, op. cit.*
50. Ryutaro Komiya, *The Japanese Economy Trade, Industry and Government*, (Tokyo: University of Tokyo Press, 1990).
51. Harry G. Johnson, *On Economics and Society*, (Chicago: University of Chicago Press, 1972).
52. Government of India, Ministry of Industry, Office of Economic Adviser, *Handbook of Industrial Policy and Statistics 1996*, New Delhi, 1996, p. 11.
53. *Ibid*, p. 12.
54. Manoj Pant, *Foreign Direct Investment In India: The Issues Involved*, (New Delhi: Lancers Books, 1995).
55. The Indian corporate sector has also been encouraged to access global capital markets through Global Depository Receipts (GDRs) mechanism as described below:
    (a) Foreign investors can invest in Indian companies through the GDR route without any lock-in period.
    (b) These receipts can be listed in any of the overseas stock exchanges and denominated in any convertible foreign currency. However, the underlying shares would be denominated in Indian rupees.
    (c) Private placement with US investors is also permissible in accordance with the US Securities Act.
    (d) Short-term capital gains are taxable at the rate of 65 per cent along with business income. Long-term capital gains (computed on holdings for more than 12 months) are taxable at the rate of 10 per cent.

    See Vijaya Katti, "India's Economic Reforms: An Assessment of the Impact on Industry and FDI", Foreign Trade Review, Vol. XXVIII No.1, April-June 1993, p. 81.
56. Kirit S. Parikh, *India Development Report*, 1997, (New Delhi: OUP, 1997), p. 134.
57. Nagesh Kumar, "Industrialisation, Liberalisation and Two Way Flows of Foreign Direct Investments: Case of India", *EPW*, Vol. XXX No. 50, December 16, 1995.
58. See *Times of India*, New Delhi, January 21, 1997.

59. Unpublished Article,"Foreign Direct Investment and Technology Transfer into India", Policy Planning Division, Ministry of External Affairs, Government of India, 1997.
60. See Nagesh Kumar, "Liberalization and Changing patterns of Foreign Direct Investments: Has India's Relative Attractiveness as a Host of FDI Improved?", EPW, Vol. XXXIII, No. 22, May 30, 1998.
61. According to an International Management Institute study, FDI into China during the period 1979-95 totalled $ 98.12 billion, but the flows really picked up from 1991, with the annual inflows touching $ 33.9 billion in 1994. Nearly 79 per cent of FDI came from overseas Chinese, with those in Hong Kong and Macao accounting for 61 per cent and those in Taiwan, Japan and South Korea sharing the remaining 18 per cent. The overseas Chinese settled in Hong Kong and Macao are businessmen while 15 to 18 million NRIs are mainly manual workers and professionals. Times of India, *op. cit.*
62. *Times of India*, December 10, 1994.
63. *Times of India*, April 28, 1995.
64. *Times of India*, April 25, 1995.
65. *Business India*, August 28 to September 10, 1995.
66. *Business India, op. cit.*
67. *Ibid.*
68. *Report on Currency and Finance 1991-92*, Vol. I: *Economic Review, op. cit.*, p. 391.
69. *Report on Currency and Finance 1995-96, op. cit.*, p. X-9.
70. *Ibid.*
71. Biplab Dasgupta, "SAP: Issues and Conditionalities; A Global Review", *EPW*, May 17-24, 1997, p. 1097.
72. Confederation of Indian Industry, Background Paper for the National Seminar on Administrative Reforms held in January 1993.
73. Interview with the former Minister of Commerce and External Affairs, Pranab Mukherjee, January 24, 1997.
74. M.M. Buchanan, R. Tollison and G. Tullock (Eds.) *Toward a Theory of the Rent-Seeking Society*, (College Station: Texas A and M University Press, 1980).
75. The lack of adequate infrastructure, particularly power, telecommunications and transportation, is also regarded as a major constraint. *World Bank, World Development Report 1994*, (Washington D.C.: OUP, 1994).
76. Confederation of Indian Industry, *op, cit.*

77. Jagdish Bhagwati and T.N. Srinivasan, *India's Economic Reforms,* (New Delhi: the Government of India, Ministry of Finance, 1993), p. (iii).
78. This researcher accompanied the delegation of Sunkyong Group from October 30 to November 7, 1995.
79. Interview with the then Director of Information and Publicity, Ministry of Railways, Mr Jatin Sarkar, Febuary 21, 1997.
80. J.N. Dixit, *My South Block Years: Memoirs of A Foreign Secretary,* (New Delhi: UBSPD, 1996), p. 392.
81. *Ibid.*
82. *The New York Times,* August 15, 1992.
83. Quoted in *India Today,* August 15, 1991, p. 31.
84. *Times of India,* September 6, 1995.
85. Charan D. Wadhva, *op. cit.,* p. 115.
86. Jagdish Bhagwati and T N Srinivasan, *op. cit.* p. 10.
87. The former Minister of Commerce under P.V. Narasimha Rao, P. Chidambaram said that he complained to the Prime Minister and Finance Minister that they do not sell the economic policy and advantages to the people. On the BBC interview, August 8, 1997. For the detail of the Prime Minister's political management of the reform, see James Manor, "The Political Sustainability of Economic Liberalization in India" in Robert Cassen and Vijay Joshi (eds), *op. cit.*
88. Pranab Bardhan, *The Political Economy of Development in India,* (New Delhi: OUP, 1985).
89. Sharad Marathe, "Issues in Fiscal Policy", second of series of three lectures delivered as CD Deshmukh Lecture at the National Insurance Academy, Pune on August 2, 1993.
90. Pranab Bardhan (1998), *op. cit.,* p. 131.
91. H. D. Shourie, "Our Government Offices Lack Work Ethos", *Times of India,* December 31, 1998.
92. G. Cornia, R. Jolly and F Stewart (eds), *Adjustment with a Human Face,* Vol.1 (New York: OUP, 1987), L. Taylor, *Varieties of Stabilisation Experience* (Oxford: Clarendon Press, 1988), Commonwealth Secretariat, *Engendering Adjustment for the 1990s,* Report of a Commonwealth Expert Group on Women and Structural Adjustment, 1989, M. Chossudovsky, 'Globalisation of Poverty', *Frontline,* March 13, 1992, and N. Chomsky, Year 501: *The Conquest Continues* (Boston: South End Press, 1993).
93. "Vulnerability in such usage implies a limited capacity to sustain and protect oneself. Translated into more direct expression, it

would mean an economic condition arising out of poor access to means of production. Members of the so-called vulnerable sections of society do not have independent and reliable access to means, such as land or tools, necessary to generate a livelihood. All they have is the capacity to labour. For the opportunity to exercise this capacity they depend on people who own the means of production." Krishna Kumar, "Market Economy and Mass Literacy: Revisiting Innis's Economics of Communication", *EPW*, Vol. XXVIII, No. 50, December 11, 1993, pp. 2729-30.

94. Economists such as Cornia, Jolly and Stewart began to pressurise the international financial institutions to evolve structural adjustment with a human face, a concept which emerged in 1985-86 and gained acceptance in 1986-87. These scholars argued that adjustment is a long-term process, the benefits reach the poor only after a long time and hence social or redistributive policies must be adopted to reduce the interim social cost. They listed out the main element of such a strategy that must be undertaken by the governments once there is an explicit acceptance of the objective of structural adjustment with a human face. G. Cornia, R. Jolly and F Stewart (eds), *Adjustment with a Human Face: Protecting the Vulnerable and Promoting Growth*, Vol, I, (Oxford: OUP, 1987).
95. *Eighth Five-Year Plan 1992-97*, Vol. I, *op. cit.*, p. 16
96. See K. Seeta Prabhu, "The Budget and 'Structural Adjustment with a Human Face'", EPW, Vol. XXIX Nos. 16 and 17, April 16-23, Table-1, p. 1017.
97. Jyotsna Jalan and K. Subbarao, "Adjustment and Social Sectors in India" in Robert Cassen and Vijay Joshi (eds.), *op. cit.*, p. 321.
98. V.K. Ramachandran, V. Rawal and M. Swaminathan, "Investment Gaps in Primary Education: A Statewise Study, *EPW*, Vol. XXXII, January 4-11, 1997, p. 40.
99. K. Srinivasan and Abusaleh Shariff, *India: Towards Population and Development Goals*, (Delhi: OUP, 1997), p. 87.
100. *Ibid.*
101. Jean Dreze and Amartya Sen, *India: Economic Development And Social Opportunity*, (Delhi: OUP, 1995), p. 123.
102. The United Nations Development Programme, *Human Development Report 1994*, (New York: OUP, 1994).
103. P.N. Tyagi, *Education for All: A Graphic Presentation*, first edition, (New Delhi: National Institute of Educational Planning and Administration, 1993), p. 82.

104. K. Srinivasan and Abusaleh Shariff, *op. cit.*, p. 86.
105. Dreze and Gazdar, "Uttar Pradesh: The Burden of India" in Jean Dreze and Amartya Sen (eds.), *Indian Development: Selected Regional Perspectives*, (Delhi: OUP, 1996), p. 66.
106. *Ibid.*, p. 67.
107. These figures are derived from the National Family Health Survey, as reported in International Institute for Population Science, 1994.
108. J. Bhagwati and T.N. Srinivasan, *op. cit.*
109. Padma Prakash, "Changing Priorities in Health Care", *EPW*, Vol. XXIX, March 19, 1994, p. 661.
110. The United Nations Development Programme, *Human Development Report 1996*, (New York: OUP, 1996), p. 76.
111. *Ibid.*
112. S.P. Gupta, "Welcome Address", in S.P. Gupta, et al., *Trade Policy Reforms*, (New Delhi: Macmillan, 1994), p. 231.
113. In many developing countries' cases, which took various stabilisation and structural adjustment programmes, social expenditure on education and health is also curtailed. See Paul Mosley, James Harrigan and Jone Toye, *Aid and Power- the World Bank and Policy-based Lending*, Volumes 1 and 2, (London: Routledge, 1991).
114. Interview with Manmohan Singh, March 6, 1997.

Four

India and the International Economic Institutions

India's foreign economic policy during the first half of the 1990s faced some major challenges from the international economic institutions. These were manifested both in the Uruguay Round of negotiations of the General Agreement on Tariffs and Trade (GATT) and in the negotiations of financial support from the International Monetary Fund (IMF or the Fund) and structural adjustment loans with the World Bank[1] (or simply the Bank). The nature of India's relations with international economic institutions underwent significant changes during the first half of the 1990s. The international economic institutions have had a significant impact on the nature and direction of India's economic and foreign policy agenda. They have also significantly affected the functioning of contemporary international political economy. In this regard, this chapter will discuss the relationship between India and the three major international economic organizations: the IMF, the World Bank and the GATT which was replaced by the World Trade Organization (WTO).

The Final Act of the Uruguay Round of Multilateral Trade Negotiations in December 1993 had far-reaching implications for the development of India at a time when India's own economic liberalization was carried forth in the direction of an open and deregulated economy, and integration of its economy with the global economy. It is not possible to analyse all the complex issues of the Final Text of the GATT and the WTO agenda in this study. Though there are many other major areas of concern for India such as the agreement on textiles and clothing, balance of payments provisions of the GATT 1994, trade and environment, trade and labour standards or the 'social clause', and competition policy, this chapter will mainly highlight four core areas, namely, the Intellectual Property Rights, Agriculture, Investments and Services in order to assess the consequences for India, in terms of her national interests. It will also discuss the implications of the establishment of the World Trade Organization for India's economic interests. How were India's interests involved in the four major issues of the Uruguay Round? What were India's reactions to the WTO regulations? This part will also discuss how India negotiated in the GATT negotiation meetings to maximise its national interests.

Generally reforms have been supported by various forms of structural adjustment lending from the IMF and the World Bank. The Government of India received financial support from mainly the Fund and the Bank, when the country faced severe economic crisis and had to initiate the economic reforms under the Congress government headed by P.V. Narasimha Rao. These reforms had involved a set of conditionalities which had been mutually agreed upon between the Government of India and the international financial institutions, primarily the IMF. In this regard, it explores the relationship between the international finance support and the nature of the economic liberalization within a political economy framework. While discussing this issue, the focus will be on how the provision of conditional resources affected the political economy of reform in India. It also tries to see how far India's economic liberalization programme followed the typical IMF - World Bank stabilisation-cum-structural adjustment package.

INDIA AND GATT/WTO

The compulsions of India's position and its ultimate inability to resist the developed countries on the new issues of the Uruguay Round negotiations were varied. Different views have been submitted by experts on the issue. These are studied at some length in order to explore the causes and consequences of India's position in the negotiations. The impact on India's foreign economic policy was vital.

Political Economy of India's Negotiations in the GATT

In order to liberalise global trade and to strengthen the multilateral trading system through the removal or reduction of tariff and non-tariff barriers, multilateral trade negotiations (or trade round) were periodically initiated to improve the framework of the GATT rules and disciplines on identified issues. Eight multilateral trade negotiations were conducted under the aegis of the GATT. However, of all rounds, the eighth round (Uruguay Round) was the most contentious.

Traditionally, the GATT was concerned with trade in goods which were mainly primary manufactured products. But the eighth round had a much wider scope as it established separate rules and regimes in the five new areas, namely, agriculture, textiles and clothing, investment, intellectual property rights and services. The jurisdiction of the new WTO would, therefore, impinge on domestic policies, legal and regulatory framework in a wide area. These fundamental changes brought about by the Uruguay Round were particularly relevant for developing countries like India with large or lucrative and growing domestic markets because a central objective of the developed countries in the Uruguay Round negotiations was that such markets should be opened up for their goods, services, investment and technology. The opening up of the big emerging markets was and continues to be a matter of high priority to them.

It is generally believed that if a country has a weak position in her economy, it has very little options to bargain for its interests in any negotiations with various international economic institutions. In this regard, we will see how India had pursued its negotiations in the GATT for its interests in the light of the economic crisis and subsequent economic liberalization.

Initially a group of ten developing countries led by India and Brazil and consisting of eight other developing countries namely, Egypt, Yugoslavia, Argentina, Cuba, Nigeria, Tanzania, Peru and Nicaragua resisted the developed countries at Punta del Este meetings held in 1989 on the new issues such as services, trade-related investment measures (TRIMS), and trade-related intellectual property rights (TRIPS). Indeed, the compromise reached at Punta del Este gave major concessions to the developing countries' demands. In the words of S.P. Shukla, the former Finance Secretary of Government of India who was a negotiator from India's side at the Uruguay Round, "the new issues did enter the" agenda but in a manner which limited the potential damage to the sovereign economic space of the Third World. The intellectual property matters and investment regimes could be brought in only tangentially, more in the nature of elaborating the disciplines already prevailing in GATT. The issue of common enforcement mechanism through cross-retaliation was kept at bay. The textile trade was brought in with a view to its ultimate integration into GATT and the industrialised countries agreed to take on the standstill and rollback commitments".[2]

As Mr Shukla himself goes on to point out, the success achieved by the group of ten in the Punta ultimately turned out to be short-lived, as one after other of its members began to withdraw from any future strategy of resistance. There was a report in India which had been used by the government of India to reassess its position for the 1989 meeting of the GATT.[3] It stated that the early months of 1989 presented a "golden chance to possibly rearrange the internal priorities of India with reference to both 'substance' as well as 'negotiating tactics'." However, India could not use the crucial time to safeguard its own interests as well as the interests of the Third World because of various international and domestic reasons.

By 1989, there was a decline of counter-hegemony efforts (diminishing coalitions of developing countries) by the Third World against the West India and Brazil too dropped their resistance. Many developing countries needed aid and support from developed countries for managing their debt-ridden economies. Also many developing countries had already gone in for loans from the IMF and the World Bank. There were also genuine differences of opinion arising from their respective economic interests. Further, the unity of the countries of the Third World broke because of bilateral pressures especially from the US under the Super and Special 301, which it continued to use all along. Besides this, the failure of the socialist system in Eastern Europe and in the Soviet Union further made frail the bargaining position of developing countries to restructure international economic relations. All these aspects weakened the developing countries' negotiating position.[4] This decline of the Third World opposition gave the US and other developed nations leverage to persuade developing countries regarding the importance of the new issues in the GATT.[5]

Though it is not clear what led to the shift in the Indian negotiating position in April 1989, one possible reason for the change was that the Government of India felt isolated in the negotiations.[6] Here a question arises as to how this isolation came about. According to Muchkund Dubey, who was directly or indirectly involved throughout the period of negotiations in the Uruguay Round, this isolation was "a part of a conscious policy" of the Government of India.[7] The Indian delegation received a word from the political level from the time of the mid-term review session of the Trade Negotiation Committee in Montreal in December 1988: "Do not appear to be ganging up against the Americans".[8] Dubey explained this in operational terms, "it meant that India should not try to be on the vanguard of the struggle of the developing countries and should leave the leadership role to some other developing country or countries".[9] As a result, at Montreal, the Indian delegation did not attempt to consolidate the developing countries' positions on various issues.

Besides the isolation factor, Manmohan Agarwal underlined other possible reasons for the change in India's negotiating position in 1989. One of the these is that the change reflected a belief that economic concessions were necessary for political support in the fight against terrorism. Another possible reason given was that India's negotiators believed that India's agreeing to negotiate might soften US action under US 301.[10]

It has been underlined that "the shift damaged India's negotiating ability: India lost its credibility in the eyes of the developing countries- by appearing to buckle under pressure. Also the impression gained ground that the diplomats negotiating on India's behalf had been insincere in their earlier stand. This points to an important organizational lacuna-lack of a forum for examining alternatives and for discussing them without involving the Government formally".[11]

During the period 1990-92 of the GATT negotiations, India did not make any attempt to renegotiate on issues of interest to India. No indication was given to the Parliament or to the public that the minimum must, which India should have taken up for renegotiation had been identified. During this period, India also stuck to its policy of not taking any initiative to mobilise the support of other developing and like-minded countries, to bolster its position.[12] For these kinds of India's attitudes, one may find a possible answer that to a large extent, India was under pressure of section 301 of the US Trade Act and the pressure of the IMF and the World Bank. The former Finance Minister, Manmohan Singh agreed with this view in an interview.[13] With India coming under the net of IMF-World Bank, it became easier for the developed countries to have their way. When negotiations were on in Brussels (December 1990), India was on Super 301 for not opening its economy to US firms in the area of insurance. This was enough to blunt the stand taken by the Indian representative during the negotiations.

It may be said that it was also due to a cautious approach in foreign policy, which would not bring any adverse effect on India's liberalization process as pointed out by Muchkund Dubey in an interview.[14] Another possible view is that India was not in a position to renegotiate on issues of interest to her due to its precarious economic situation during the period as we have seen in Chapter-II. This proposition was supported by the former Minister of Commerce and External Affairs under the Rao regime, Mr Pranab Mukherjee.[15] In this context, one may say that when a country faces a precarious economic condition and thereafter initiates economic liberalization which is supported by outside forces, its economic aspect of foreign policy becomes vulnerable to foreign pressure. This was the case with regard to India.

It was only at the end of 1992 that under pressure of nation-wide agitation against some of the key provisions of the Dunkel Text,[16] the Government of India tried to find out a few issues in which her interest should be protected. But it was too little and too late to safeguard India's interest as the Dunkel text was finally adopted without substantial change.[17] Thus, one of the strong critics opined that "the consequences of India signing the Uruguay Round of the GATT at Marrakesh in April 1994 are truly momentous, not only with respect to its economic impact on India but in the disarming of India's capacities to resist imperialism in the future on the terrain it is most concerned about-the economic".[18]

Four core issues are focussed upon here as they are directly linked with India's foreign economic policy in a substantial manner.

(1) Trade-Related Intellectual Property Rights (TRIPs)

The TRIPs was the most sensitive, complex and controversial issue in the Uruguay Round of negotiations from the developing countries' point of view. Most of the developing countries had a utilitarian view to Intellectual Property Rights (IPRs) stressing the role of innovations in promoting industrialisation by local diffusion of knowledge.[19] Until the mid-term review of the Uruguay Round Negotiations in Montreal in December 1988, they regarded any discussion of norms and standards of IPRs as beyond the competence of GATT. As we have discussed earlier, due to pressure from the developed countries and the weakening of coalitions among them, the developing countries resiled from their position at the resumed mid-term review meeting in Geneva in April, 1989 and agreed, for the first time, to discuss norms and standards of IPRs. On the other hand , the developed countries had the natural rights view of the IPRs, best encapsulated in the Hegelian dictum that "an idea belongs to its creator because the idea is a manifestation of the creator's personality or self".[20]

The final outcome of the Uruguay Round represents a definitive victory for the developed countries' viewpoint. The subject of the IPRs was crucial for the industrialised countries as they have a near monopoly of knowledge and technology. The TRIPs Agreement internationalises the national IPR systems of developed countries and provides for an enhanced scope and higher level of protection of IPRs, not for the purpose of stimulating invention and innovation but basically in order to enable these countries, particularly their transnational corporations, to retain their control over technology which is the main factor creating competitive advantages in the world market.[21]

The TRIPs agreement covers seven types of intellectual property: patents, copyrights, trademarks, trade secrets, industrial designs, geographical indications and integrated circuits. Except in case of patents, in all other areas, the Indian law and regulations are not different from those obtaining in the rest of the world. So, the main issue affecting India is that of patents. In the final text, both products and processes could be patented now which meant that by producing some product through a new process the producer could not escape from obligations towards original patent-holder of the product.

In India social obligations are of crucial importance unlike in the West. In India patents are not granted to enable patentees to enjoy monopoly in the market. Patent in India is granted to encourage inventions but it should in no way preclude the achievement of socio-economic goals like access to health care and availability of food at cheap rates for the poor. The act protects the interests of both the inventor and the consumer. The patentee is not allowed to establish absolute monopoly of his patented products through importation or through domestic production and sale of his products at exorbitant price.

According to Indian Patent Act, 1970, only process patents are granted in the areas of food, chemicals and pharmaceutical with patents limited to a period of seven years from the time of filing or five years from the date of granting whichever is shorter. In the Dunkel proposal, the time limit of product patent is 20 years. And the protection of IPRs provided in the Agreement will be enforced through the common Dispute Settlement Mechanism of the WTO, which provides for retaliation and cross-retaliation. No distinction is made between developed and developing countries. As a result, two sectors in which TRIPs issues are particularly relevant for India are pharmaceutical and agricultural seeds.

It is generally believed that patent protection in the third world is weak, with some countries (like India) providing only process patents and others (like Mexico and Zambia) having no patents at all. This weak protection is alleged to have imposed substantial losses on pharmaceutical industries in the developed countries. According to one estimate, the US loses annually $1.4 billion from the sale of copied drugs in the four developing countries- Argentina, Brazil, Mexico and India, with India accounting for about $ 0.92 billion of such losses.[22]

It has been seen that the drug prices in India are the lowest in the world because India goes by process patent and Indian drug companies thrive on inventions elsewhere thus avoiding a lot of expenditure on research and development. Countries like Pakistan which go by product patent cannot make medicines available at Indian prices. For example, Zantac produced by Glaxo is a drug used in the treatment of ulcers which costs Rs. 29 for ten tablets in India. The same drug in Pakistan is available for Rs. 220, in the US for $ 24 and the UK £ 9.[23]

In a country like India with massive poverty, it is extremely important to make drugs available to the people at low prices. Thus, it was feared that the drug prices will shoot up manifold if India adopts product patents in the pharmaceutical sector. However, if the product patent is finally granted in this sector, prices of drugs would shoot up immediately and the unbridled growth of prices can not possibly be checked with the existing machineries. This would certainly affect sections of the poor who will then not have the generic option open. The consequences will be particularly serious since a National Health System is not in effective operation in India.[24] Furthermore, due to India's own economic liberalization, the subsidies for health care were cut as discussed in Chapter-III.

The TRIPs Final Text provides pipeline protection to the owner of a patent in pharmaceutical and agricultural chemical products to register in India from day one after the entry into force of the WTO Agreement, and to claim exclusive marketing rights for five years, thus rendering ineffective the process patent mechanism. To give effect to the provision on pipeline protection through the grant of exclusive marketing rights, the Government of India introduced the Patent Amendment Bill, 1995, in the

Parliament. The Bill was passed by the Lok Sabha but was blocked in the Rajya Sabha by a determined opposition as the Congress did not have a majority in the Upper House. The bill came in for stiff criticism from the entire opposition, which said that the legislation would only serve to strengthen MNCs by giving them rights over the product rather than process.

One of the most far-reaching provisions in the TRIPs Agreement is that relating to the patenting of plant varieties. The TRIPs provide for protection of plant varieties either by patents or by an effective sui generis system or any combination thereof. India has opted for the sui generis system. These provisions have been essentially aimed at protecting the interests of the plant breeders and the seed companies on the rationale that they would have spent huge resources on research and development.

The *sui generis* system commonly refers to the system of Plant Breeders Rights (PBRs) and it is in operation in Europe and other Western countries. Under this system, the holders of PBRs are conferred the exclusive right to produce and distribute the protected variety of seeds for the duration of patent period. Codified in Union for the Protection of New Varieties (UPOV), the PBRs offer monopoly on the production and commercial marketing of the produced varieties. The PBRs will be conferred to only those new varieties which satisfy the four basic criteria of novelty, distinctness, uniformity and stability. Considerable research and development as well as investment is required to develop commercially viable new varieties that could meet these stringent conditions.

The farmers in India had the right to save, modify, multiply and sell seeds from their harvests. These rights were threatened under the new GATT proposed patent regime extending to seeds. One section of the farmers fear that the proposals suggested in the GATT would stop farmer-to-farmer sale of seed which was an important factor in the spread of new varieties during the Green Revolution era. This might cause a disruption in the agricultural system because of the prevailing practice among farmers in India, of obtaining a large proportion of their seeds requirement from other farmers. According to one study, of the six lakh tonne seeds requirement of Indian agriculture, not more than 32 per cent is met by formal agencies like the National and State Seed Corporations. The remaining 68 per cent are provided by inter-farmer sales.[25]

There was growing concern that the cost of agriculture may increase significantly if the plant breeders and the seed companies create a monopoly or oligopolistic market for seeds. Multinational seed companies can prop up prices by creating artificial shortages. Perhaps India's small and marginal farmers would never be able to afford high yielding varieties. They will have to restrict themselves to the traditional varieties, and may not be able to meet their own food requirements. So, India's food and agricultural export were threatened.[26]

(2) Trade in Services

In the September meeting of the GATT members in Punta del Este in 1986, it was agreed that services[27] would be discussed, but on a parallel track among the GATT contracting parties outside the legal framework of the GATT. According to one analyst, both the US (because talks on services were started) and India and other developing countries (the integration of services into the GATT had been stalled) were able to see this compromise as a victory.[28]

Initially, the developing countries feared that the demand of developed countries in services area would be for an across-the board market access. This fear has been substantiated by the fact that the developed countries run huge surpluses on the services trade account while the services trade account of the developing countries, in general, show deficits. For example, in 1992 while the US had a deficit of over $ 96 billion on the merchandise trade account, it had a surplus of over $30 billion on the services trade.[29] Thus, recognising the growing importance of trade in services in their economic growth and development, the developed countries, particularly the US, included the subject of services in the GATT negotiations at the Uruguay Round.

A more fundamental factor of the developing countries' fear was a virtual explosion in technology. Technology permits the rapid expansion of trade in services either as the substance of such trade or as the medium that makes international trade in services possible. There is increased demand from producers for industrial and agricultural goods as well as of services for specialised knowledge, hence increasing the importance of the producer service sector. The TNCs are the major generators of new technologies supported by their home governments. The mastery of advanced information and communication technologies had provided them with an advantage in production of and trade in both goods and services (facilitated by mutual support of these sectors and their domination of modes of delivery of information and capital-based services). Given the link between goods and services exports, they are able to control markets through dominance of services sector.

Under the final agreement of the General Agreement on Trade in Services (GATS) only the obligations of Most Favoured Nations (MFN) treatment and transparency are applicable to the entire universe of services, while national treatment and market access commitments are applicable only to the specific services negotiated.

In this context, the important point for consideration in case of India is that GATS does not by itself impose obligation of providing access across the board to foreign service providers. This has to be negotiated by individual countries on a reciprocal basis. The ability of a developing country not to offer any significant commitment of access or to lay down restrictions on access, very much depends upon its bargaining power. Since India had to overcome its economic crisis and reduce its dependence on the financial supports from the IMF and World Bank, it was and in further may not be easily pressurised by the TNCs of the developed countries to liberalise its large service market.

One of the important demands of the Third World during the GATT negotiations was for the free movement of labour to seek employment in the developed countries. This is the only service sector in which the developing countries have distinct competitive advantage. They demanded that commitments be made for independent professionals to work abroad without the requirement of commercial presence. Very few developed countries responded to this demand, and its attainment became the main objective of the extended negotiations on movement of persons.[30]

In the final offers made on 28 July, 1995, some modest

improvements were made by the developed countries. In the light of some improvements, having rich manpower with good English skills, a huge comparative advantage, India has secured major gains in the supply of professional services providers to the key markets of the US and the European Union in the WTO agreement on financial services and movement of natural persons. On the other hand, India has given away very little in terms of commitments to liberalise its financial services sector for foreign companies. This is so because India has no obligation under the agreement to liberalise the financial sector any further than what has been already done. It has no obligation to open up the insurance sector. The US decision to opt out of the multilateral agreement on liberalization of the financial services trade will not be to India's disadvantage. India has no stake in the financial services market of the US.

In 1995 the US agreed to undertake as many as 64,000 personnel covering all professions globally every year. This market access concession was not linked to the financial services agreement. According to one report, India has a share of 20 percent of all professional services providers who go to the US.[31] With the US decision on short-term movement of natural persons, India has had the additional advantage of being able to move personnel even without having a business establishment in the US.

Unlike the US, the European Union has not imposed an annual ceiling on the number of personnel who would be allowed in. It has undertaken to allow skilled personnel to provide services in 15 sectors including computer software, architecture, engineering, tourism, entertainment and legal services. The schedules of concessions vary from one European Union member country to another, But, the major markets that India is most interested in such as the UK, Germany, France and Italy- the market access concessions are substantial. Computer software, which is an area that offers tremendous potential for India's exports, is perhaps the most important area where greater access for the cross border movement of skilled and professional people can be of benefit to India.

Besides this, the enlarged opportunities for the services sector for Indian suppliers would arise mainly from two specific identifiable opportunities that have emerged. First, due to its own economic liberalization in the early 1990s, India has attracted remarkable foreign investments as has been shown in Chapter-III. This in turn would result in a much larger volume of projects to come in the future. This will require engineering and design services to be followed by construction services on a very large scale. Early action taken would result in a substantial part of the consultants which will also eventually lead to a large part of engineering design services to be provided in the country. Since many new investors have entered India for the first time, this opportunity could be taken full advantage of by Indian services system. It is also possible to visualise that once such contracts are established with new foreign investors Indian consultancy services would also more easily find acceptance in other countries where the same investors are likely to take part.

Secondly, since the contribution of the services sector to the GDP in many countries is increasing and services constitute the fastest growing part of the world economy, India with its large scientific and technically qualified manpower would be able to mobilise a sizeable part of this for enlarging services.

(3) Trade-Related Investment Measures (TRIMs)

India and other developing countries suffered a setback in their campaign to keep the TRIMs out of the agenda of the GATT. Developing nations tried to have freedom to devise and apply investment measures that would oblige foreign investors to observe their national priorities; to make foreign investment supportive of transfer of technology and industrialization; and to control anti-competitive and trade-restrictive business practices of foreign investors.[32] However, due to the vulnerabilities in the economies of developing nations to foreign influence in the 1980s, the US and other developed countries found their way to pin the investment measures to the Uruguay Round of the GATT. The objective was to benefit their multinational companies who were anxious to invest in the developing countries.

The agreement on TRIMs prohibits member countries from

applying any TRIMs that is inconsistent with provisions of Article III or Article XI of the GATT 1994.[33] Article III is on national treatment. Article XI deals with general elimination of quantitative restrictions. The agreement compels every member country of the GATT to give national treatment to foreign capital. It obliges the nations not to discriminate against foreign investors. It also says that foreign investors will not be obliged to use local products and material. Export of part of the output will no longer be mandatory. Restrictions on repatriation of dividend, interest and royalty will be eliminated.

The Final TRIMs agreement states that all specific measures in the Article III and XI categories being applied by any member will have to be notified within 90 days of the entry into force of the Agreement establishing the WTO. Developing countries have five years to implement the agreement. Once the agreement comes into force, developing countries including India will be robbed of their power to regulate the import of technology and to restrict imports in the interest of their development. Even though some of the concessions and privileges of the agreement have been already enjoyed by the foreign investors under India's economic liberalization measures, this may impede India's self-reliant development and accentuate the balance of payments situation. This creates a fear that dependency on foreign investment and technology will increase resulting in strengthening the hegemony of foreign multinational companies in India. In the light of there being no provision in the agreement to deal with the restrictive business practices of foreign investors, it has been argued that "in order to make the agreement balanced from the point of view of developing countries, provisions for elimination of TRIMs should have been accompanied by international rules for controlling restrictive business practices. There is very little evidence to show that developing countries made even an effort in this direction".[34]

In the agreement, there are provisions that a country with a balance of payments crisis can have recourse to some of the prohibited measures and policies to protect their balance of payments. However, such restrictions should be imposed in the least trade-disruptive manner and should favour price-based measures like import surcharges and import deposits, rather than quantitative restrictions. Moreover, the restrictions will be only for a temporary period. The applying country has to enter into consultations with other members in the balance of payments committee. The committee shall have the power to review all the restrictive import measures taken for balance of payments purposes. And once the host country improves its own balance of payments position, it has to eliminate the identified measures even if it justifies to maintain the restrictions on its broader macro-economic and strategic grounds.

Thus, the TRIMs part took away the rights of the host countries to put restrictions on the incoming investment. Earlier host countries had the right to regulate foreign investment in their land in a manner they considered necessary for safeguarding their national interests. After the conclusion of the Uruguay Round, these rights were to be superseded by the global laws governing cross-border investments.

(4) Agriculture

Agriculture had been the most contentious of all issues- a major reason for the collapse of multilateral trade negotiations at Brussels in December 1990 due to acrimony over agricultural subsidies among different participating countries, especially the US and the EU. On 13th January 1992, the then Director General of the GATT Secretariat Arther Dunkel put forward the compromise proposals, the Dunkel Draft to the member nations for final consideration. The proposals contained in the draft were finalised by December 1993 which generated all-round concern throughout the globe.

Agriculture plays an important role in India's economic development. Two-thirds of India's population still depends on agriculture. Therefore, during the run up to the GATT agreement, fears were expressed that India's interests in agriculture will be adversely affected as a result of the proposed agreement on agricultural issues in the Uruguay Round. There were apprehensions that India may be forced to reduce the subsidies available to her farmers; phase out the public distribution system and compulsorily open up to agricultural imports.[35] However, Mr Pranab Mukherjee, the then Commerce Minister told Rajya Sabha that the Dunkel proposals would not obliterate the farmers' interests, and the economic sovereignty of the country as contended by the opposition parties.[36]

The basic objective of the Agreement on Agriculture is to initiate a process of agricultural trade reforms in three main areas, viz (i) market access, (ii) domestic support, and (iii) export competition with a view to establishing a fair and market oriented agricultural trading system while taking into account the particular needs and conditions of the developing country members.

Market Access

Under market access commitments all member countries of the GATT are required to replace all type of non-tariff barriers, and reduce the level of tariffs under a time bound programme. These levels are to be reduced by 24 per cent in case of developing countries and by 36 per cent in case of developed ones. The period during which these reductions are to be taken up varies from six years in case of developed countries to 10 years in case of developing countries. In addition to these commitments, this measure also calls for maintaining current access opportunities and the establishment of minimum access tariff quota. Countries with closed farm markets will have to import at least 3 per cent of domestic consumption of the product, rising to 5 per cent over six years.

The implementation of these measures will not have any adverse effect on Indian agriculture during the implementation period. This is because imports of various agricultural commodities in India are subjected to mainly quantitative restrictions for balance of payments reasons. The special provisions of agreement allow any country to maintain import restrictions up to the end of the implementation period. In any case, India does not have to compulsorily import 3 per cent of its domestic consumption.[37] However, it is argued that due to vastly improved position of foreign currency reserve, India may not be able to escape for too long the commitment for providing minimum access. Once its balance of payments protection is removed, it will then have to import agricultural commodities, even if it does not need to do so.[38]

Domestic Support

Under domestic support commitments all forms of subsidies in favour of agricultural producers, except direct or indirect government assistance to encourage agricultural and rural development including subsidies to resource poor producers in developing countries, shall have to be reduced to the level of 5 per cent of the value of the product in developed countries and to 10 per cent in developing countries. A method of computing the farm subsidy is also given, known as the Aggregate Measurement of Support (AMS).

According to the calculations made by the Ministry of Commerce, for the non-product specific, the AMS works out 2.9 to 6.0 per cent depending on the assumptions made. Even the higher figure of 6 per cent is much below the limit of 10 per cent stipulated in the Dunkel Draft below which no reductions have to be made. As for product specific AMS, in most products, the AMS is negative. In one or two products, it is positive but less than 10 per cent.[39] Thus, the then Commerce Secretary, Mr Tenjendra Khanna stated that India has already filed a statement in GATT that India is not obliged to make any reduction at all of agricultural subsidy because it is far below the ceiling.[40]

Dunkel proposals required India to maintain the public distribution system only through purchase at market price. This means that the Government of India cannot interfere with the price settlement mechanism, like it can do now. The consequences of buying at market price may not be so apparent in times of plenty, but in times of shortages, compulsion to buy at market prices can mean suicidal for the country's ability to procure and stock food and release for consumption at subsidised rates. This in itself would be enough to push India into a dependence on imports. The buffer stocks have been critical in stabilising the prices of essential food grains.

Export Competition

In the area of export competition, the GATT agreement calls for reducing direct export subsidies to a level of 36 per cent below 1986-88 level in case of developed countries over a period of six years. The quantity of subsidized exports by the developed countries is to be reduced by 21 per cent during the same period. In case of developing countries direct export subsidies are to be reduced by 24 per cent and the quantity of subsidized exports is to be reduced by 14 per cent. These reductions in case of developing countries are to be carried out over a period of 10 years as against six years in case of developed countries.

In order to see the impact of these commitments on agricultural exports from India, one has to look at the nature and extent of these subsidies. Indian exports of agricultural commodities do not get direct export subsidy. The only subsidies available to exports of agricultural commodities are in the form of: (i) exemption of profits from export sales from the income tax, and (ii) subsidies on costs of freight on export shipments of certain products like fruits, vegetables and floricultural products.[41]

According to one estimate developed countries' export subsidies amounted to $ 16.4 billion during the base period.[42] These countries could be required to gradually reduce their export assistance programme. In this regard, Vijaya Katti argues that India's rice competitiveness in the world market is expected to increase, specially with the opening of Japanese market under the GATT agreement.[43] The Government of India stated that the reduction in export subsidies on agriculture by developed countries will make Indian agricultural exports more competitive in world market. This argument is already supported by the fact that as we have seen in the Chapter-III, agricultural products exports in India like rice have increased 254.5 per cent during 1995-96 over the previous year. The exports of non-basmati rice has increased about 1,000 times during the same year over the previous year. Of course, it was made possible by the removal of the stipulation of minimum export price on these items as a part of the ongoing liberalization programmes. But it has improved the prospects for India's agricultural competitiveness in the world market.

The World Trade Organization (WTO)

The Uruguay Round of GATT (1986-93) gave birth to the WTO. The members of the GATT signed on an agreement of the Uruguay Round in April 1994 in Morocco for establishing a new organisation named the World Trade Organization. It was officially constituted on January 1, 1995 which took the place of GATT as an effective formal organisation. The GATT was an informal organisation which regulated world trade since 1948.

Contrary to the temporary nature of GATT, the WTO is a permanent organisation which has been established on the basis of an international treaty approved by participating countries. It achieved international status like the IMF and the World Bank but it is not an agency of the United Nations Organisation (UNO). The WTO shall provide a common institutional framework for the conduct of trade relations among its members in matters related to the agreements and associated legal instruments included in the Annexes to the text of the WTO. This means that the WTO provide facilities for implementation, administration and operation of multilateral and bilateral agreements of the world trade.

To be a member of the WTO, a country has to accept all the agreements in their totality; there is no discretion either for reservation or for picking and choosing parts from the agreements, which a country might wish to follow. A member country of the WTO has to adjust its domestic legislation according to the relevant WTO agreements. If a member nation fails to do so, it can be expelled from the membership of the WTO by a two-thirds majority.

One of the most important implications of the WTO is that it provides for cross-retaliation. By administering the Understanding on Dispute Settlement, the WTO promotes the practice of cross-retaliation. Since all the agreements under the Final Text of the GATT have cross linkages, retaliation can be imposed not only in the identified area in which the offending distortion of trade had taken place, but also in any other area. It means that if India violates the US patent right, it can be retaliated by the US in the field of commodity trade. Therefore, it is pointed out that the cross-retaliation of the WTO in a sense legitimizes and universalizes the unilateral trade action of the Super 301 of the US Trade and Comprehensiveness Act which also provides for cross-retaliation.

In this context, one analyst pointed out that "the developing countries should not be under any illusion that they can also use the cross-retaliation provision of the WTO. Because of the lower stage of their economic growth, with its associated need to import from developed countries in order to keep up the tempo of economic growth, and also due to their weak bargaining position, the developing countries were seldom able to retaliate under Article XXIII of the GATT. It is indeed a wishful thinking to believe that they would now be able to retaliate simply because there are now alternative sectors of retaliation".[44] Thus, it is held that the Understanding on Dispute Settlement of the WTO is weighed in favour of the developed nations, especially the US.

One of the functions of the WTO is to assist the International Monetary Fund and the International Bank for Reconstruction and Development and its affiliated agencies for establishing coherence in global economic policy design. In this regard, it was thought that "global economic policy-making in the present context carries the unfortunate implication of conditionalities, fashioned mainly by the IMF and the Bank. The decision of the WTO to single out the IMF and the Bank for co-operation in ensuring coherence of global economic policy-making appears to be a move towards collaborating with these institutions for applying cross-conditionalities in the areas of money, finance and trade".[45]

The Uruguay Round was finalised when both domestic and world opinion were weighing India as a potential high growth economy. When some semblance of consensus on GATT started emerging in mid-1993, the Indian economy was showing an all-round improvement due to the economic reforms programme. Realizing the reality of the new emerging world economic system and some positive aspects of its own economic liberalization, India ratified the Final Act of the Uruguay Round in December 1994, and has, thus, become a founder member of the WTO. The opposition parties held a rally in New Delhi to protest against the GATT saying that the Congress government surrendered interests of the country by approving the GATT treaty on December 15,

1994.

In contrast to the view of the opposition parties, the ruling Congress party took a positive attitude in the light of the reality of the WTO. Making a statement in the Lok Sabha in December 1994, the then Union Commerce Minister, Pranab Mukherjee said that while perceptions differed on one or the other aspect of the Uruguay Round results, the government is of the view that India's continued participation in the multilateral trading system will be in the national interest. He said the government carefully examined the agreement, establishing the WTO and found that reductions in tariffs will contribute to an increase in trade flow.[46]

There is no doubt that with the advent of the WTO, world trade has become more globalised than ever before. This has helped in the unprecedented integration of the world economy with which India has sought to integrate through trade, investment and technology flows by launching a far-reaching economic liberalization programme. To facilitate this aim of aiding India's economic development, it was considered wise to stay with the new international trade system.

INDIA, THE IMF AND WORLD BANK

Facing a precarious economic situation, India launched the liberalization programme. For this, India received financial support from the IMF and the Bank. This raised a lot of questions: Was India forced to dilute its non-aligned stand to get financial support, especially during the Gulf War?, How far did India benefit from the IMF and the World Bank loans?, How and in what way did the Fund and Bank react to the progress of the economic liberalization programme in India? How did India agree to the conditionalities of the loans?, and what were the opinions within India on the loans and its conditionalities? To answer these questions, this part is divided into four categories, namely, loans from the IMF during the Gulf War, economic liberalization programme, the IMF and the World Bank loans, conditionalities, and critique and defence of the conditionalities and loans.

Loans from the IMF during the Gulf War

As we have seen in Chapter-II, the crisis in the balance of payments during 1990-92 necessitated IMF support for mobilisation of external funds to fill the substantial gap arising due to mainly heavy withdrawals from NRI deposits and the drying up of the sources of commercial credits. After the completion of drawings under the Extended Fund Facility (EFF)[47] arrangement in April 1984, India had not taken any recourse to the IMF till December 1990. On 31 December 1990, foreign exchange reserves declined to $ 1.2 billion, equal to about two weeks' imports. It was only in January 1991 that the Chandra Shekhar government was forced to borrow Special Drawing Rights (SDR)[48] of 551.93 million from the IMF, under a first credit tranche stand by arrangement for 3 month.[49] In the same month, the government of India also received the Compensatory and Contingency Financing Fund (CCFF)[50] loan from the IMF.

In this context, it is interesting to note what Mr Subramaniam Swamy, the former Commerce Minister under the Chandra Shekhar government said about the relation between the Fund loans for India and the US planes refuelling facilities in January 1991. According to one report, Mr Swamy confirmed that the action of his government in permitting the US planes refuelling facilities during the Gulf War (This issue will be discussed in detail in Chapter-V) facilitated the one billion dollar loan from the IMF in early 1991. He said that it so happened that the Indian government was requested to provide landing facilities. The IMF loan figured during a discussion of India's economic problems and the loan was cleared "within 48 hours" with no restrictions, no conditionalities. [51]

It is said that the interests of the IMF and the World Bank management complemented the Cold War requirements of the rich countries led by the US.[52] Even after the end of the Cold War, the West, particularly the US, has been using the IMF and the World Bank loans facilities to promote the interests of their foreign policies. Evidences can be found in various countries. The loans for Russia after the collapse of the Soviet Union serves as the best example. The question is whether India also received the loan from the IMF after it tilted towards the US. If Mr Swamy's statement holds, India appears to have compromised its pursuit for an independent non-aligned foreign policy orientation by materially assisting the US planes. In this respect, one may argue that as the US has leverage with the IMF, the US goodwill and friendship were helpful to India in stemming the economic crisis. The Gulf War clearly established the unequivocal supremacy of the US on the international scene. The socialist bloc, following its capitulation to the capitalist world, was no longer a countervailing power in the world economy.

In early 1991, the government also initiated discussions with the World Bank for utilisation of the undisbursed IDA loans ($ 3.3 billion). But the Bank indicated that important bases for fast disbursing assistance could be "reform measures contained in the 1991-92 budget, and in any policy related... statements".[53] Nevertheless, it organised an informal donors' meeting in April 1991 to mobilize support on the conditions that the country adopt a structural adjustment programme. However, since the caretaker government with Chandra Shekhar as the Prime Minister was not able to decide on policy reforms, neither the Bank released any proportion of the undisbursed credit nor did any donor provide new loans.

The Government of India along with other oil importing developing countries had asked the Fund to modify the CCFF by including oil import element in it. This modification was approved by the IMF Board in mid-November, 1990. As a result, the Government of India received the CCFF loan during January-September 1991, totalling SDR 1.35 billions equivalent of about $ 1.88 billions or Rs. 4108 crores. This loan was treated as a contingency loan to offset the fiscal disruption caused to the Indian economy resulting from high oil prices, a temporary loss of export markets and remittance earnings from the Gulf region as shown in Chapter-II.

Economic Liberalization Programme, the IMF and World Bank Loans

After the mid-term poll, when the new government led by the Prime Minister, P.V. Narasimha Rao took office in June 1991 with Manmohan Singh as the Finance Minister, a grave economic crisis was inherited by the Congress minority government. The crisis could be avoided only if it received loans from international financial institutions and dramatic corrective actions were undertaken in the direction of its past development strategy.

In the first week of July 1991 the Rupee was devalued by as much as 22.5 per cent (in two phases, in the course of three days). Here it must be emphasised that since 1983 devaluation had become a compulsory requirement for having the assistance from IMF.[54] The World Bank's Report of October 1990 had also advocated a 20 per cent devaluation of the rupee to correct the balance of payments problem.[55]

The Union Commerce Minister, on 4th July, 1991, announced a radically liberalized trade policy. Coupled with the supplementary measures announced in August 1991, it aimed at significantly reducing the quantitative restrictions on imports of intermediate and capital goods, lowering the tariff rates, substantially eliminating the state monopoly on imports and exports and so on. On July 24, 1991 the New Industrial Policy was announced drastically changing the hitherto policy regime in terms of liberalization and openness. The government announced three major initiatives, namely, the virtual abolition of the complex system of industrial licensing; measures to strengthen competition between private sector and public sector enterprises and a significant liberalization of foreign investment.

The provisions of industrial policy were incorporated into the Central Budget of 1991-92. The Union budget announced the Central Government's intention of reducing its fiscal deficit by as much as two percentage points of GDP to 6.5 per cent level by the end of 1991-92. This was agreed upon with the IMF as per the economic programme of the Government of India. The Finance Minister Manmohan Singh sent on August 24, 1991 the first, 'Memorandum on Economic Policies' setting out the 'Economic Program' of the Government of India to the Managing Director of the IMF. The 'Program' set out targets, quarterly monitoring mechanism and reviews by the Fund. The second and revised Memorandum of Economic Policies for the year 1992-93 was sent to the IMF by the Government of India on June 2, 1992.[56]

From time to time a country predicts conditionalities and launches policy reforms even before the formal negotiation with the International lending institutions begins. It helps the government concerned to claim that its policy reforms have not been dictated by the funding agents and have preceded loan negotiations.[57]

In this regard, though it is not clear as to whether India consciously undertook some major policy reforms prior to signing the agreement with the IMF for the stand-by loans, it is very interesting to note what the managing director of the IMF, Mr Michel Camdessus said in 1991. He mentioned that the prior change in policies by the Government of India was one of the reasons that he supported the economic liberalization of India. He said that a number of measures, including those in the structural areas, had already been taken. So they are no longer just intentions expressed in the letter of intent but they are facts in the past tense. So the government can say in the letter of intent: "We already have, for instance, abolished industrial licensing. We already have reduced some tariffs. We already have simplified import procedures and so on".[58]

As expected the IMF came to India's help. On October 31, 1991, the IMF approved a stand-by credit for the government of India authorizing drawings upto the equivalent of SDR 1656 million (US $ 2262 million) in support of the government's economic and financial programmes 1991/92-1992/93.[59] The stand-by credit was disbursed to India over a period of 20 months in quarterly instalments, after periodic assessments of the Indian economy.[60] The stand-by credit's first instalment was to be made available in November 1991 itself in order to enable New Delhi to meet certain debt repayment requirement. The gross drawings from the Fund during the stand-by credit between November 1991 to January 1992 amounted to SDR 2.2 billion equivalent to $ 3 billion or Rs. 6500 crores as shown below the table-1.

TABLE - 1

DRAWALS FROM THE IMF DURING JANUARY 1991 TO JANUARY 1992*

Period	*Name of Facility*	*Amount* *SDR bn.*	*$ bn.*	*Rs. hun. cr.*
January 1991	First Credit Tranche	0.55	0.79	14.50
Jan.-Sep. 1991	CCFF	1.35	1.88	41.08
Nov.1991-Jan.1992	Stand-by Credit**0.27	0.38	9.88	

* The drawal of SDR 487 million July-September 1990 of the reserve tranche[61] is not regarded as the use of Fund credit as it is treated as part of the country's external resources which can be drawn up to its full amount at any time without conditions.

** A total of SDR 1,656 billion ($2,262) to be disbursed in 8 tranches over a 20-month period from November 1991 to June 1993.

Source: Economic Survey 1991-92, Table 5.12.

In April-December 1992 SDR 924 million ($ 1306 million) were drawn. India drew the last tranche of $ 325 million under the stand-by arrangement in June 1993. It may be mentioned that the Fund, by releasing the last tranche of $ 325 million, virtually accepted the validity of the Indian reform programme and confirmed that the Government of India was on the right track in so far as identification and implementation of the programme were concerned. The implication of the economic policies and the performance of the economy during the period of the loan arrangement was subject to continuous review and monitoring by the IMF. If the Fund is not satisfied with the policies, subsequent phases of the loan might attract more stringent condition or might not be made available at all.

According to Economic Survey 1995-96, India drew a total amount of SDR 3560 million under the CCFF and Stand-by Arrangements from the IMF between January 1991 and June 1993. In 1992 some discussions had been undertaken with the IMF for a medium-term arrangement under the EFF[62] with a blend of resources under the Enhanced Structural Adjustment Facility (ESAF). With the marked improvement in the balance of payments, the Government of India, as contemplated earlier, did not approach the Fund for a medium term EFF. Instead, the country made advance repayments of $ 1.1 billion to the Fund in April 1994. This was scheduled for payment in instalments over 1994-95.[63]

After the IMF approved the second drawing of the CCFF in July 1991, the World Bank subsequently organised a lending programme spread over the next four year period, 1992-95 comprising the following:

1. World Bank lending of up to $ 2.0 billion per annum.
2. IDA resources of approximately $0.9 billion per annum.
3. IDA resources of $ 0.65 billion from replacement of funds cancelled from the current IDA portfolio as proposed in the Board Paper R 91-241 [IDA/R 91-149], dated 12 November 1991.[64]

It is noted that the last facility constituted about 20 per cent of the undisbursed IDA credit that was denied earlier[65] and was extended after the Finance Minister of India wrote a letter to Mr Preston, the then President of the Bank on November 11, 1991 in which the Minister elaborately explained the package of policy reform to stabilise the economy and restore growth momentum. At the end, he solicited "continued support" of the Bank for attaining policy objectives.[66]

This was the Bank's first policy-based loan, amounting to $ 12.25 billion spread over four years, to India. Traditionally, the Bank has been giving loans to specific projects of the member countries. India also has been taking mostly project loans from the Bank because it did not want the Bank or any outside agency to use lending as a medium to dictate changes in its policies.

While there were significant differences between the IMF and the World Bank, they narrowed their mode of operating and managements. Earlier the Fund was concerned with short-period remedies to the problems of balance of payments and stood for demand side. It has started offering 10 year term EFF since 1974 and structural adjustment loans since 1986. On the other hand, the Bank usually associated itself with long term remedies and operated on the supply side. Through its structural adjustment loans, it has turned from projected-based lending to policy-based programme. It is also concerning with macro-economic management.[68] As a result, it is mentioned that "the former distinctions between the roles of the Fund and the Bank- macro versus micro, demand versus supply, adjustment versus development, financial versus real, programme versus project loans, short term versus long term- have been severely eroded".[69]

The World Bank approved its first Structural Adjustment Loan (SAL) to India in December 1991, for an equivalent of $ 500 million, with one half of it in the form of IDA soft credit. This loan was completely delinked from projects and disbursed quickly against commitment to carry out major economic policy changes. According to the World Bank's source, its objectives were to support "the initial phase of India's programme of industrial deregulation, liberalization of international trade, and increasing the efficiency of public enterprises".[71]

To support India's transition to a more open and competitive economy, the Bank approved in June 1993, an adjustment loan (i.e. the Liberalization of the External Sector and Investment Regime) for the equivalent of $ 300 million in a single release operation.[72] This loan was cleared by an official letter of May 31, 1993 written by the then Finance Minister, Dr Manmohan Singh to the World Bank President, Mr Lewis Preston. The Finance Minister in the letter provided a blueprint on the government's medium term programme for liberalising the external sector and investment regime.[73]

As soon as the Bank agreed to lend, other creditors took their cue. The Aid India Consortium[74] of Western donors of which the World Bank is a member pledged an enhanced aid package of $ 7.2 billion for 1992, including $ 3.3 billion fast disbursement assistance, to help India tide over the difficult balance of payments situation.[75]

The World Bank and the Aid India Consortium of Western donors outlined a 10 point programme of action on which they expect India to take "further early and significant progress" for the success of the reform process. These points are: (1), The balance of payments situation. (2), The recovery of growth on a non-inflationary basis. (3), The social aspect of the adjustment process. (4), Skilful debt management. (5), Further reduction of tariffs. (6), Unify the exchange rate. (7), Restore growth momentum as early as possibly, thus minimise the social cost of adjustment. (8), Decline in public expenditure. (9), Reform public enterprises, the financial sector and tax system. (10), Improve performance of agriculture sector.

These points were highlighted by Mr Joseph Wood, the World Bank Vice President who presided over the two-day Aid India Consortium meeting in 1992.[76]

Conditionality

The conditionality associated with the use of Fund's resources require the member to undertake a programme. This requirement is designed to ensure that the Fund's financial assistance supports the implementation of economic policies that give a substantial assurance of a viable balance of payments position within a reasonable period of time; in most instances, it involves restoring of a sustainable balance between the aggregate demand for, and the aggregate supply of resources in an economy.[77]

The conditions of the Fund vary from country to country. The choice of policies and the nature of policy mix in the programme result from extensive negotiations between the country's authorities and the IMF.[78] But generally one may say that there are broadly three conditionalities of the IMF.[79]

1. The first condition: a member country borrows from the Fund only when it is faced with serious balance of payments problems. In such a situation the IMF directs the borrowing country to restore and maintain fiscal balance. This balance can be restored and maintained only if the borrowing country reduced or removed altogether the budgetary deficits. To fulfill this objective, the Fund puts forth the conditions that private enterprises are encouraged, the openness of the economy is facilitated, the subsidies given in different items be stopped, the government expenditures be curtailed, industrial output be increased, the labour law be strictly

enforced and so on.

2. The second conditionality of the IMF is related to imports and exports with the view to balancing the payment position. The balance of payments problem, in a way, is a foreign exchange crisis. The balance of payments position deteriorates when there is sharp decline in foreign exchange reserves of the country so much so that these reserves become inadequate to meet the exchange needs. These foreign exchange reserves have to be increased some how and the best and the most important way of increasing these reserves is to earn foreign exchange by increasing the exports both in value and the volume. For an increase in exports, the IMF insists on the devaluation of the currency of the borrowing country.

3. The third condition of the IMF is related with the liberal industrial policy and the opening of the foreign investment so that capital investments would increase and the inflationary trends are arrested. The foreign investors would be given the maximum appropriate facilities for investments in the country concerned.

Though the World Bank's conditionalities are less specific, which aim at reorienting the incentive structure in tune with a market-oriented economy, the three main components of its conditionalities, which seek to achieve liberalization, privatisation and globalisation, come very close to the IMF conditionalities of structural adjustment facilities.[80] Whether designed by the lenders or suggested by the borrower, the Indian attempt at stabilisation and adjustments on the basis of the loan from the Fund and the Bank appeared to follow more or less the lending institutions combine programme during the first half of the 1990s as we have seen in Chapter-III.

There is considerable debate as to whether the Fund-Bank combination imposes those conditions on countries that turn to it for support under crisis situations. Also, the attempt by external actors to exercise policy influence has been the subject of a growing literature.[81] Paul Mosley, Jane Harrigan and John Toye, for example, argue that conditionality can be modeled as a bargaining game consisting of three steps: a negotiating process that sets the conditions, an implementation process in which the government decides how far to honour the promises made in the first step, and a response by the external aid and lending agencies to the government's actions.[82]

It is difficult to tell exactly how far the Government of India succeeded in its negotiations with the IMF and other agencies. Judging by the conditionality attached to the loan, according to Manmohan Agarwal, the government was quite successful in its negotiations with the IMF. As in the case of the previous loan in 1980, the conditionality attached to this loan was, in spite of India's weaker bargaining position, relatively mild. The rate of reduction of the fiscal deficit was lower than had been negotiated, for instance, with many Latin American countries. He concluded that the government handled the negotiations fairly well, getting assistance with conditionality- milder than one had expected.[83]

It seems that the IMF and the World Bank were satisfied with the implementation of their conditionalities by the government of India and therefore released the last tranche of $ 325 million of the Fund and $ 300 million adjustment loan of the Bank in June 1993.The IMF appreciated the progress made by India so far on its post-1991 economic reforms and urged India to accelerate the pace of required reforms.[84]

Conditionalities of IMF and World Bank Loans: A Critique

There were criticism within India on the economic liberalization during the Rao government, which was supported by the international economic institutions. The major criticism by the politicians in the opposition, some of the left-wing economists and news media was that the liberalization programme was dictated by the Fund and the Bank and consequently the sovereignty of India was bartered away.

Leakage of budget proposals in February 1992, through a letter addressed to Michel Camdessus, the managing director of the IMF, received severe critique. The content of the letter included the significant proposals of the budget before it was presented to the Indian Parliament. Thus, the direct role of the IMF in defining the budget proposals came to light. This was considered a serious attempt towards undermining Indian economic sovereignty. It was also pointed out by Bharat Bhusan that people took exception when the Bank commented on the Eighth Plan much before it was submitted to the Indian Parliament which is a sovereign body.[85] It was also mentioned that the silent and shrewd whispering to India for framing the budget proposals has been considered offensive.[86] To add to it, the government had promised to reach an understanding on the 1992-1993 budget and present a medium-term time-bound programme for tax reforms along with the usual performance criteria involving short-term fiscal and monetary target. It is in the light of the above critical remarks that the conditionalities imposed by the Fund and the Bank had been construed as an infringement on nation's sovereignty.

Another criticism was that the governments (borrowers) must give them signal that they were moving in the direction desired by these institutions. Thus, Amit Bhaduri and Deepak Nayyar pointed out that "the most costly aspect of this capitulation to the blueprint designed by the IMF and the World Bank was that it reduced the degree of freedom of the government in policy formulation, as it shaped not only priorities but also objectives. It is only natural that the priorities of the multilateral financial institutions are different from national priorities in developing countries such as India. The economic priorities of the people and the development objectives of the country were forgotten in the process".[87] Therefore, the IMF-Bank economic programme was considered as anti-poor and aimed at making the economy more import-prone, which differed from the national priorities. As we have seen in Chapter-III, structural adjustment programme were not in conformation with social priorities like health and education. The Central Malaria Control budget was reduced by 43 per cent, which affects malaria itself, a disease which disproportionately afflicts poor people.[88]

While receiving the stand-by loan from the Fund, the government appeared to give up much more freedom than was necessary in the area of balance of payments management and trade policy. It promised that "during the course of the program (sic), the government will refrain from imposing new or intensifying existing restrictions on payments and transfers for current international transactions, or introducing or modifying multiple currency practices, or concluding bilateral payments arrangement with the Fund members inconsistent with Article VIII, or imposing new or intensifying existing import restrictions for balance of payments".[89] It was criticised that this limits the independence of government in conducting economic policies of the balance of payments, trade and industry.

Another criticism was that these institutions interfere in the borrowing country's domestic affairs so much that such interference amounts to interference in sovereignty of the debtor countries. For instance, the IMF had been putting pressure on India for substantial cut in defence expenditure as a major condition for the loan.

In Defence of Loans from the IMF and World Bank

The reform programme supported by international economic institutions was heavily criticised. But it would be wrong to say that the process of policy reforms were externally imposed by the lending bodies on unwilling policy makers. There is no rationale in lending to a government that lacks the political interest or capacity to pursue a programme to its conclusion. "These institutions do not force themselves on the member developing countries if the latter choose not to approach them for assistance. Also the member countries are free to abort the mutually agreed and necessary conditionalities as judged by any lender to ensure full repayment of the loan in reasonable time. Aborting of such programmes too is not without cost; but this can be done by a sovereign country after giving due notice if it strongly feels that is must be done".[90]

In an interview, Manmohan Singh said that "these programmes were programmes which responded to India's needs and the Fund and the Bank agreed with us...It would be wrong to say that they dictated these policies. These were our autonomous response to the crisis." He further argued that "what happened was that we wrote into the conditionalities what we felt had to be done. It was not a question of the conditionalities being imposed from outside. The Fund and the Bank agreed with what we could do and then it was a mutual consultation and so it is not something imposed on India".[91] Charan D. Wadhva concluded that in retrospect, the conditionalities on macro-economic variables like the ratio of fiscal deficit to the GDP and ceilings on the rate of growth of money supply have proved to be beneficial to the government in enforcing discipline on itself which it has found difficult to maintain in the absence of such conditionalities. Most of these conditionalities have a deflationary impact in the short run. It is desirable to control inflation as part of reforms as inflation hurts the poor and also adversely affects the competitiveness of the concerned nation's exports. Besides, hyper-inflation is inimical to sustained high growth in the long run.[92]

External assistance also allows the country to sustain a higher level of investment, which in turn should lead to greater economic benefits in later years. As a consequence of the economic liberalization, there was a huge increase in non-debt private capital inflows. It was $ 4.1 billion in 1993-94 and $ 4.9 billion in 1994-95.[93]

At another level, these capital inflows helped to revive the economy. The flows contributed to resolving the liquidity crisis of 1991 and in to assisting the Central Bank to build up sizeable foreign exchange reserves; the latter reached a high point of nearly $20 billion in 1994-95. As pointed out by Ajit Singh, ironically, these foreign exchange reserves helped to reduce the government's dependence on the IMF, giving it greater freedom to pursue a more independent economic policy which was politically necessary.[94] This was proved as we have seen earlier. Considering the substantial improvement in the foreign currency reserves of the country and acquiring a greater degree of maneuverability in managing the economy, the Government of India eliminated the need for negotiating any fresh loans from the IMF.

In this context, one may argue that some of the arguments presented by the left-wing intellectuals and economists against the economic liberalization as anti-national and a violation of its sovereignty to the international financial institutions have lost their sharp edge due to improved performance of the Indian economy, especially success achieved in the external sector and overcoming of the balance of payments crisis. It rather proved that lack of external support can weaken its sovereignty in the economic crisis situations.

While Jagdish Bhagwati and T.N. Srinivasan[95] agreed that conditionality played a role in strengthening India's will to launch the economic liberalization, they emphasised that the driving force behind the reforms was equally, even overwhelmingly, India's own conviction that India had lost time in the past to reform its economy, and that the new strategy was finally its only option. At the same time, they rejected the claim that the ideas and policies of the reforms under the Rao government were foreign and therefore ill-suited to India. Because, as they argued, that in fact, the ideas and policies of the reforms, which were rejected by Indian authorities in the past, had been advocated since the early 1960s by many Indian economists including themselves and that those very ideas have been recycled back to India. Thus, it is wrong to say that the ideas were dictated and imposed.

Dani Rodrik[96] also expressed a similar view that Indian economic liberalization cannot be credited to the Bretton Woods institutions. He observed that India has had a long history of avoiding and evading World Bank conditionality on liberalization. He argues that external actors have played at best a modest role in initiating the economic liberalization. The bulk of the credit must go instead to the dire economic circumstances. It was felt that under the continued deterioration in economic conditions, the need to seek the international financial support was the only viable and preferred shot-term alternative available at that time.

Saxena in his assessment of IMF loans justifies the conditionalities imposed by the Fund. To him the conditions are not only confined to India alone but to every county in the world. He argued that it will be an extreme view to say that the conditionality clause on the IMF loan to India amounts to sell out of economic sovereignty.[97] Bhagwati also pointed out that the spread of reforms worldwide, before India was getting to them, meant that the IMF-World Bank conditionality could no longer be plausibly dismissed as ideological; it had been legitimated as a sensible prescription that only reflected what they had all learned in the three decades of experience.[98]

In concluding the above responses, one may say that while the critics have valid points that need to be seriously considered by the Government of India as they refer to shaping and directing the various socio-economic development programmes of the country, at the same time, enthusiastic reception of the financial supports from the international financial institutions along with conditions was inevitable, even worthwhile under the crisis situation of the economy. It brought in a fresh wave of dynamism and competitiveness in the economy.

REFERENCES

1. The term World Bank is being used collectively to refer both to the International Bank for Reconstruction and Development (IBRD) and to its soft lending affiliate, the International Development Association (IDA). H.N. Ray, *The World Bank: A Third World View*, (New Delhi: Indus Publishing Company, 1996), p. 52.
2. S.P. Shukla, "The Emerging International Trading Order: A Story of the Uruguay Round" in G.S. Bhalla and Manmohan Agarwal (eds.), *World Economy in Transition*, (Shimla: Indian Institute of Advanced Study, 1992).
3. S.S. Saxena and R. K. Pandey, *The Uruguay Round of Multilateral Trade Negotiations Under GATT: Mid-Term Review at Montreal - Main Outcome - an Appraisal*, (New Delhi: Indian Institute of Foreign Trade, 1998), pp. 50-57. The report was actually completed in January 1989.
4. In this regard, see Sumitra Chishti, *Restructuring of International Economic Relations*, (New Delhi: Concept Publishing Company, 1991) and Manmohan Agarwal, "Implications of Economic Liberalization for India's Foreign Policy", *International Studies*, 30, 2, 1993.
5. See, Stephen D. Mcdowell, "India, the LDCs, and GATT Negotiations on Trade and Investment in Services" in Richard Stubbs and Geoffrey R.D. Underhill (eds.), *Political Economy and the Changing Global Order*, (London: Macmillan, 1994).
6. *Ibid.* and Muchkund Dubey, *An Unequal Treaty: World Trading Order*

After GATT, (New Delhi: New Age International Publishers, 1996).
7. *Ibid.*, p. 8.
8. *Ibid.*
9. *Ibid.*
10. Manmohan Agarwal, *op. cit.*, p. 138.
11. *Ibid.*
12. Muchkund Dubey, *op. cit.*
13. Interview with Manmohan Singh, March 6, 1997.
14. Interview with Muchkund Dubey, January 18, 1997.
15. Interview with Pranab Mukherjee, January 24, 1997.
16. For instance, in December 1992, the Karnataka Rajya Ryota Sangha (KRRS) launched what it called 'Seeds Satyagraha' to protest the farmers rights to produce multiple seeds. They attacked on the office of Cargill Seeds India Ltd. in Bangalore.
17. Muchkund Dubey, *An Unequal Treaty, op. cit.*, p. 10.
18. Achin Vanaik, *India in a Changing World*, (New Delhi: Orient Longman, 1995), p. 66.
19. U. Anderfelt, *International Patent Legislation and Developing Countries*, (The Hague: Martinus Nijhoffs, 1971).
20. J. Hushes, "The Philosophy of Intellectual Property", *Georgetown Law Journal*, Vol. 77 (2), 1988, pp. 287-366.
21. Muchkund Dubey, *op. cit.*, pp. 32-33.
22. J. Nogues, *Patents and Pharmaceutical Drugs: Understanding the Pressures on Developing Countries*, PRE WP Series No. 502, The World Bank, Washington D.C., 1990.
23. Public Interest Research Group, *GATT Strophe*, Delhi, 1994.
24. For a detailed argument, see D.M. Nachane, "Intellectual Property Rights in the Uruguay Round: An Indian Perspective", *EPW*, Vol. XXX No. 5, February 4, 1995, pp. 262-64.
25. Suman Sahai, "Dunkel Draft is Bad for Agriculture", *EPW*, June 19, 1993.
26. For a positive aspect, see G. Omvedt, "Three Sides of Every Story", *Down to Earth*, July 31, 1993.
27. Services are generally defined as intangible, as opposed to tangible commodities and goods, and therefore difficult to trade. See Orio Giarini (ed.), *The Emerging Service Economy*, (Oxford: Pregamon Press, 1986); Raymond J. Krommenacker, *World-Traded Services: The Challenge for the 1980s*, (Dedham, Mass.: Artech House, 1984); Ronald Kent Shelp, *Beyond Industrialization: Ascendancy of the Global Service Economy*, (New York: Praeger, 1981).
28. Stephen D. Mcdowell, *op. cit.*, p. 501.
29. Francis Cherunilam, "Trade in Services" in G.S. Batra and Narinder Kaur (eds), *GATT: Implications of Dunkel Proposals*, (New Delhi.

Anmol Publications, 1994), p. 229.
30. Muchkund Dubey, *op. cit.*, p. 57.
31. *Times of India*, July 28, 1995.
32. Muchkund Dubey, *op. cit.*, p. 68.
33. See the results of the Uruguay Round of Multilateral Trade Negotiations; *The Legal Texts*, GATT, Geneva, 1994.
34. Muchkind Dubey, *op. cit.*, p. 71.
35. Government of India, Ministry of Finance, *Economic Survey 1993-94*, (New Delhi: Government of India Press, 1994), p. 127.
36. *Financial Express*, March 21, 1994.
37. See P. Thomas, *et. al.*, "Implication for Rural Sector", EPW, March 26, 1994, pp. 452-53.
38. Muchkund Dubey, *op. cit.*, p. 78.
39. Government of India, Ministry of Commerce, The Uruguay Round of Multilateral Trade Negotiations: A Paper for Discussion, Monthly Commentary, July 1992.
40. *Financial Express*, March 21, 1994.
41. Ashok Gulati and Anil Sharma, "Agriculture Under GATT: What It Holds for India", *EPW*, Vol. XXIX, No. 29, July 16, 1994, p. 1860.
42. GATT Secretariat, *An Analysis of the Proposed Uruguay Round Agreement with Particular Emphasis on Aspects of Interest to Developing Countries*, Geneva, November 29, 1993.
43. Vijaya Katti, "GATT Proposal: Implications for India's Rice Exports", in K.R. Gupta (ed.), *GATT Accord and India*, (New Delhi: Atlantic Publishers, 1998).
44. Muchkund Dubey, *op. cit.*, p. 106.
45. *Ibid.*, p. 109.
46. *Times of India*, December 10, 1994.
47. The EFF was introduced in 1974 under which the IMF could provide loans for structural adjustment in case of serious imbalance in production and trade resulting in slow growth and poor foreign exchange reserves in member countries.
48. The IMF has its own currency in all practical terms. This is called the SDR. This is a kind of international money issued by the IMF just like the Central Banks issuing their national currencies. Since January 1, 1981 the value of SDR has been determined by the basket of currencies of 5 largest exporting member countries: US Dollar, Deutsche Mark, Yen, Franc and Pound Sterling. In 1991, the weight to these five currencies in SDR price determination was as follow: US Dollar 40 per cent, German Mark 21 per cent, Japanese Yen 17 per cent, British Pound 11 per cent, and French Franc 11 per cent. The value of SDR is determined by the IMF each day by summering the values in US dollars, based on market

exchange rates of a basket of five currencies. The country can use SDRs to buy hard currency from the IMF whenever needed.

49. *The IMF Survey*, February 4, 1991, Washington D C., pp. 45-46.
50. This is a special facility, initially provided to assist the member countries experiencing balance of payments deficits caused by a fall in exports earnings and worker's remittances resulting from factors beyond the member's control. Since 1981, the facility was extended to member countries faced with a rise in the import cost of cereals. The CCFF, as modified by the IMF's Executive Board in November 1990, is available to meet balance of payments problems created by temporary shortfalls in export earnings, receipts from workers' remittances and tourists and sharp increase in the price of cereal and oil imports. The Fund expanded the scope of the CCFF in December 1990 to include losses resulting from shortfalls in other services, such as receipts from pipeleins, canals, shipping, transportation, construction and insurance.
51. The Public Interest Research Group, *The Great Surrender*, Delhi, 1995, p. 7.
52. Graham Bird, *IMF Lending*, Overseas Development Institute Working Paper, London, No. 64, 1993, p. 22 and Tony Killick, *Continuity and Change in IMF Programme Design 1986-92*, ODI Working Paper, No. 69, London, 1992, p. 25.
53. World Bank, *India: Structural Loan/ Credit*, Washington D.C. 1991, p. 5.
54. Graham Bird, *op. cit.*, p. 20.
55. C.T. Kurien, *Economic Reforms and The People*, (Delhi: Public Interest Research Group, 1996), pp. 11-12.
56. Charan D. Wadhva, *Economic Reforms in India and the Market Economy*, (New Delhi: Allied Publishers, 1994), pp. 103-4. A Letter of Intent, or Memorandum, is first submitted by the country when it applies for a loan; it indicates how the country proposes to deal with the problem with the support of the loan. What eventually turns out to be conditionalities are often contained in the document; hence in a formal sense, the conditionalities are suggested by the country concerned. But, of course, those who seek the loan are fairly familiar with the conditions acceptable to the lender. C.T. Kurien, *op. cit.*, p. 16.
57. Steven B. Webb and Karim Shariff, "Designing and Implementing Adjustment Programs" in Vittorio Corbo, Stanley Fischer and Steven B Webb (eds.), *Adjustment Lending Revisited- Policies to Restore Growth*, A World Bank Symposium, World Bank, 1992, p.82 and Paul Mosely, James Harrigan and John Toye, *Aid and Power-the World Bank and Policy-based Lending*, (London: Routledge,

1991), p. 45.

58. *Business Standard*, September 13, 1991.
59. *The IMF Survey*, December 2, 1991, Washington D.C., pp. 364-65.
60. The total quantum of loan is usually sliced into a number of tranches, each specific to a time period, and payment for each tranche is conditional on the fulfilment of the preceding period. See Paul Mosley et al 1991, *op. cit.*, p. 45.
61. Since half of the quota contribution comes in terms of the member's domestic currency and the balance in convertible currency, the first facility available to a member country is a repurchase of its own contribution made in convertible currency. This is known as the reserves tranche. The access of the reserve tranche is more or less automatic since it basically amounts to merely taking back what has been contributed by the member country itself.
62. The rationale for the EFF was explained by the then Finance Minister, Dr. Manmohan Shigh. He said that "for the next three years, we do need the support of the international financial institutions... Therefore, we should be asking for the support of the IMF for an Extended Fund Facility (EFF) arrangement. That will give us a greater sense of confidence. Because we do not know, although we should do everything to increase our exports, we do not control the international environment. If the international economy goes into a recession, we can do nothing. Therefore, to deal with those shocks, which are not of our own making, we do need the Extended Fund Facility". *Economic Times*, July 5, 1992.
63. *Economic Survey 1994-95, op. cit.*, pp. 88-89.
64. World Bank, *India: Structural Loan/ Credit, op cit.*, p. 32.
65. Dalip S. Swamy, *The Political Economy of Industrialisation: From Self-Reliance to Globalisation*, (New Delhi: Sage Publications, 1994), p. 252.
66. *Times of India*, February 28, 1992.
67. This was started to provide long term concessional credit to low income countries. The requirement to obtain assistance from the facility is to develop medium term policy frame for a three year period and detailed annual programmemes.
68. Tony Killick, *op. cit.*, p.17 and Paul Mosely *et al, op. cit.*, p. 37.
69. Jone Williamson, "The Lending Policies of the International Monetary Fund", in Jone Williamson (ed), *IMF Conditionality*, (Washington D.C.: Institute for International Economics, 1983), p. 619.
70. Paul Mosley *et al, op. cit.*, p. 56.
71. World Bank, *The World Bank in India*, New Delhi, 1993, p. 26.
72. *Ibid.* p. 27.

73. The text of this letter was published in several leading newspapers and magazines in India around July 20, 1993. For a quick review of the contents, see newspaper report: "For promise Preston interest cut, import licence abolition", *Business Standard,* July 20, 1993.
74. It has been called as Indian Development Forum (IDF) since 1994. Earlier, the participants in the IAC were donor countries led by the World Bank. For the first time, the transnational corporations and Indian private sector representatives were invited by the World Bank to the IDF meeting at Paris during June 29-July 1, 1994. In this meeting, over 90 representatives of big corporations and banks from the US, Britain, Japan, Canada, Hong Kong, Germany and Switzerland were joined by other 15 from India. See Public Interest Research Group, *The World Bank and India,* Delhi, 1995.
75. *Financial Express,* June 27, 1992.
76. Ibid.
77. A.W. Hooke, "The IMF-Its Evolution, Organisation and Activities", The IMF, Pamphlet, No. 37, Washington, D.C., 1982, p. 46.
78. M.S. Khan and M.D. Knight, "Fund Supported Adjustment Programmemes and Economic Growth", IMF Occasional Paper, No. 4, Washington D.C., 1985, p. 2.
79. Shridhar Pandey, "The IMF Conditionalities and India", in Rama Shankar Singh (ed.), *IMF Policies Towards Less Developed Countries (LDCs): With Special Reference to India,* (Delhi: Deep & Deep Publications, 1996), pp.165-66.
80. Tony Killick, *op. cit.,* pp. 21-22.
81. Sidney Dell, *On Being Grandmotherly: The Evolution of IMF Conditionality,* (Princeton: Princeton University, International Finance Section, 1981); Jone Williamson (ed.), *op. cit.;* Elliot Berg and Alan Batchelder, "Structural Adjustment Lending: A Critical Review", *World Bank,* CPD 8521, Washington D.C., 1985; Stephan Haggard, "The Politics of Adjustment: Lesions from the IMF's Extended Fund Facility", in Miles Kahler, (ed.), *The Politics of International Debt,* (Ithaca: Cornell University Press, 1986); Paul Mosley, *Conditionality as Bargaining Process: Structural Adjustment Lending, 1980-86,* (Princeton: Princeton University, International Finance Section, 1987); Albert Fishlow, "Conditionality and Willingness to Pay: Some Parallels from the 1890s", in Barry Echengreen and Peter Lindert, (eds.), *The International Debt Crisis in Historical Perspective,* (Cambridge: M.I.T. Press, 1990); Paul Mosley *et al, op. cit.*
82. Paul Mosley *et al, ibid.*
83. Manmohan Agarwal, *op. cit.,* pp. 136-7.

84. The International Monetary Fund, *World Economic Outlook 1994,* (Washington D.C.: IMF, 1994).
85. Bharat Bhusan, "World Bank Comments on Plan Draft Before Parliament Sees It", *Indian Express,* July 16, 1992.
86. See *Sunday Observer,* March 2, 1992.
87. Amit Bhaduri and Deepak Nayyar, *The Intelligent Person's Guide to Liberalization,* (New Delhi: Penguin Books, 1996), pp. 55-56.
88. Robert Cassen, Vijay Josh and Michael Lipton, "Stabilization and Structural Reform in India", *Contemporary South Asia,* 2(2), 1993, p. 191.
89. Quoted in "IMF Stand-By Loan Conditions", *EPW,* December 28, 1991, p. 2977.
90. Charan D. Wadhva, *op. cit.,* p. 111.
91. Interview with Manmohan Singh, *op. cit.*
92. Charan D. Wadhva, *op. cit.,* p. 112.
93. Vijay Josh and I.M.D. Little, *India's Economic Reforms 1991-2001,* (Delhi: OUP, 1996).
94. Ajit Singh, "Liberalization, the Stock Market, and the Market for Corporate Control: A Bridge too Far for the Indian Economy?" in Isher Judge Ahluwalia and I.M.D. Little, *India's Economic Reforms and Development: Essays for Manmohan Singh,* (Delhi: OUP, 1998), p. 180.
95. Jagdish Bhagwati and T.N. Srinivasan, *India's Economic Reforms,* (New Delhi: Government of India, Ministry of Finance, 1993), pp. 8-9.
96. Dani Rodrik,"The Rush to Free Trade in the Developing World: Why So Late? Why Now? Will It Last?", in Stephan Haggard and Steven B. Webb (eds.), *Voting For Reform: Democracy Political Liberation, and Economic Adjustment,* (New York: OUP, 1994), p.79.
97. P.R. Saxena, *The IMF Loan to India: An Economic Assessment,* (Delhi: Anmol Publications, 1986).
98. J Bhagwati, The Design of Indian Development", in I J Ahluwalia and IMD Little, *op. cit.,* p. 35.

Five

Impact on India's Foreign Relations

A marked feature of global relations in the post-Cold War era is the absence of the ideological confrontation between the East and the West. In a post-Soviet world, economics began to dominate the foreign policy agendas of most of the states including that of India's. As underlined by an eminent analyst, "the economic struggle had taken primacy over the political struggle".[1] Accordingly, many countries adjusted foreign policies to maximize their national interests in the emerging new global equations and relations. So did India. The former Prime Minister, Narasimha Rao said in the early 1990s, "now the Cold War is over. There is an element of cooperation instead of confrontation. It is a new situation. And we have to respond to that also. So certain policy reorientations will take place to ensure that our national interest does not surffer".[2]

It was inevitable that India adjusted the style and substance of her diplomacy to keep pace with the global changes. There emerged a moderate, pragmatic and more flexible style of diplomacy. The former ambassador to the US, Abid Hussain interestingly stated, "we are now using language which is less offensive and jarring".[3]

As seen earlier in the study, the collapse of the Soviet socialist bloc had fuelled the urgent need for a pragmatic and flexible foreign economic policy. Economically, the collapse of the Soviet Union had shaken one of the main pillars of India's international economic relations. It also threatened India's strategy of economic self-reliance through a diversification of foreign economic relations, when India desperately needed to increase its exports at a fast rate.

The drastic collapse in India's trade with the former USSR and Eastern Europe had compelled New Delhi to seek suitable compensatory markets. In this context, the markets of leading capitalist countries assumed added significance and urgency from the Indian standpoint. Also, India's economic crisis during 1990-91 and the Rao government's efforts to fundamentally reform the Indian economy along free-market lines had forced New Delhi to seek the assistance of capitalist countries. The need for foreign capital, technology and market access for exports required the creation of new economic relationships.

Thus, with the end of the Cold War, the collapse of the Soviet Union and liberalization of economic policies in India consistent with global trends, a new agenda in external relations became urgent. This chapter reviews the major developments in India's foreign relations during 1990-95, focusing on the economic aspects of India's foreign relations. How did the economic liberalization of India influence India's diplomatic style? How did it influence in the shaping of India's bilateral relations? The adoption of economic liberalization also created new incentives to join regional preferential trade associations. In this regard, this chapter focuses on India's approach to regional blocs such as the European Union (EU), the Association of South-East Asian Nations (ASEAN), the Asia Pacific Economic Community (APEC), the South Asian Association for Regional Cooperation (SAARC) and the Indian Ocean Rim Association for Regional Cooperation (IORARC).

ECONOMIC DIMENSIONS IN DIPLOMACY

Changes in the international economic environment in the post-Cold War era and India's own economic liberalization programme in 1991 suggested that dramatic reform should immediately be made in India's foreign economic policy. According to the former foreign secretary under the Narasimha Rao government, J.N. Dixit, the Prime Minister issued instructions to the foreign office late in 1991 to concentrate more on the economic aspects of India's foreign relations.[4] Naturally the Rao government's conduct of foreign relations continued to be guided by a desire to increase the volume of exports and the inflow of high technology and investment.

In the post-bipolar world, the economic crisis and the subsequent economic liberalization of India during the first half of the 1990s had profound implications for India's relations with other countries. The economic liberalization of India changed its equations with many countries. The economic dimension became the most important dimension of India's foreign policy. It also became the most far-reaching aspect of India's diplomacy.

India's economic liberalization and globalization attracted the attention of many nations. Narasimha Rao's visits to many leading capitalist countries and the visits of important leaders of the world to India during this period could be considered within this context. In each summit, the economic aspect of the relationship with India was on top of the agenda. The Rao government sought to utilize the visits as an international political support for its economic liberalization programme. The leaders naturally backed India's new economic liberalization policies and to that extent these visits must be considered successful.[5]

This new thrust in Indian diplomacy was also reflected in the appointment of ambassadors in target countries like Japan and Germany with the commerce secretary being a part of the panels that decided foreign postings. Besides translating the implications of the country's new economic stance for governments and investors abroad, India's ambassadors were being increasingly called upon to sell India as a lucrative option.

With this in mind, about two dozen heads of missions were called to India in March 1992 to attend an orientation course in the Foreign Service Institute (FSI), New Delhi, to be briefed about the new economic policy and its ramifications. Another such 10-day course was convened in December for 27 more heads of missions. Unfortunately, the Ayodha crisis occured before the session could start on December 7 and the ambassadors rushed back to their bases to manage the crisis at hand.[6] These steps indicated the new economic dimensions that Indian diplomacy had acquired.

The former external affairs minister under the Rao government, Mr Dinesh Singh, stressing on economic diplomacy stated "the work is cut out for our missions abroad. They will not only act as sales offices for marketing India's new economic environment but will also be responsible for communicating the feedback from the local government and business community. Above all, they should actively seek foreign investment and new markets for Indian exports".[7]

P.M.S. Malik, the former additional secretary in-charge of economic affairs in the ministry of external affairs again mentioned India's new dimension of diplomacy. He described in the early 1990s that "today in our major missions, the highest priority is being attached to economic issues. Earlier economic negotiations were not considered to be the normal functioning of an ambassador. Now it is".[8] Regarding the above aspects of India's foreign policy, one may refer to James Manor,[9] that in contrast to not making much effort to generate support for the economic liberalization within India, the Rao government tried to sell the liberalization of the economy outside India.

In the post- Cold War era, more than ever before, there has been increasing economic competition among the leading capitalist countries. It is, therefore, not surprising that the Western nations and other leading capitalist countries have been interested in developing closer business ties with emerging economies like India's. Since the Indian Government started the liberalization process in June 1991, most embassies in the Capital had found it important to keep their country's business community informed about the major policy changes in India. In the field of foreign policy, economic potential is undeniably a major factor for a country's room for manoeuvre, albeit not its sole determination. In this context, this chapter also tries to examine whether India was able to obtain any policy leverage vis-a-vis other countries, specially the US, as a result of its own economic liberalization programme.

INDO-US RELATIONS

The dynamism of the Indo-US relationship, specially the economic relationship, during the first half of the 1990s was certainly facilitated by India's economic liberalization programme. The outward-looking market oriented policy under the Rao government had paved the way for a reorientation in US perceptions of India. From the Indian point of view, in the era of the economic liberalization and greater integration with the world economy, India had to rebuild its relations with the US, which has the most powerful economy in the world. The influence of the end of the Cold War and the disintegration of the Soviet Union, however, could not effectively change the political content of the relationship between the two states. So, before we turn to the economic dimensions of Indo-US relations, it is necessary to analyse the political aspects of relationship between the two states during the period.

Political Aspects of the Relationship

The end of the Cold War and later the Soviet collapse had substaintially removed the irritations in Indo-US relations which had been caused by bipolarity and India's close ties with the former Soviet Union during the Cold War era. These provided for more amicable relations between the two nations. India needed to find new partners who could compensate for the former Soviet Union's status with regard to its economic as well as political support. (The importance of the USSR for India during the Cold War period has been discussed in Chapter-II.) Newly independent Russia was keen to reformulate its foreign policy keeping in mind its own interests. Russia was strongly drawn towards the Western capitals. Therefore, developing countries such as India were not considered significant for Russia's foreign policy. The US emerged as the pre-eminent world power in the post-Cold War period. Its economy remained the world's largest economy although its share in the world economy declined. In contrast, India's foreign policy options, its manoeuvring space, and bargaining power resources had become more limited. This fact could be tested by India's attitudes during the Gulf War of 1990-91.

As discussed earlier in Chapter-IV, India's decision to refuel American aircrafts during the Gulf War needs to be seen in the context of US help in getting the IMF loans for New Delhi's economic crisis. In this regard, one may argue that the state of the Indian economy during this period influenced the formulation of foreign policy to the extent of affecting its credibility.

It is also necessary to view the refuelling issue against the background of the perceptible improvements in Indo-US relations in the post-Cold War era. Since the former USSR was too busy with its own internal problems in the field of politics as well as economics, the US was left unchallenged in the Gulf War operations as the only remaining super power. Hence, policy-making circles in the ministry of external affairs were convinced that India had to adapt to a changed international system in which only one superpower existed. According to an expert, the reason that India as a non-aligned member country tilted towards the US by giving the refuelling facilities during the Gulf War was in response to the new realities that emerged on the international scene as a result of the end of the Cold War. This argument was pointed out by the then Indian Secretary of the Ministry of External Affairs, Mr Muchkund Dubey, who had played a major role in getting the decision of the Government of India in giving refuelling facilities to the US. He said in an interview that "the change was deliberately and consciously introduced in order to meet the challenge of the post-Cold War situation. It was clearly realized that after the Cold War, United States has emerged as the only superpower. It was felt that it was important to deal with United States without the blinkers of ideology which used to be the case before".[10]

This kind of new policy towards the US in the post-bipolar world continued during the Narasimha Rao government period. The former Indian foreign secretary, J.N. Dixt revealed that "it was acknowledged that India, having lost the leverage of its relationship with the Soviet Union, should develop positive equations with new power centres in the wold, out of which the United States was the most important one".[11] This was a new dimension for India's foreign policy in the post-Cold War.

The US strategic perceptions towards the subcontinental region had been changed by the exit of the Soviet forces from Afghanistan and the subsequent collapse of the Soviet communism. These developments provided an added incentive for closer Indo-US relations. The Bush government decided not to consider old resolutions calling for plebiscite in Jammu and Kashmir as relevant to resolve Kashmir tangle. It had affirmed its commitment to India's twenty year old Shimla agreement with Pakistan which stipulated a peaceful and bilateral resolution of all disputes. The US had also cut off its military and economic aid to Pakistan in October 1990 for the first time under the Pressler amendment originally passed in 1985.[12]

India's intention to be closer with the US, however, did not have a reciprocal response from the US soon after Bill Clinton took office in Washington in 1993. The US again took the traditional approach with its pro-Pakistan tilt. The Assistant Secretary of State in charge of Bureau for South Asia Affairs in the State Department, Robin Raphel questioned the legitimacy of the very accession of Kashmir to the Indian Union when she gave an informal briefing to the Indian press in Washington in 1993. She said that the US considered Jammu and Kashmir as a disputed area. She further stated that the US did not consider the Instrument of Accession (signed by the Maharaja of Kashmir in October 1947 making Jammu and Kashmir part of India) politically or legally valid.[13]

This question on Kashmir provoked many Indian sentiments, which made a negative impact on Indo-US relations. According to one source,[14] Robin Raphel's expression on the Kashmir issue was caused by the series of events. They were the demolition the Babri mosque on 6th December, 1992, heightened tensions in Kashmir, bomb blasts in Bombay in early 1993 and thereafter, communal conflicts in India. The President Clinton himself compared the Kashmir situation with other ethnic religious conflicts in his speech of 27 September 1993 in the UN. He mentioned that "bloody ethnic, religious and civil wars were raging from Angola to the Caucasus to Kashmir". The President also referred to Sikh rights and the human rights abuses in Punjab in a letter to the US Congressman, Mr Gary A Condit.[15]

In this regard, for the first time, six former Foreign Secretaries of India took strong exception to a series of comments by high US officials, including the President's, against India. In their joint statement, they stated that "A number of recent pronouncements by high US officials in Washington have given cause for concern in this country. They show complete disregard to the facts and have resulted in a setback to Indo-US relations, at a time when there have been signs of improved understanding and cooperation between the two countries".[16]

The Indian expectations from the US were totally thwarted during the year 1993. The Clinton Administration did not focus much on India as an economic and strategic ally in Asia. Only Japan and China were regarded as the most important countries in Asia in terms of the US economic interests. During the year, American foreign policy was pre-occupied with Russia and Eastern Europe. The US was generally interested only in contentious issues such as Kashmir, human rights and non-proliferation as mentioned by Robin Rahpel. She said to the then Indian Foreign Secretary, J.N. Dixit that "You must realise that India is not on his (Clinton) radar screen. His attention is not focused on India except in situations where critical developments or conflicts may take place in the region. In this context, India should be more forthcoming on non-proliferation matters, on finding a compromise on Kashmir and agreeing to confidence-building measures in South Asia suggested by the USA".[17]

However, from early 1994 onwards, the US began to adopt a non-controversial approach on political issues, while they took pragmatic and flexible positions on economic issues. This change manifested a US desire to forge a new partnership with India in order to benefit the US economy and business. There were important reasons for this change. One was the fact that by this time the state of the Indian economy had stabilised. It had clearly recovered through its liberalization programme after the crisis induced low growth of 0.9 per cent in 1991-92. The year of 1993-94 recorded 4.3 per cent economic growth, and, further the next year showed an acceleration of growth to 5.3 per cent led by its industrial growth of around 8 per cent and supported by a robust agricultural performance. Beside, the Indo-US bilateral trade and the US investments in India began to show a steady increase. Another was the US economic compulsion to revitalise its own economy, especially when global economic giants like Japan and Germany threatened its competitive edge in the world economy.

In this background, Ms Raphel came on her first visit to India in February 1994 which was described as aiming to remove "some misunderstanding and work to place Indo-US relations on a sound footing".[18] In the meanwhile, there was also an invitation to the Indian Prime Minister, P V. Narasimha Rao to visit America. From 1994, the US clearly showed its emphasis on economic aspect of foreign policy towards India as the former Ambassador of the US to India, Mr Thomas Pickering had predicted. Mr Pickering mentioned, before he left India in 1993, that trade and economic ties will be the catalyst that would drive future Indo-US relations.[19]

During Rao's visit to the US in 1994, there was a mood that the bilateral agenda of political dissatisfaction ought not to cloud the reality of working together for mutual gains. Kashmir, human rights and the nuclear programme issues that had dominated the Indo-US agenda for the past year, were discussed in private backrooms to cement the way for a successful summit between the two leaders. On the nuclear issue, both agreed that the most acceptable method would be to change the agenda from a bilateral one to a large multilateral forum to endorse the proposed global comprehensive ban on nuclear tests and fissionable weapons production, both issues which India supported.[20] On the Kashmir issue, the President, Clinton clearly supported the Indian view point that the Pakistan government was supporting the Kashmiri militants. Mr Clinton stated that "based on our best evidence, official Pakistani material support to the Kashmiri militants has dropped".[21] This indicated that the US now officially acknowledged that it was Pakistan that was cultivating Kashmiri terrorism.

At the defence level too, there was closer relationship between the two countries. A major Indo-US naval exercise, the second in two years, took place off the coast of Ratnagiri, Maharashtra, in mid-September 1994. It was believed to have been a marine commando-training exercise and lasted for ten days.[22] This was followed by an important visit by Defence Secretary William Perry on 10-12 January 1995. The defence connection received a significant boost as Perry signed with the Indian Minister of State for Defence, an agreed minute on defence relations seeking to enhance the level of bilateral defence cooperation. In the first-ever defence pact signed between India and the US at the political level, this contract was expanded to cover not only civilian officials in the two defence ministries but also the defence research establishments.

Perry, however, made it clear at a press conference that a deepened security relationship with India would not mean tilting away from Pakistan or from the principle of a balanced US approach towards the two countries. He also ruled out joint technology development and arms transfer to India in the immediate future.[23] This kind of US policy was shown in the Brown Amendment, which was considered as being inimical to India's interest. Thus, in general, one may say that Indo-US political relations were marked by both highs and lows during 1990-95 period.

Economic Aspects of the Relations

Economic compulsions faced by India and the US constituted the main forces that brought New Delhi and Washington closer to one another. In fact, from the Indian point of view, closer economic relationship with the US was an important imperative of India's foreign economic policy under the Rao government, which tried to reform its economy along free market lines.

While threatening India that Washington will have to keep Super-301 as a punitive option against New Delhi regarding intellectual property rights and the ongoing Uruguay Round of negotiations, Americans generally welcomed India's economic liberalization policy as a positive aspect of Indo-US relations.[24] In 1992, the US Import-Export Bank doubled its lending profile in India to over $ 500 million and expected India to be its fastest growing portfolio.[25]

A senior US administration official at the White House briefing said "the dynamism in the US-India relationship is that Americans are more interested in India now as an economic player, and therefore that is what is driving, creating a larger constituency in this country for a relationship with India".[26] The US Under Secretary of Commerce for International Trade, Mr Jeffery E. Garten, also expressed a similar view that as the economic reforms gathers momentum, India may be "in a position to provide significant commercial opportunities for US firms throughout the 1990s".[27] The Clinton Administration has recognised India as a major player in the economic field. The US Commerce Department identified India as one of the top ten big emerging markets in the world.[28]

It was clearly indicated that during the former Prime Minister, Mr Narasimha Rao's visit to the US for six days, he wanted to push the economic agenda on the centre stage instead of political issues. According to one report, one of the remarkable features of Rao's visit was that mention of Pakistan was deliberately left out of a majority of the official level discussions. The only reference was when Rao questioned Clinton on the F-16 sale. This strategy clearly helped in imparting the dialogue far more flexibility.[29] In this regard. one may say that the adoption of sweeping economic liberalization programme by the Rao government compelled India to adopt more flexible and business oriented attitude towards the US.

During the visit, Rao spent maximum time on business talks with politicians as well as the business community in the US. At New York and Houston, Rao held several meetings with the US business community. As a result, Rao generated interest amongst the US chief executive officers (CEOs) to invest in India.

By attracting American investors, Rao was also able to establish an 'India Interest Group' including AT & T, Coca Cola, Enron, IBM, Ford, General Electric, International Equity Partners, Morgan Stanley, Raytheon and Unisys, which can act as a pressure group in favour of India. In 1995, however, the Indian embassy in Washington had not yet organised these allies against Republican Congressman Dan Burton who moved an amendment to the US foreign aid bill demanding a cut of 25 per cent aid to India as punishment for its human rights violations.[30]

During Rao's visit to the US in 1994, it was decided to resurrect the Joint Economic Trade Commissions. It was a significant step between the two countries in the context of the new emphasis on economic diplomacy. As a follow-up to the Rao-Clinton Summit, the US Energy Secretary, Hazel O'Leary's visited India in mid-July 1994 along with a high-powered business delegation. During the visit, India and the US signed 17 agreements including 11 joint ventures agreements in private sector and five more official Memoranda of Understanding (MOUs), broad MOU on bilateral consultation and cooperation in the energy sector.[31] In November 1994, it was followed by five energy technology agreements with total investments of around $800 million[32] which opened the door for transfer of technology which hitherto was closed due to its sensitive and dual use.

In early 1995, the then US Commerce Secretary, Ron Brown, visited India accompanied by 26 CEOs of US corporations. During the visit the then Commerce Minister of India, Mr Pranab Mukherjee and the US Commerce Secretary signed an agreement for the establishment of an Indo- US Commercial Alliance aimed at forging closer business-to-business link to promote trade and investment, which was formally launched in both countries on 14 May, 1995. The US delegation focused only on the business achievements and played down contentious political issues. The Government of India was also careful not to link the improvement of the overall bilateral relationship with the differing views such as nuclear non-proliferation.[33] In this context, B. Bhattacharyya pointed out that "creating an institutional mechanism for getting the direct involvement of industry in the management of the country's foreign economic policies can also help to create a buffer between the fallout of political decisions and maintaining normal commercial relations".[34] As a result, the two sides produced eleven business collaborations, six in power, four in telecommunications and one in the insurance sector-envisaging US investment of about $1.4 billion. Many of the collaborations, however, related to old projects.[35]

U.S. Investments in India

As we have seen in Chapter-III, during the period 1991-95, the US was the single largest investor in India accounting for nearly 29 per cent of the investments approval. The amount of investment approvals of the US was Rs.15422 crores almost half of which came in 1995 itself. This showed that the US was clearly the best responder to the economic liberalization of India.

The US was particularly interested in the sectors of power,

finance and banking, telecommunication, insurance and consumer goods. In response to the US, the Government of India gave positive response to the power and telecom sectors, but was reluctant to liberalise its banking and insurance sectors. For example, It was for the first time that the Indian government gave the counter-guarantees for a state project to the Dhabol Power Company, promoted by American companies Enron, General Electric and Bechtel. The deal unfortunately became a victim of the domestic politics of Maharashtra as discussed earlier in Chapter-III. Furthermore, just before the Prime Minister, Narasimha Rao's visit to the US, the government of India announced a new telecommunication policy permitting 100 per cent foreign participation, in which the US was most interested.

As a result, the majority of foreign direct investments (FDI) of the US during 1991-95 were in priority sectors such as telecommunication and power. The US Energy Secretary said that "the only projects that will be financed are those which are robust".[36] In this context, one may guess that a major intention of the US investments in India was to capture the domestic market of India rather than the export markets, despite the advantage of operational low cost of India.

Trade with the US

The US was also India's single largest trading partner accounting for 19.8 per cent of India's total exports and 10 per cent of India's total imports during 1994-95.[37] Since the end of the Cold War, the US replaced the former Soviet Union as the single largest country for India's trade. Although India's exports have registered a persistent rise, looking from the global view point, the Indian share in the US imports continued to be insignificant, especially when compared to the magnitude of the US trade with other countries of the Asia-Pacific region. Out of total US import amount of 690 billion dollars in 1994, India's share stood at a meagre $ 5.2 billion, i.e., 0.75 per cent. On the other hand, of the total US exports of $ 513 billion, India's share was $ 2.2 billion, i.e., 0.4 per cent.[38] India enjoyed a favourable balance of trade with America from 1990 to 1994. America's trade deficit with

India which was $ 0.7 billion in 1990 rose to $ 3 billion by 1994.

Essentially, the problem on the export side for India seems to be narrow base of products and services sold to the US. The export basket was dominated to a large extent by gems and jewellery, especially polished diamonds, and garments and textiles, with relatively minor contributions from a host of traditional exports such as tea, cashew nuts, seafood products, handicrafts, and leather goods. The two major non-traditional exports included engineering goods and, increasingly after the new economic liberalization policy, computer software. Even in these two fields, the optimistic projects have not materialized.

India's imports from the US consisted primarily of fertilizers, which constitute the largest product group, transport equipment, metal scrap, pulp and waste paper, organic / inorganic chemical, and scientific and precision instruments. India also imported small quantities of some US agricultural products, such as California almonds.

Economic Liberalization as a Political Leverage?

When one looks at the Indo-US relationship during the period of 1990-95, especially for 1994 and 1995, one may say that the economic recovery of India and its huge domestic market prompted the US to downplay some of politically contentious issues such as Kashmir, human rights and nuclear proliferation. It is true that in the field of foreign policy, economic potential is a major factor for a country's room for manoeuvre, albeit not its sole determination. Then, here a question arises as to whether India had a leverage against the US on the issue of security by liberalising its economy during the 1991-95. The answer was negative, especially on the issue of India's missile programme.

In the absence of diplomatic support of erstwhile Soviet Union and circumstances under which it opted for economic liberalization, India was fully susceptible to external pressure. This was clear from the then Chairman, House Committee on International Relations, Lee Hamilton's public admission just before PM's visit, that US can pressurize India to give up the missiles programme since she has newly initiated the policy of economic liberalization. At the same time, he admitted similar policy has not worked against China.[39]

In this regard, it is interesting to note one report that the US assured Mr Rao that the US would do nothing to embarrass him, nor would it spring any surprises when Rao visited the US. In return, the US requested Rao to make some conciliatory gestures. This happened during the meeting between the Prime Minister of India and the US Deputy Secretary of State, Strobe Talbott.[40]

According to some critics, apparently there were certain concessions made by India in the field of its own security. It was evident from the fact that though India conducted a user test of Prithvi in June 1994, soon after the PM returned from his US trip, until the end of 1995 India did not conduct any further tests of Agni or Prithvi missiles. New Delhi also did not take any action to deploy these missiles. In this regard, one study has argued there must have been a private assurance from Prime Minister Rao to Bill Clinton on non-deployment of the Prithvi. This led US officials to conclude that India's Agni project is in "a period of suspended animation", while Prithvi is in "a period of hibernation".[41]

In May 1995, a multiparty defence committee of Parliament urged the Congress government led by Narasimha Rao to pursue the deployment of Prithvi. Dr Murli Manohar Joshi, leader of the then main opposition party BJP, insisted that both the Prithvi and the Agni should be integrated into the country's defence system.[42] In response, the then Prime Minister Rao said that the deployment of Prithvi was under consideration, and that the decision would not be influenced by foreign pressure.[43]

But, some analysts[44] have argued that Indian policy makers should have taken note of the economic compulsions of the US as well, while deciding the extent of accommodation they were willing to accept on security perceptions. Indian economic liberalization came about at a time when the US was in a state of economic decline. Hence the US needed to penetrate into newly industrializing countries like India for her own economic recovery. Moreover, the revolutionary nature of economic reforms initiated by India's Prime Minister Narasimha Rao (since July 1991) seemed quite tantalizing for the US which was seeking new overseas markets and investments.

But, it is commonly accepted that India needed the US much more than Washington needed New Delhi. For India, one of the urgent matters was to invite the US capital and technology to improve its economic situation. In this context, it is worth noting what the former Secretary of External Affairs, Muchkund Dubey pointed out in an interview. He mentioned that because of the increasing dependence of India on the Western markets and capitals, particularly the US, she was more cautious about what would be reaction of Western countries to any thing that she did. As a result, sometimes, India compromised some of its security policies. Citing the example of stopping the test of the Agni missile he argued it was influenced by the US pressure.[45]

As we have discussed earlier, Indo-US economic relationship was still a very asymmetrical one, though the US direct investments in and trade with India were steadily increasing. Only a small fraction of the global American investments was in India. India's share of America's global trade was less than one per cent.[46] Moreover, India' s economic potential to compete with the US interests was comparatively limited. As we have said, after the end of the Cold War and the disintegration of the Soviet Union, the focus of American foreign and economic policies was on Eastern Europe and the Russian Federation. In Asia, its focus was on Japan, China and in some respect, on South Korea. In this regard, it is interesting to note that the US media reportedly almost ignored the then Indian Prime Minister's presence in June 1994 in America.

Considering the above factors, one may say that India was still not in a position to get any substantial concessions with regard to the security matters. In other words, India could not utilize its economic liberalization programme as a leverage against the US on the issue of its own security.

INDO-EUROPEAN UNION RELATIONS

During the Rao government, India had a "twin-track policy"[47] towards Western Europe. First, it focussed on larger and more important nations individually like the U.K., Germany and France, which were visited by the Prime Minister Rao for expanding bilateral relations. Secondly, India emphasised economic cooperation between her and the European Union (EU).[48] Without doubt, one of the main reasons for focusing on the three major countries of the EU and on the EU as a whole was India's economic compulsion, and the economic challenge faced by the Congress government.

In the context of the growing importance of economic diplomacy with the EU, Prime Minister Rao called a meeting of the Indian Ambassadors to the West European countries while stopping in Paris on the way to Caracas to participate in the G-15 summit in 1991. In the Ambassadors meeting, the Prime Minister stressed on economic aspects of Indian diplomacy. Further, with the structural changes in the EU, India paid additional attention for greater cooperation with the region as a whole. On 1 January, 1993, the Single Market of the EU was formally launched, removing internal frontiers for the 12 separate national markets. A significant landmark in the process of European integration was the signing of the Treaty on European Union on 7 February, 1992, at Maastricht in the Netherlands. The Treaty came into force on 1 November 1993, after it was ratified by the 12 member states and the European Community was renamed the European Union. On 1 January, 1995, Austria, Finland and Sweden became members, taking the membership from 12 to 15. The 15 countries' union was the world's biggest free trade area, offering the largest market in the industrialised world with a population of nearly 370 million. It was the world's biggest importer of agricultural products. It is also mentioned that these developemnts of EU and India's economic liberalization process had almost simultaneously occurred.

In this regard, India made some efforts towards better understanding, and responding effectively to the Union in order to activate contact with the major individual countries and upgrade its relationship with the EU. For instance, in 1994, the Government of India institutionalised bi-annual meetings of Heads of Indian Missions in Belgium, Germany, France, Italy, Netherlands, Sweden, Austria, the UK and Spain. The first meeting was held at Paris in April 1995 under the chairmanship of the then Minister of External

Affairs, Pranab Mukherjee.[49]

The EU also made efforts to upgrade relations with India. The EU 'troika'[50] had been formed to interact with India on both economic and political issues. In this context, V.P. Dutt argues that "there is no doubt that Europe's interest in India was rekindled by New Delhi's economic reforms. The political importance was being rediscovered only when it appeared that India would be emerging as a major economy in the world".[51] The individual governments, business and industry of the EU reacted positively to India's economic liberalization programme initiated by the Rao government. The EU recognized India as a major partner in the fields of trade, investment, technological and scientific cooperation. It was assured by the troika of EU foreign ministers in 1992.[52] It was confirmed by the then Finance Minister of India. He said that the Europeans recognized India as "wide awake, determined to march ahead to emerge as a strong internationally-competitive economy, and to gain its rightful place in the community of nations".[53]

As a result, India and the EC established the Indo-EC Business Forum for regular interaction between the businessmen and the Government of India with the EC and the European business leaders. Their relationship was further strengthened as a "third-generation" agreement on partnership and development was signed between India and the European Union on 20 December 1993 (in force since August 1994). By this time, India's own approach on its economic liberalization had more or less crystallized. On the issues of human rights and nuclear non-proliferation, unlike the US, the EU took a more moderate approach towards India, even though they also had certain reservations on these issues. They continuously hoped that India would sign the NPT, and that the human rights conditions in India would be improved.

In fact, the then Prime Minister of India was aware of the European countries' reservations on these issues. As a result, when the Foreign Ministers of the EC Troika called on Rao on 4 March 1992, he underlined that while India was desirous of substantively expanded relations with the EC, the EC countries should be sensitive to India's political concerns and security interests. He stressed that they should not expect India to compromise on these issues for the sake of furthering economic relations.[54]

However, at a general level, there was a mutuality of interests as both India and the EC desired to expand their relationship, especially the economic relationship in the wake of India's economic liberalization policy. India needed cooperative relations with the EC for capital, technology and markets and the need from India's side was perhaps greater than the EC's need of India. This was reflected in the fact that in Asia as a whole, the EC was more interested in the growing economies such as China and East and South East Asian countries. The European Union's growing interest and focus on the booming economies of Asia were reflected in its New Asia Strategy,[55] adopted at the Essen Summit (December 1994), which sought to raise EU's profile in Asia, strengthen its economic presence, promote an enhanced political dialogue and generate a sense of urgency about Europe lagging behind in exploiting Asia's potential.[56]

The EU also complained about some of India's economic policies, despite substantial changes in these policies. It pointed out that India's tariffs remained high. Furthermore, many of the reductions had not been bound with the WTO. India, it saw, had also been using the Balance of Payments protection clause to retain extra protection for certain sectors, especially consumer goods, where taxes substantially increase import prices. Even major export sectors like textiles and clothing are still protected. Naturally, the EU is keen for these barriers to be tackled in a multilateral context.[57]

From India's point of view, nevertheless, the EC as a whole remained one of India's most important international economic partners, while India had only a modest presence in the external economic relations of the EC, which will be discussed below. In this regard, Jorgen Dige Pedersen describes the relationship between India and EU as "a case of 'asymmetrical interdependence' with India being at the same time more sensitive and more vulnerable to changes in Europe than vice versa".[58]

Trade and Investment Patterns

The EU as a whole was India's largest trading partner, being the destination for 26.7 per cent of its exports and the origine of 24.8 per cent of its imports in 1994-95. In 1990-91, Indian exports to the EU was Rs. 8,951 crores. It became more than doubled to Rs 22,075 crores in 1994-95. Indian imports into the EU also showed a similar rise. They rose from Rs. 12,680 crores in 1990-91 to Rs. 22,339 crores in 1994-95.[59]

Nevertheless, if one looks at the Indo- EU trade relationship from the EU point of view, trade with India was only marginal, though India's share in the EU's imports improved from 0.98 per cent in 1991 to 1.43 per cent in 1995. As a result, while the EU stood prominently in Indian foreign economic policy priorities, the same did not hold true for the EU. Thus, it is said that there was an asymmetric trade relationship between India and the EU.

A major chunk of India's exports to the EU was constituted by traditional items such as textiles, leathers, gems and jewellery, which together accounted for 56.6 per cent in 1994. In contrast, India's imports from the EC consisted of sophisticated industrial goods such as machinary and other forms of engginer goods and pears and stones. They constituted for 51 per cent in 1994-95.

A major problem in the Indo-EU economic relationship was that only few countries accounted for the bulk of India's trade with the region. Three countries, namely, Belgium, Germany and the UK accounted for over 60 per cent of Indian exports in the first half of the 1990s. These three countries accounted for around 70 per cent of Indian imports for the region in the same period. On the other hand, France registered mere 8 per cent of Indian exports and 9 per cent of imports.

While there was a continuous growth of Indo-EU trade in the first half of the 1990s, India's trade balance with the EU remained negative. India's trade deficit recorded Rs. 3729 crores in 1990-91. This figure of trade deficit continued till 1993-94. In 1994-95 the deficit, however, fell significantly to Rs. 264 crores.[60]

On a bilateral level, an MOU concerning the export of Indian textiles to the EU was agreed in December 1994. This increased the flexibility of the phase-out period agreed under the Uruguay

Round's agreement on textiles and clothing. The EU also revised its Generalized System Preferences (GSP) and under the new regime India is likely to lose some of the benefits it held in the textiles and leather goods, but will gain market opportunities in a number of other sectors, as more developed countries, such as South Korea, were excluded. India was the second largest user of the EU's GSP.

As we have discussed earlier in Chapter-III, the EU countries were major sources of FDI inflows in India until 1991. Their importance, however, declined during 1991-95. Compared to the US and other Asian countries, the EU did not show much of its enthusiasm for the various liberalising measures taken by India in the FDI front. The EU's share in actual total FDI inflow in India went down substantially from 39.8 per cent in 1991 to 11.6 per cent in 1995.[61] Now we shall turn into the relations between India and the major countries of the EU, namely, the UK, Germany and France.

Indo-UK Relations

The economic content of Indo-British relations witnessed a qualitative improvement during the first half of the 1990s. It was largely due to India's stabilisation-cum-structural adjustment programme. In this regard, the Prime Minister of England, John Major's visit to India in January as the chief guest of the Republic Day parade on 26 January, 1993 was perhaps the most significant development in the relations between India and the UK. Mr Major was accompanied by a 17-member delegation comprising chief executives and chairman of multinationals like Guinness, Cadbury Swepps, Rolls Royce and British Gas. He described the business delegation as "the most prestigious group of British businessmen ever to accompany a British Prime Minister abroad".[62] During the visit, both the governments institutionalised the interaction between the private sectors of the two countries, which was called the Indo-British Partnership Initiative (IBPI) supported by the two governments. The IBPI had a task to expand Indo-British economic and technological cooperation. The co-chairmen of the IBPI were to report to the respective Prime Ministers once every six months or so.

It was during this visit that India and the UK signed the

Indo-British Extradition Treaty, which could reduce anti-Indian activity within England. Mr Major did not overtly insist that India sign the NPT. On the issue of Kashmir too, the UK understood India's stand which was that the problem should be solved under the Shimla agreement.[63]

The British Prime Minister clearly focused on the economic dimension of diplomacy with India. It was evident from the fact that speaking during the question hour in the House of Commons, the Prime Minister stressed that "I have earned 20,000 jobs for the country and initiated contracts worth billions of pounds".[64]

Indo-British economic relationship was further strengthened by the visit of the Indian Prime Minister to London in mid-March 1994. During Narasimha Rao's visit to Britain, the two countries signed a ten-year agreement to promote and protect investments. The UK was the first country with which India concluded such an agreement.[65] They also extended the IBPI for another year with the intention of focusing on small and medium companies to boost trade links between the two countries. This was recommended to both the Prime Ministers in 1994 by the co-chairmen of the IBPI.

During Rao's visit, the UK did not raise the nuclear non-proliferation issue paying heed to India's sensitivities. The Indian Prime Minister was satisfied with his visit to the UK as he described the outcome of the visit as "one of my most successful visits abroad".[66]

As a result, the bilateral economic cooperation between the two countries increased substantially. A report submitted by the co-chairmen of the IBPI to the two Prime Ministers in May 1995 pointed out that bilateral trade increased by 50 per cent over the last two years; 350 new collaborations had been agreed upon; and British investments in India increased ten fold since 1992.[67]

Indo-German Relations

Given the importance of Germany both in political and economic aspects in the post Cold War era, one of the first foreign trips undertaken by Narasimha Rao after coming into power in June 1991 was to Germany. During his visit, Mr Rao spent most of his time with German leaders and businessmen to explain the initiative of his government's economic liberalization, and called for economic cooperation between the two countries.

In response, German Chancellor, Helmut Kohl praised India's efforts at the liberalization of its economy. The German government also pledged to India a DM 400 million of concessional aid for the current year 1991-92 when India faced difficult economic situation. Most of this assistance was for the fast disbursement track.[68] During Rao's visit in 1991, it was decided to set up the Indo-German Consultative Group, which was to advise both the governments for enhancing the bilateral cooperation in various fields.

Yet another significant step in the development of economic relations between the two countries was taken when Chancellor Kohl visited India from 18 to 22 February 1993. The focus of attention was on economic matters. Mr Kohl brought a large business delegation with him. According to the then Indian foreign secretary, J.N. Dixit, Kohl assured the Indian Prime Minister that he would resolve those problems related to defence supplies and augmentation of economic assistance as distant from investment and trade.[69]

Of course, there were some difference on global issues such as the NPT between the two countries. During his discussion with Indian leaders, Kohl expressed the hope that India would soon sign the NPT. Kohl even maintained that signing the NPT "would be beneficial to Indo-German economic and technical cooperation".[70] But, the issue did not directly affect the improving economic relations.

The Indian Prime Minister visited Germany again within three years when Bonn attached new importance to India in the context of her new Asia policy. During the second visit, the German government did not raise the issue of the NPT, instead Bonn focussed on economic cooperation. For instance, the German government requested Mr Rao for further expansion of Lufthansa airline services to India and permission for a direct Lufthansa flight to Madras.[71]

However, despite all these efforts, unlike the American business community, German companies did not immediately respond to India's liberalization programme, especially in the field of foreign direct investment. As we have seen in Chapter-III, in 1995, the amount of investment approvals of Germany was Rs. 1339 crores. From the fifth largest investor in India in 1991, Germany had slid to the tenth position. In the field of trade too, German share of India's total exports declined from 7.79 per cent in 1990-91 to 6.62 per cent in 1994-95. In terms of India's total imports, German share fell from 8.0 per cent in 1990-91 to 7.6 per cent in 1994-95.

One may say that one of the reasons behind the lack of interests of German companies in India was India's bureaucratic red tapism. In fact, the German Chancellor pointed out, during his visit to New Delhi, that India's bureaucratic problem as a hurdle should be removed to attract more of his country's investment.[72] But, perhaps a mol important reason could be that Germany that Germany was preoccupied in Russia, Eastern Europe and the Balkans. In Asia, the focus of German foreign economic policy was mainly in China and East Asian countries.

Nevertheless, Germany was the most important trading partner of India in Europe. According to Economic Survey 1995-96, in 1990-91 India exported goods worth Rs. 2549 crores rising to Rs. 5488 crores in 1994-95- the highest to any country in Europe. Its imports from that country totalled Rs. 3473 in 1990-91 to over Rs. 6,867 crores in 1994-95, again the highest from any European country.

Indo-French Relations

India's economic relations with France proved to be the most problematic amongst the three major countries in the EU, mainly because of controversies relating to three specific Indo-French projects which had run into difficulties. Three controversies were Dulhasti hydroelectric project in Jammu and Kashmir, payments to the French companies for the construction of a pipeline, and a project undertaken by a French-Japanese consortium to produce an oral polio vaccine for distribution in India.[73] In this regard, the then French Foreign Secretary-General Beaude Vieux pointed out that "while the potential for Indo-French economic cooperation was immense, forward movement to realise this potential would be handicapped by the controversies that dogged the ongoing projects".[74]

Meanwhile, in the era of its own economic restructuring process, India continued to emphasise on economic dimension of its foreign policy towards France. Indian Prime Minister, Narasimha Rao visited France three times during the period of 1991-95. The focus of all the three visits was expansion of bilateral trade and economic cooperation with France. French government and business community also expressed full appreciation about the new economic policy under the Congress government and hoped for greater economic cooperation with India.

Nevertheless, French direct investment approvals in India during the first half of the 1990s were considerably lower compared with Germany and British. During the period of 1991-95, the total approved investments of France in India was only Rs. 688 crores whereas those of Germany were Rs. 2212 crores and of England Rs. 3797 crores. The bilateral trade relations between the two countries were also not fully satisfactory. Of the total Indian exports amounting to Rs 82674 crores in 1994-95, France's share stood at a meagre Rs 1828 crores, i.e. 2.2 per cent. On the other hand, of the total Indian imports of Rs 89971 crores, French share was Rs 1933 crores, i.e. 2.1 per cent.[75]

In explaining France's comparatively low interest in India's economic liberalization, one may consider two main reasons while keeping in mind the controversies of the three projects mentioned earlier.

First, France was cautious, being concerned about both a slowdown in the economic liberalization as well as political stability of India. In this regard, it is significant that the then Indian Commerce Minister, Pranab Mukherjee told a gathering of French industrialists and political leaders that there was a national consensus on economic reforms and the question of whether the Congress remained in power should not make any difference.[76] In his third visit to France accompanied by Indian business delegations representing FICCI, ASSOCHAM and CII. in June 1995, Rao also stressed to the French industrialists that India's economic reforms process was irreversible.[77] Second, France was too preoccupied with the post- Soviet collapse situation in Europe. Further, its foreign policy in Algeria and the rest of what is called Francophone Africa continued to be major French preoccupations. In Asia, its attention was taken up by China and the ASEAN countries, with which India also wanted to improve its relations.

LOOK EAST POLICY: INDO-ASEAN RELATIONS

Despite historical, cultural ties with and geographical proximity to the Association of South-East Asian Nations (ASEAN),[78] India had, during the Cold War era, focused its attention mainly on the West and the former Soviet bloc. In fact, India got the support of the Communist Soviet bloc while the ASEAN (with the notable exception of its newest member Vietnam) had vested interests with the US and leaned towards it. During the Cold War, there was a period of mutual suspicion between India and the ASEAN. Moreover, India's growing maritime strength created some concerns in countries like Malaysia, Indonesia and Singapore. On the economic strategy front, the ASEAN countries have generally been following export-oriented strategies of capitalist economies, whereas India's economy prior to the 1991 was largely based on inward-looking import substitution strategies. As a result, there was limited scope for developing close relations between India and these countries during the Cold War era.

However, in the post-Cold War era, with a new international situation and India's economic liberalization programme initiated in 1991, there was a turning point in India's foreign policy and perspectives. The Congress government led by Rao adopted a "Look East" policy[79] which received favourable attention in the ASEAN region both bilaterally and collectively. In fact, the Congress manifesto in 1991 had already stated that the Congress will pay "special attention to the faster growing Newly Industrializing Countries of Asia such as the member countries of ASEAN and the Republic of Korea".[80]

Since the ASEAN had emerged as one of the fast growing trade blocs in the world, the region could provide various opportunities on cooperation with India in trade, investment and technological spheres. It is, therefore, natural that India identifies these countries as thrust economic partners for its economic development. In the era of new economic regionalisation in the post-Cold War period, India also tried to be part of the ASEAN. New Delhi hoped that the region as a bridge may also lead to eventual linkages with the APEC or other important world trade groupings. Trying to be part of the ASEAN was a logical extension of the new language of Indian diplomacy in the economic liberalization era of 1990s.

From the ASEAN point of view, mutual suspicions fostered by being on the opposite sides of the Cold War divide, were almost swept away in the new economic environment. The reason for ASEAN states' renewed interest towards India was the positive signs shown by the new Indian government to liberalise the economy and move towards fewer government controls leading to a more competitive and open economy. Yet another reason which stimulated ASEAN states' interest towards India was that the ASEAN countries relied on foreign markets as much as they did on foreign investments. Naturally, they were keen on getting a foothold in the vast Indian market following the liberalization measures. Given these factors it was not surprising that the ASEAN states sought to revitalise economic relations with India.

The Rao government's new economic policy, which increased its economic potentiality, qualitatively changed the perceptions of the region on India. As a result, India was offered a "sectoral dialogue partnership" status of the region in 1992. It is also clear from the fact that, according to one source, the then ASEAN Secretary-General, Ajit Singh openly mentioned that "the decision to initiate sectoral dialogue with India was an acknowledgement of the vast potential for cooperation resulting from the liberalisation of economic and trade policies by the Narasimha Rao government".[81] Therefore, it is considered that economic imperatives were nudging both India and ASEAN towards a pragmatic relationship.

The identified sectors between India and the ASEAN were in the areas of trade, tourism, agriculture and investments including industrial and technological cooperation.[82] Initial patterns of cooperation were to be forged through government channels. As agreed, in March 1993, the two parts held the first Indo-ASEAN sectoral dialogue in New Delhi which formally institutionalised India's linkage with the region. An institutional linkage like sectoral relationship bestows benefits such as regular contacts and frequent communications but it cannot, by itself, guarantee an upswing in trade and investment. It functions more as a facilitator. The actual task of pursuing business ventures and trade lies with the business groups who have to take the initiative to translate hopes into reality.

In this context, the meeting also agreed to call the private sector representatives in the both sides in future dialogue. India also offered to set up a fund under the Indian Technical and Economic Cooperation (ITEC) programme for the implementation of projects in the agreed upon areas.[83] This was followed by the establishment of the ASEAN-India Business Council (AIBC) comprising the private sector representatives in the both sides.

With the growing regionalism of world trade in the post-bipolar era, in 1992, the ASEAN countries took a major step in economic cooperation in the region with the signing of the agreement of ASEAN Free Trade Area (AFTA)- to be realised by 2003. This agreement reaffirmed the ASEAN commitment to a liberalised market and its willingness to integrate in the global economic system. The aim of AFTA is to remove obstacles to free trade among member states. The decision on the creation of AFTA also responded to the announced strengthening of Europe and to the creation of the North American Free Trade Agreement (NAFTA) in 1992 (Since January 1, 1994, it has operated among USA, Canada and Mexico). In this new global economic environment, India expressed its hope to be member of the ASEAN or the ASEAN security forum officially known as the ASEAN Regional Forum (ARF).[84] But unfortunately, the ASEAN rejected India's request till 1995.

In this regard, it is considered that the improving economic potentiality of India was not enough for her to be a part of the ASEAN or the ASEAN Security Forum until 1995. In other words, India's economic strength resultant from its liberalization measures could not alone be a 'sufficient condition' to be a part of the

ASEAN, but it could be viewed as a useful and possibly a 'necessary condition' for such a process to be initiated.

Yet another reason behind India's exclusion from the membership of the region or the forum till 1995 was perhaps related to India's size and regional problems. The ASEAN states had their own anxieties in having a large country like India as their member which could break their equilibrium. The region felt that India could be a source of disturbance bringing the political conflicts between India and Pakistan to its own territories.[85] Another possible reason was the basic difference in the pace of decision-making and implementation process in India vis-a-vis the ASEAN.

Meanwhile, India consciously attempted to strengthen relations with the ASEAN countries both collectively and bilaterally. This was evident from the fact that Indian Prime Minister, Narasimha Rao accompanied by business delegations visited five out of seven countries during 1991-95 - Indonesia in 1992, Thailand in 1993, Vietnam and Singapore in 1994 and Malaysia in 1995. As a part of India's efforts of the "Look East" policy, New Delhi also cultivated key personalities in the ASEAN countries. It was also reflected in the invitations sent to a large number of high-level governmental and private sector delegations. The Singapore Prime Minister's presence as the chief guest of the Republic Day in 1994 was part of this diplomatic exercise.

As a result, there was a quantitative increase and qualitative improvement in India's bilateral relations with the individual countries of the region, especially with Singapore and Thailand. This improvement was reflected in the expanded trade and investment volume between the two.

Trade and Investment Patterns

As mentioned earlier in Chapter-III, there was dramatic increase in trade and investment between India and the ASEAN countries. The region emerged as important sources of FDI and markets for India during the first half of the 1990s.

In 1991, the ASEAN countries invested in India only a meagre Rs. 1.5 crores. This drastically increased to Rs 144 crores in 1992. In 1995, it recorded Rs. 5,731.5 crores.[86] In terms of Indian joint ventures abroad as on November 1995, the ASEAN states attracted a bulk of these in Asia as a whole as we have discussed in Chapter-

III. The presence of Non-Resident Indians (NRIs) in the region was one of the reasons that the region hosted a volume of Indian joint ventures.

In the trade field too, there was notable increase of the trade relations between India and the ASEAN region. The share of the ASEAN in India's global exports had steadily increased. It was 4.2 per cent in 1990 which increased to 5.6 per cent in 1991. Then it reached 7.4 per cent in 1993-94. India exported its goods to the area worth $ 748 million in 1990. In 1993-94, India exported $ 1643.9 million, while it imported $ 1050.9 million from the region.

As a result, while trade balance between India and ASEAN was mostly in favour of the region during the 80s, from 1991 India enjoyed a trade surplus with the region which in 1993-94 went upto $ 593 million.[87] However, India's economic cooperation with the ASEAN was mainly on bilateral basis. India increased its economic cooperation notably with Singapore and Thailand among the ASEAN countries, which were continued to be major markets for India's exports. There was almost no bilateral trade with Brunei.

India and Singapore

The Prime Minister of Singapore, Goh Tok-Chong was actively involved in furthering Indo-Singapore economic cooperation and technological relations. He visited India in January 1994 as the Chief Guest of the Republic Day celebrations. He was accompanied with 36 CEOs of major business houses in Singapore. Within a short span of eight months of the meeting in January 1994, the two Prime Ministers met again in Singapore in September 1994 during a visit by Mr. Rao to Singapore. The Singapore Prime Minister visited India again in January 1995 in connection with the Centenary celebrations of the CII in Calcutta.

During all the meetings between the two Prime Ministers, the focus was primarily on economic cooperation in which both sides saw immense potential. Public housing, power generation, telecommunications, in addition to tourism and civil aviation, were identified as sectors for possible cooperation with Singapore in India.[88] Singapore fully supported India's quest for a deeper involvement with South-East Asia, whether in the form of full dialogue partnership with the ASEAN, or membership of the ASEAN Regional Forum and APEC. It was mainly India's vast economic market that attracted a small country like Singapore.

Singapore's capital, technology and expertise could complement India's agricultural and mineral wealth, skilled technical manpower and cheap labour. A phenomenal interest in augmenting economic interaction between India and Singapore occurred with the economic liberalization initiated in 1991. Prior to that, investments were modest and, in fact, showed a decline in 1990-91. In 1991 Singapore companies were tied up in 17 Indian ventures, rising to 34 in 1992 and 42 in 1993, amounting to S$ 152 million. In the first six months of 1994, Singapore was involved in 24 projects in India. During Rao's visit to Singapore in September 1994, deals for 12 joint venture projects worth S$ 800 million were signed.[89] Investment proposals from Singapore worth Rs. 991 crores were approved during the year of 1995 making it the eleventh largest investor as we have seen in Chapter-III.

Among the important projects in India in which Singapore involved were the Information Technology Park in Bangalore for computer, electronic and telecommunication industries, shipbuilding plant at Alang in Gujrat and the Madras industrial park.[90] For Singapore, Indian liberalization programme especially in the high-tech area has meant a great deal as this complements the contemporary phase of economic development in Singapore with its emphasis on high value added capital and technology intensive goods and services.

India's bilateral trade with Singapore continued its upswing with growth of around 20 per cent per annum. The share of Singapore in India's total trade volume was about 3 per cent, which was the highest among the ASEAN countries. India exported Rs. 1,705 crores in 1992-93. It increased to Rs. 2,359 crores in the subsequent year. The amount of India's exports further increased to Rs. 2,419 crores in 1994-95 and registered an upswing with Rs. 3,048 crores in 1995-96. India's imports from Singapore also increased from Rs. 1,830.71 crores in 1992-93 to Rs. 1,966 crores in 1993-94, Rs. 2,825 crores in 1994-95 and Rs. 3,692 crores in 1995-

96.[91]

As a result, the trade balance between the two countries was in favour of Singapore. India had Rs. 125 crores deficit in 1992-93. This increased to Rs. 404 crores in 1994-95 and further jumped to Rs. 644 crores in 1995-96. Among the key exports from India to Singapore were cut diamonds, non-electrical machinery, marine products, transport equipment, spices and cashew kernels. Indian imports include refined petroleum products, mineral fuels, chemicals, animal and vegetable fat, machinery and transport etc.

Indo-Thailand Relations

Indo-Thai relationship was further strengthened by Prime Minister, Rao's visit to Bangkok in April 1993. During the visit, both the countries agreed on the need for high level political direction to augment bilateral trade and commerce by at least 20 per cent each year. Specific areas such as fisheries, aquaculture, tourism, agriculture, and science and technology including peaceful uses of atomic energy were identified for time-bound cooperation.[92]

As a result, India's bilateral trade with Thailand continued to expand with overall value reaching Rs 1808.67 crores during the year 1994-95 as against Rs. 1297.56 crores in 1993-94.[93] Throughout the period of first half of 1990s India had a trade surplus. In 1992-93, India had Rs. 566 crores surplus against Thailand. It jumped to Rs. 942 crores in the subsequent year. During 1995-96, Thailand's trade deficit with India further widened at Rs 1024 crores.[94] Therefore, Thailand was concerned about the continuing deficit in its trade with India, while it was also keen on developing economic relations with India. Bangkok was also hoping that India would be a gateway to markets in other countries in South Asia and Middle East.

In the field of direct investment, Thailand sharply showed up and down pattern. Investment proposal from Thailand was nil in the year of 1991. But, the approved amount suddenly jumped up to Rs. 368 crores during the year of 1993. Then, it was sharply decelerated to Rs. 10 crores in 1994 but again dramatically jumped upto Rs. 1968 crores in 1995 making it the fifth largest investor (see Chapter-III, table-6).

India ranked as the fourteenth largest investor in Thailand. The number of Indian joint ventures in operation in Thailand in mid-1994 amounted to about forty with a capital of $ 24 million but representing only about 0.6 per cent of the total foreign investment in the country. There were ten joint ventures under operation and fourteen under implementation with equity of Rs. 1,559 lakh and Rs. 2,503 lakh respectively by the end of 1995. Fisheries sector seems to receive the bulk of the attention.[95]

Look East: JAPAN AND SOUTH KOREA

Indo-Japan Relations

In the wake of economic crisis and subsequent economic liberalization, India tried to woo Japanese investment, technology and market. Japanese GNP accounted for about 15 per cent of the world's GNP, as well as 15 per cent of world trade. Japan has been the biggest provider of official development assistance (ODA) worldwide.

India was making a sustained effort, both officially and non-officially, to attract Japanese corporate interest in the economic liberalization programme launched by the Congress government in mid-1991 and to raise Indo-Japanese relations to a new level. Soon after the Congress government came to power at the centre in mid-1991, the Government of India took coordinated action among the concerned ministries in consultation with the leading economic chambers of India like the CII and the FICCI to woo the Japanese.[96]

As a result, Japan sent a large high-level business delegation to India led by Rokura Ishikawa, chairman of the Japan Chamber of Commerce, late in 1991 and early in January 1992. During the visit, the Japanese delegation submitted a 23-point memorandum, in which they wanted the Government of India to pursue some more additional measures to attract foreign investment and technology. The Japanese demands included the lifting of the restrictions on foreign equity participation pegged at 51 per cent, delinking profit repatriation from export earnings, early revision of India's Foreign Exchange Regulation Act (FERA), etc.[97]

The then Foreign Secretary, J.N. Dixit felt that the Japanese suggestions lacked understanding of India's socio-cultural and socio-economic dimensions. The proposals mainly concerned their own interests.[98] In this context, it is interesting to note that during his visit to Japan in mid-1992, the Indian Prime Minister informed the Japanese business leaders that the pace of the economic liberalization would be accelerated. At the same time, he pointed out that a consensus in the country had to be evolved and for that he needed some time.[99]

Thereafter, the architect of the Indian economic liberalization of 1990s, the then Finance Minister, Dr Manmohan Singh visited Japan in April 1992 to convince the Japanese about the continuing of reforms and urged them to take advantage of new opportunities in India. In the same year in June, the Indian Prime Minister visited Japan. The main purposes of the visit was to introduce India's new economic policy and attract Japanese business community. During the visit, while there were no official agreements between the two governments, a number of economic projects were finalised.[100]

India's efforts to convince the Japanese about the continuity of economic liberalization and to attract Japanese investment in various sectors in India were continued at both official and unofficial level in 1993. At the official level, Indian dignitaries like the Finance Minister Manmohan Singh, Minister of Power N.K. P. Salve and Minister of State for Petroleum Satish Sharma visited Japan at different stages to urge the Japanese to take advantage of India's new economic policy. At the non-government level, Indian business organisations like the CII sent several delegations to Japan.[101]

In March 1994, a 46-member Japanese Economic Mission visited India to study and exploit possible areas of economic cooperation with India. Again in November, a 24-member of delegation from Japan visited India. During their visit, the delegation signed an MOU with the CII for a wideranging trade cooperation.[102]

As part of Japan's growing interest in India, in Indo-Japan Joint Business Council meeting in New Delhi in January 1995, Japanese minister for international trade and industry, Ryutaro Hashimoto revealed a seven-point action plan of his government to enhance Indo-Japanese economic cooperation. For example, the plan included $ 1 billion Japanese lines of credit for two years to support economic development in India in view of the reforms initiated by the Indian government. It also included that a further lowering of export-insurance and investment-insurance premium rates for India in April 1995, in addition to the reduction announced in July in 1994.[103]

Japanese Investments in India

Despite all these efforts, the Japanese continued to drag their feet with regard to investment in India. This was evident from the pattern of Japanese investment in India. During 1981-91, the share of Japan's investment in the overall foreign investment approvals in India was 7.7 per cent.[104] During 1991-94, Japan's share was only 6.3 per cent compared to 34.5 per cent for the US and 10. 3 per cent for the UK. India received only around 0.1 per cent of Japan's overseas investments. The amount of investment approvals of Japan in India was lower than South Korea's. Investment proposals from Japan worth only Rs. 401 crores in 1994 and Rs. 1514 crores in 1995, whereas, South Korea had Rs. 1069 crores and 3142 crores respectively (see Chapter-III, table-6). They talked about many roadblocks such as high tariffs, lack of infrastructure facilities, bureaucratic red tapism, and so on. They also mentioned about the political instability and centre-state relations, especially after the Enron case.

During the discussion with Indian officials, the head of the Japanese delegation mentioned privately that "...India spends too much time in theorising and on discussion of long-term plans. It would be good if your able businessmen concentrate on actual projects and actions and on short- and medium term planning".[105]

According to one source,[106] the Japanese business community had made three core demands to the Government of India. One of them was the freedom for full and unrestricted repatriation of the profits earned by the Japanese companies, which required the full convertibility of the rupee. Another demand was the relaxation of the equity ratio for foreign participation pegged at 51 per cent. And yet another and the most contentious demand was the formulation of an exit policy which means the freedom to fold up in case of failure. Fulfillment of this demand could further social tensions by aggravating the problem of unemployment.

In this regard, the then Finance Minister Manmohan Singh told the 29th joint meeting of the Indo-Japan Business Cooperation Committee that "India could not sanction an outright exit policy that would allow companies to hire and fire workers at will. The government could not afford large-scale political backlash. Workers needed the assurance that liberalization was not a conspiracy against them, but rather it aimed to create more job opportunities. For that an appropriate climate needs to be created and a social safety net firmly established".[1071]

As we have seen in Chapter-III, none of the three core demands met with any concrete response from the Government of India till 1995. In this regard one may also point out that dissatisfaction of the Japanese business community on their core demands was considered one of the reasons behind Japan's 'wait and watch' approach towards investment in India.

Yet another possible reason why Japan did not enter Indian market with great enthusiasm was that "South-East Asian countries were much quicker in responding to India's love-call".[108] For Japan, relations with India was a secondary priority. Japanese foreign relations were pre-occupied with the US and the major European countries. Japan's diplomatic activism has been primarily focused on China, South Korea, member states of the ASEAN, and Russia with India figuring lower down in the scale.

While Japan had still kept a 'wait and watch' approach towards India for its investments, it had continuously increased its official development aids to India. It may be said that Japan was looking for future investments in India when there could be a better economic environment.

Indeed Japan's official developmental assistance continued to rise. In 1991 when India faced the full scale macro-economic crisis, Japan quickly extended an emergency loan of 30 billion yen.[109] Tokyo announced 119,640 billion yen (equivalent of Rs 3250 crores) loan assistance for the year 1993-94- a rise of some 7 per cent over the previous year. Japan continued to be largest bilateral donor of development assistance. In 1994-95, Japan's commitment was Rs. 3,920 crores. The aid pledge covered twelve projects in the power, transport, drinking water and sewage system, environment and afforestation sectors.[110]

Japan did not take a keen interest in India's participation in the APEC or in the ARF. India asked Japan to support its effort to become a member of the APEC, an 18-country grouping of the region-from Australia to the US of which Japan is an important member. But, Japan expressed some anxieties about India's participation in the APEC.

One of the reasons for Japan's reservation about actively inviting India into this region was that in most Japanese perceptions, "the Asia-Pacific region" does not include South Asia even if it extends as far as Australia. Just a week after Indian Prime Minister, Rao's visit to Japan, Japanese Prime Minister said that Asian security should be promoted by utilising existing fora such as ASEAN Post-Ministerial Conference and APEC and that in the future, Russia and China should be included in a political dialogue of the region. But, the Japanese Prime Minister did not mention India.[111] Yet another obstacle to be member of the APEC was possibly that India might bring the Indo-Pakistan conflict into Eastern Asia.

The bilateral trade relationship between India and Japan was an asymmetric one. Japan was India's third largest trading partner, i.e., Japan took 8 per cent of the share of India's foreign trade; yet India did not even account for one per cent of Japan's global trade. During the period of first half of 1990s, the trade balance between India and Japan was zigzag. The growth percentage of India's exports to Japan during the period of 1990-95 was only 6 per cent per annum. India's exports jumped from Rs. 3039 crores in 1990-91 to Rs. 5460 crores in 1993-94. It further increased Rs. 6363 crores in 1994-95. The import picture showed a figure of Rs. 3245 crores in 1990-91 increasing to Rs. 4774 crores in 1993-94, Rs. 6405 crores in 1994-95.[112]

India and South Korea

Perhaps one of the closest economic relationships which

India established after it launched the economic liberalization programme was with South Korea. In September 1993, the first ever Indian Prime Minister's visit to South Korea was a crucial milestone in growth of bilateral relations between the two countries. It materialized as a result of India's new "Look East" policy and South Korea's new "Look South" policy in the age of economic competition in the changed post-Cold War international situation.

During the Cold War era, both India and South Korea were not in a position to take an active role in promoting their bilateral relationship due to their different geopolitical perspectives, geo-security compulsions and strategies of economic development.[113]

Both the nations, however, readjusted their foreign policies towards a new friendship in the post-Cold War and economic liberalization era. South Korea had many charms for India's economic development. South Korea has been a newly industrialized country. It had an important place among advanced trading nations. It ranked only next to Japan among Asian countries in terms of trade volume. Seoul also interested India in terms of its membership in an economic bloc. As a member of the APEC, South Korea played a leading role in the group. During the visit to Seoul in September 1993, the Indian Prime Minister, Rao requested the government of South Korea to lend support for his country's efforts to join the APEC. Seoul gave India a positive assurance to support its membership of the APEC. The former Finance Minister, Manmohan Singh said in an interview that India had great admiration for what had been achieved in South Korea. He said that Seoul's achievement is a real saga of great adventure.[114]

Besides the economic importance of South Korea, there were other respects in which Seoul was important for India as a new partner in the post-Cold War era. First, there had been dramatic changes in the Korean peninsula, thanks to the end of the Cold War, the collapse of the Soviet Union and Seoul's full fledged diplomatic relations with Russia and China. In this changed situation, Seoul tried to be more independent in its relations with the US, though it was still dependent on American military for its security. It attempted to readjust its foreign policy to accommodate greater globalisation. It also paid more attention to developing countries like India which had been marginalised in the framework of Seoul's foreign policy during the bi-polar world era.

It is clear that India shifted its earlier foreign policy of equidistance on the Korean peninsula after the end of the Cold War. This was justified by the improvement in Seoul's political and economic positions in international society. South Korea witnessed significant political changes, when the new non-military President, Mr Kim Young Sam restored parliamentary democracy. The end of the Cold War enabled Seoul to join the UN in September 1991. Recognising the United Nations' importance in the post-Cold War era, South Korea had actively participated in many UN organisations, especially in peace-keeping operations. These activities further enhanced the nation's stature in the community of nations. To make things better, South Korea has been member of the Organization for Economic Cooperation and Development (OECD).

Acknowledging Seoul's growing international position, the former Indian Ambassador to South Korea, B.M. Oza stated that "India decided to set up a mechanism of annual bilateral consultative talks between the foreign ministers of the two countries. Also, it was decided to activate the joint trade committee which had remained dormant for many years".[115]

From South Korean point of view, India also had a great merit for its economic development. India's economic liberaization in 1990s came at the time of a new internationalization strategy of the South Korcan economy. Seoul had been greatly attracted by India's immense potential and the new economic policies in the 1990s which brought about "a radical and comprehensive change by Indian standards".[116]

South Korea was witnessing a sagging economy. Its economic growth rates were only 4 per cent in 1992 and 2.5 in the first quarter of 1993, the lowest in 12 years. These figures were reflective of a steady decline in production activity over the past few years.[117] As it survived as a trading nation, South Korea, however, faced various trade difficulties due to rising incidence of protectionism of the West. It also suffered from a huge trade deficit with Japan because of its heavy dependence on the latter's technology.

Yet another reason behind Seoul's "look India policy" was that the competitiveness of labour intensive products, which was South Korea's traditional strong field, had declined because of jumping of labour cost. As a result, many South Korean labour intensive companies shifted to South East Asia and China to survive in the age of tough international competition. Added to this, South Korean business community did not get good results from their investments in China as they had expected earlier.

Thus, it had to find a breakthrough for easing the economic difficulties. As one of the solutions, Seoul paid more attention on economic relations with the developing countries like India which has huge markets and great economic potential.

Bilateral Trade Relations

As mentioned earlier, India's direction of trade had significantly changed in the first half of the 1990s. Perhaps one of the most significant changes that took place was towards South Korea. Before India launched the new economic liberalization in 1991, the bilateral trade between India and South Korea remained at a very small volume. However, with the ongoing economic liberalization and market reforms initiated by India since July 1991, the scope of Indo-South Korea trade apparently increased. Specially in 1993, the total trade account between the two nations recorded the highest volume touching $ 2327 million. Compared to the previous year's total trade of $ 916 million, it increased more than double times, thanks to India's massive imports from South Korea. India's imports from South Korea sharply increased from $ 438 million in 1992 to $ 1804 million in 1993, i.e. by more than four times.[118]

Although South Korea's exports sharply rose in 1993, looking from the global viewpoint, the South Korean share in India's imports continued to be insignificant, especially when compared to the importance of India's trade with the advanced countries like the US, Japan and England. Of India's total imports amounting to $ 23306 million in 1993, South Korea's share stood at a meagre 2.4 per cent. On the other hand, of the total India's exports of $ 22238 million, Seoul's share was 0.9 per cent.[119]

India's total exports to South Korea had not increased substantially. In 1993, it exported $ 523 million increase of 45 million compared to the previous year. Essentially, the problem on the export side for India seems to be the narrow base of products sold to South Korea. The export basket was dominated to a large extent by primary items and industrial raw materials such as iron ore, oil seed extraction and iron and steel accounting for 61 per cent of the total volume. India's major import items from the South Korea were articles of steel, plastics and polymers and ships that accounted for 81 per cent of the total imports from South Korea in 1993.[120]

Since 1993, South Korea had been showing a favourable balance of trade with India. Indian government policy of easing imports-restrictions was partly responsible for the trade deficit. India's trade deficit with South Korea was $ 1281 million in 1993. However, this continuously declined to $ 328 by 1995. This narrowed trade deficit gap was contributed by declining of South Korea's traditional export items to India like vehicles, steel products, ship tankers. This narrowing trade deficit between India and South Korea was also effected by India's growing export items like textiles and oil products that became more competitive in South Korean market.[121]

Foreign Direct Investment

As a result of New Delhi's liberalization of foreign investment policy, South Korea's direct investment picture in India had undergone a significant change as reflected in the higher value of approvals and the rising trend in the actual inflows. South Korean firms' total value of direct investment approvals by India was meagre worth $ 4.7 million of 14 cases from 1982 to June 1991. However, from 1992 to 1995, the investment surprisingly jumped to 110 projects worth $ 117.3 million.[122] In 1995 alone, investment proposals from South Korea were approved worth Rs 3142 crores ranking it third.

One of the reasons behind South Korea's persistent rise in direct investment in India was the changing investment strategies of South Korea's companies which faced problems of direct investment in China and tried to find a new huge market like India. If one looks at the pattern of South Korean investment in India from the global point of view, South Korea's investment concentrated mostly on financial collaborations.[123]

INDIA, SAARC and IORARC

To understand India's high desire to be member of the ASEAN or other regional groups as a result of its own economic liberalization, it is useful to examine India's own regional group-the South Asian Association for Regional Cooperation (SAARC), and India's role in it. It is equally necessary to understand how far economic liberalization and the emphasis on exports by the Rao government created interests in regional economic cooperation within the context of the SAARC. This part also discusses how far problems of SAARC changed India's attitude towards Indian Ocean cooperation.

The SAARC was formally launched in 1985,[124] with the member countries being Bangladesh, Bhutan, India, Maldives, Nepal, Pakistan and Sri Lanka. One of the main objectives of the Association[125] is to "promote mutual assistance in the economic, social, cultural, technical and scientific fields". However, up to the middle of the nineties, the SAARC could not give rise to open economic regionalism, which was in marked contrast to the evident trend towards free-trade agreement in several parts of the world as discussed earlier. As a result, SAARC was excluded from the list of one of IMF studies on regionalism.[126] It was only in April 1993, the SAARC countries signed a framework agreement on South Asian Preferential Trade Arrangement (SAPTA), which was ratified by all the member states. It came into force only in December 1995.

The SAPTA was the result of the Eighth SAARC conference held in New Delhi in 1995 where this new concessional trade system was approved. It was a stepping stone towards eventual free trade arrangement within South Asia by the beginning of twenty first century. Among the SAARC countries, concessional tariff rates have been introduced for 226 trade items. These concessional rates range between 10 per cent to 100 per cent. India gave this concession to 106 items, which is the highest among all the countries. Similarly, other member countries also gave concessional rates- Pakistan (35 goods), Sri Lanka (31 goods), Maldives (17 goods), Nepal (14 goods), Bangladesh (12 goods) and Bhutan (11 goods). However, most of these items notified by various states of the SAARC either do not have a demand in the potential importing countries of the region, or the items are such that they do not have exportable surplus which could be traded within SAPTA, after domestic needs are met and after exports to the developed countries generating hard currencies have been made.[127]

What then were the main causes for the slow progress of economic cooperation in the SAARC, while other regional groups consolidated their organisations towards great economic cooperations. There were many reasons for the lack of enthusiasm among the SAARC countries including India towards intensified economic cooperation within the region.

South Asia is an Indo-centric region in terms of its power and geographic position. India alone has 72 per cent of its area, 77 per cent of its total population and 77 per cent of its GDP.[128] India alone shares borders- by land or sea- with all the other SAARC countries. Further, none of the other states share borders with any other state. These factors endow India with a position of near hegemony within the region. In other words, India's concerns and policies are crucial in determining the shape and scope of regional cooperation in South Asia. Due to the geographical, historical and cultural inter linkages and affiliations of the South Asian countries, domestic conflicts of these countries often spill over into other states of the region and affect bilateral relations. These have been obstacles for the smooth functioning of the SAARC. For instance, the VII SAARC Summit in December 1992 had to be postponed due to the religious and social conflicts in India after the demolition of the Babri Mosque on 6 December 1992. Large-scale violence followed in Pakistan and Bangladesh which vitiated the atmosphere for the summit. Eventually the Summit was convened in Dhaka in April 1993. India's position has been also a source of hidden fear among other countries in the region.

The smaller countries are worried about India utilizing the SAARC to consolidate its own economic dominance. There were restrictive trade policies towards Indian goods on the ground that a liberalised trade regime would swamp their markets with Indian goods which will hinder their own industrialisation.

Apart from this, according to Sumitra Chishti, if one carefully looked at the conditionalities of the IMF and World Bank under which India and Pakistan liberalised their economies, one may find that the international financial institutions did not encourage regional cooperation among the SAARC countries. They rather promoted economic linkages with the developed countries for their capital, technology and markets. She further argued that the Uruguay Round of multilateral trade negotiations discouraged South-South cooperation but promoted globalisation of their economies.[129]

Economically, as we have seen earlier, India mainly depended on outside economies, especially the West, for her economic development. This dependency on Western and other industrialised economies increased during the first half of the 1990s due to India's economic crisis and subsequent economic liberalization policy. As some said,[130] this dependency led India to shy away from the region, though India's trade within the region increased in terms of trade volume. India's economy was more competitive with other South Asian countries than complementary to each other. As a result, there had been limited progress in India's economic interaction with other SAARC countries. It is evident from the fact that the total SAARC countries' share in India's global exports on an average per annum during the first half of the 1990s was less than four per cent. The ratio for imports was even smaller, i.e. less than one per cent.[131] Among SAARC countries, Bangladesh accounted for a major share in India's total exports, i.e., about 2 per cent on an average per annum, whereas Pakistan accounted a significant for major share in India's total imports, i.e., around 3 per cent on an average per annum, during the first half of the 1990s. In terms of intra-regional trade among the SAARC countries too, the ratio had been less than 4 per cent of its global trade.[132] Compared with other regional groups, it was a very low share. For instance, in 1990 about one fifth of ASEAN trade was intra-trade, about 70 per cent of EC and 23 per cent of the NAFTA trade were among the member states.[133]

In the field of foreign direct investment, India attracted only marginal direct investments from her neighbouring countries due to lack of capital available with them. The region has been struggling with basic developments problems such as poverty, illiteracy, malnutrition etc. Four of India's neighbouring countries- Bhutan, Bangladesh, the Maldives and Nepal- have been designated as the Least Developed Countries.[134] The largest investor in India among the SAARC countries was Sri Lanka. The amount of investment approvals of Sri Lanka was 7 crores during 1991-95. Maldives accounted only 0.6 crores and Nepal recorded 2 lakh.[135]

In terms of India's joint ventures in South Asia, they were mainly limited in two countries- Sri Lanka and Nepal as discussed in the Chapter-III. Sri Lanka held the maximum number of joint ventures, namely thirty seven, out of which 17 were in operation and 20 were under implementation. Assessing prospects for Indian investment in the SAARC region, India Today described Sri Lanka as "the best hope for Indian investors".[136] Nepal attracted 30 Indian joint ventures of which 8 were in operation and 22 were under implementation as on 30 November 1995. Here one may raise a question on the nonexistence of investment between India and Pakistan, though there was scope for joint venture in the area of cement, fertilizers, sugar, edible oils, iron and steel, textiles, etc between the two countries. The reason could be the existence of political problems between India and Pakistan, which had also been a source of differing perceptions for a common economic agenda in the SAARC.

Many argue that bilateral political issues like Kashmir between India and Pakistan were largely responsible for slow progress not only in Indo-Pakistan bilateral economic cooperation but also in regional economic cooperation in South Asia as a whole. Whenever there was a chance, Pakistan always tried to raise bilateral political issues with India in the SAARC meetings, though the SAARC charter rules out taking any bilateral problems among the member countries in the meetings. Pakistan continuously resisted opening up its markets to Indian goods on the ground that this would harm its local industry.

It seems that so far as India's trade relations with Pakistan are concerned, India has taken a functionalist approach towards Islamabad. Both the functionalists and neofunctionalists argued that expanding areas and habits of cooperation in economic and technical sectors would have a spill over effect on political relations and help create conditions for regional political stability and peace.[137] Though Pakistan did not treat India on an MFN basis, India has accorded Pakistan with the same MFN status. India imported the most from Pakistan among the South Asian countries. In this respect, it is interesting to note what an Indian officer said, "It's true that we don't need or want trade that badly with Pakistan on economic grounds, but we think it is fundamental to a real process of normalisation- it is a principle with us...We accept imports from Pakistan on an MFN basis: they can sell us anything on our schedule of acceptable imports. But they don't treat us on an MFN basis".[138]

But, it seems in reality that a functional approach of India towards Pakistan did not work smoothly throughout the first half of the 1990s. Several rounds of bilateral talks at the Prime Ministerial as well as Foreign Secretary levels between India and Pakistan bore no fruits. For example, in early 1992, the two Prime Ministers agreed to solve their bilateral political problems through dialogue so that they could divert their energies towards economic development. However, this commitment was soon wasted by Pakistan, when the Jammu and Kashmir Liberation Front (JKLF) under Amanullah declared its intention to cross the line of actual control (LAC). This was supported by the Pakistan Prime Minister, Nawaz Sharif, who called for a nation-wide strike to express solidarity with the people of Kashmir. Thereafter, there was no sign of any improvement in the bilateral relations due to several events such as lightening sponsorship of terrorism by Pakistan in Kashmir, the demolition of the Babri Masjid by the Hindu extremists in India in December 1992, the Bombay blasts in early 1993, occupation of the Hazratbal Mosque in Srinagar by Pakistani trained terrorists along with mercenaries in late 1993 amongst others. Even after the new government came into power in Islamabad led by Benazir Bhutto in late 1993, the two countries could not work together for the betterment of the relations. For most of the period between 1994 to the end of 1995, Pakistan rejected any talks with India. Islamabad insisted that the disputed territory-Kashmir should be solved before talks on any other issues began, while India insisted that legally and constitutionally Kashmir was a part of its territory.

This kind of political problem between India and Pakistan has been perhaps the most critical hurdle in the path of greater economic cooperation in the South Asian region, because for any meaningful regional economic cooperation, cooperative bilateral relationship is essential. In this regard, one may say that this disappointing factor of the SAARC provided both positive and negative aspects for India's foreign economic policy.

In a positive sense, India changed its earlier perceptions on Indian Ocean cooperation. During the 80s India had kept itself out of the Indian Ocean Marine Affairs Cooperation (IOMAC). This was mainly because of geo-strategic and geo-political imperatives during the Cold War era. When the then Foreign Minister of South Africa, Mr Botha suggested the idea of a Indian Ocean Rim (IOR) trade bloc during his visit to India in November 1993, the Government of India took a positive approach though with caution. With the visit of the President Nelson Mandela to New Delhi in January 1995, India actively involved itself in the formation of the Indian Ocean Rim Association for Regional Cooperation (IORARC), which focussed on economic cooperation among select and like-minded states of the Indian Ocean region. Australia, India, Kenya, Mauritius, Oman, Singapore and South Africa were the seven promoters of the IORARC idea and notionally they represented the seven sub-regions of the Indian Ocean. The first concrete step in the direction of implementing the idea was taken by the seven states in Mauritius in March 1995. The working group of the

IORARC held its meeting at Port Louis in August 1995. During the meeting, the Indian Ocean Rim Business Forum (IORBF) and IOR-Academic Network (IOR-AN) were also formed. It was also recommended that the membership of the IORARC be expanded from seven to fourteen with the inclusion of the following new members: Madagascar, Malaysia, Mozambique, Indonesia, Sri Lanka, Tanzania and Yemen. Pakistan tried its best to join the group but India and Mauritius proposed to postpone any further induction in the group which was accepted by all the members.

The limitations manifested in the SAARC, could be one of the factors for some countries like Japan having reservations for including India in the APEC. In this respect, it may be said that the problems of economic cooperation in the region in general and conflicts between Indian and Pakistan in particular imposed limitations on the success of India's "Look East" policy.[139] It indicates that with spreading regionalisation of global trade in the post Cold War era, India's foreign economic relations with other SAARC countries are crucial for it to join the Asia-Pacific economic groups, like ASEAN and APEC.

To sum up the above discussion about the impact of economic liberalization on India's foreign relations during the first half of the 1990s, one may conclude that the liberalization certainly contributed to the changes in the direction of India's diplomatic focus. The economic aspects of diplomacy were greatly emphasized. This was clearly shown in India's external relations at both the bilateral and the mutilateral levels. India began to focus on capitalist countries and regional blocs. This readjustment in India's foreign policy which was affected by the post Cold War and post-Soviet international environment saw significant changes in relations with the US and with the major countries in the European community. It was manifested, especially in India's relations with Asian countries and with the region as a whole. However, India's policy of economic liberalization could not act as a leverage to gain concessions on its security issues. It was also unable to gain a membership for India in any of the existing regional blocs. Together with the tardy progress of SAARC, this appears to have given an impetus for greater Indian interest in evolving an economic grouping in Indian Ocean Region.

REFERENCES

1. V.P. Dutt, *India's Foreign Policy In A Changing World,* (New Delhi: Vikas Publishing House, 1999), p. 15.
2. *Sunday*, September 29, 1991.
3. *The Sunday Times of India,* "Special Report: From Talking Shop to Talking Business", February 7, 1993.
4. J.N. Dixit, *My South Block Years: Memoirs of A Foreign Secretary,* (New Delhi: UBSPD, 1996).
5. Manmohan Agarwal, "Implications of Economic Liberalization for India's Foreign Policy", *International Studies,* 30, 2, 1993, p. 136.
6. *The Sunday Times of India, op. cit.*
7. *Ibid.*
8. *Ibid.*
9. James Manor, "The Political Sustainability of Economic Liberalization in India", in Robert Cassen and Vijay Joshi (eds.), *India: The Future of Economic Reform,* (Delhi: OUP, 1995).
10. Interview with Muchkund Dubey, January 24, 1997.
11. J.N. Dixit, *op. cit.,* p. 177.
12. After a six-year US military freeze on Pakistan, imposed over Islamabad's nuclear programme, Pakistan received the first shipment of US arms on August 26, 1996 out of a batch worth $360 million released by Washington under a one-time waiver to a 1990 embargo. A Pakistan navy ship arrived at Karachi carrying 262 items worth $6.78 million. *Competition Success Review,* New Delhi, 1997, p. 18
13. J.N. Dixit, *op. cit.,* p. 193.
14. *Ibid.,* p. 195.
15. *Times of India,* January 23, 1994.
16. Quoted in Rajan Kumar Mishra, *India and International Relations,* (New Delhi: Kanishka Publishers, 1996), p. 65.
17. Quoted in J.N. Dixit, *op. cit.,* p. 192.
18. Krishan D. Mathur and P.M. Kamath, *Conduct of India's Foreign Policy,* (New Delhi: South Asian Publishers, 1996), p. 154.
19. *Economic Times,* February 21, 1993.
20. *India Today,* June 15, 1994, p. 47.
21. *Ibid.,* p. 51.
22. *Times of India,* September 15, 1994.

23. *The Statesman,* January 13, 1995.
24. It was expressed by the US Special Trade Representative Carla Hills. See *Times of India,* April 30, 1992 and *Sunday Times,* May 3, 1992.
25. US Embassy, *May 1992 Economic Trends Report,* Cable No. 11319, New Delhi, June 1995, p. 5.
26. Rajan Kumar Mishra, *op. cit.,* p. 76.
27. *Ibid.,* p. 66.
28. These are China, South Korea, Indonesia, India, Turkey, South Africa, Poland, Argentina, Brazil and Mexico.
29. *India Today,* June 15, 1994, p. 51.
30. But lobbying by India Interest Group of American corporate was the major reason for India's triumph on human rights in the US Congress in 1996 and 1997, victories that made Pakistan green with envy. See Swaminathans Anklesariaaiyar, " US Corporations, Our New Foreign Policy Allies", *The Times of India,* New Delhi, September 7, 1997.
31. Sushma Ramachandan, "Indo-US ties on Even Keel", *The Hindu,* July 21, 1994.
32. Ramesh Thakur, "India and the United States: A Triumph of Hope over Experience?", *Asian Survey,* Vol. XXXVI, No. 6, June 1996, p. 579.
33. Walter Andersen, "India in 1995: Year of the long Campaign", *Asian Survey,* Vol. XXXVI, No. 2, February 1996, p. 178.
34. B. Bhattacharyya, "India's Foreign Economic Policy: Evolving Context and Tasks" in Foreign Service Institute, *Indian Foreign Policy: Agenda for the 21st Century,* Vol.-I, (New Delhi: Konark Publishers, 1997), p. 212.
35. *The Statesmen,* 17 January, 1995.
36. *The Pioneer,* 28 May, 1994.
37. Government of India, Ministry of Finance, *Economic Survey 1995-96,* (New Delhi: Government of India Press, 1996).
38. Based on data provided by the World Bank, *World Development Report 1996: From Plan to Market,* (New York: OUP, 1996) and United States International Trade Commission, *International Trade Review,* Washington, D.C., June 1995.
39. Krishan D. Mathur and P.M. Kamath, *op. cit,* p. 155.
40. *India Today,* 15 June 1994, p. 43.
41. Krishan D. Mathur and P.M. Kamath, *op. cit,* p. 155.
42. Ramesh Thakur, *op. cit.,* p. 583.
43. But by 1996, Rao was vulnerable to charges of giving in to US

pressure on national security, and on January 27 India successfully carried out the 15th test firing of the Prithvi. Ramesh Thakur, *op. cit.*, p. 584.

44. Krishan D. Mathur and P.M. Kamath, *op. cit.*, p. 156.
45. Interview with Muchkund Dubey, January 18, 1997.
46. B. K. Shrivastava, "Indo-American Relations: Search for a New Equation", *International Studies*, 30,(2), 1993, p. 228.
47. J. N. Dixit, *op. cit.*
48. For the sake of transparency to the wider public, the term EU is systematically used. In some case the term European Community would be legally more exact.
49. Government of India, Ministry of External Affairs, *Annual Report 1994-95* and *1995-96*, (New Delhi: Government of India Press, 1995 and 1996).
50. The Troika consists of the Foreign Ministers of past, present and future Presidents in the Council of the European Union and the responsible European Commissioner.
51. V.P. Dutt, *op. cit.*, p. 332.
52. Government of India, Ministry of External Affairs, *Annual Report 1992-93*, (New Delhi: Government of India Press, 1993).
53. Speech by the former Finance Minster, Manmohan Singh at the Euromoney India Conference, New Delhi, 22 March 1994, Euromoney, April 1994, p. 166.
54. J.N. Dixit, *op. cit.*, p. 276.
55. Commission of the European Communities, Communication from the Committee to the Council, "Towards a New Asia Strategy", Com (94) 314 final, 13 July, 1994.
56. Despite strides in India's "Look East" policy, India was excluded from the inaugural Asia-Europe Meeting (ASEM)- the Asia-Europe Summit of 15 Europe and seven ASEAN nations along with Japan, China and South Korea held at Bangkok from 1-2 March 1996.
57. Commission of the European Communities, Communication from the Commission, *EU-India Enhanced Partnership*, Com (96) 275 final, Brussels, 26 June, 1996, p. 7.
58. Jorgen Dige Pedersen, "India and the EC in a New World Order", *Contemporary South Asia*, 2 (3), 1993, pp. 275-76. The author brought the concepts of 'asymmetrical interdependence', 'sensitivity' and 'vulnerability' from Robert O. Keohane and Joseph S. Nye, *Power and Interdependence*, second edition (Glenview, Illinois: Scott, Foresman and Company, 1989). Sensitivity refers to the cost for one part in a interdependent relationship of adapting to changes

within a given policy framework. Vulnerability refers to the ability to change the policy framework in order to reduce costs caused by the changes.

59. *Economic Survey 1995-96, op. cit.*
60. *Ibid.*
61. O.P. Sharma, "India, UK and EU: Trade, Investment and Joint Ventures" in H.S. Chopra (ed.), *India and the European Union into the 21st Century*, (New Delhi: Indian Council of World Affairs, 1998).
62. *Times of India*, Special Report: From talking shop to talking business, February 7, 1993.
63. J.N. Dixit, *op. cit.*
64. *Times of India, op. cit.*
65. Ministry of External Affairs, *Annual Report 1994-95, op. cit.*, p. 67.
66. Quoted in Rajan Kumar Mishra, *op. cit.*, p. 177.
67. Ministry of External Affairs, *Annual Report 1995-96, op. cit.*, p. 72.
68. *The Hindu*, September 7, 1991.
69. J.N. Dixit, *op. cit.*, p. 285.
70. Annpurna Nautiyal, *India and the New World Order*, (New Delhi: South Asian Publishers, 1996), p. 115.
71. *Times of India*, February 4, 1994.
72. *The Statesman*, February 21, 1993.
73. J.N. Dixit, *op. cit.*, p. 287.
74. *Ibid.*, p. 288.
75. *Economic Survey 1995-96, op. cit.*
76. *Economic Times*, April 7 and 12, 1995.
77. *Indian Express*, June 13, 1995.
78. ASEAN was formed on August 8, 1967, in Bangkok by Indonesia, Singapore, Thailand and the Philippines (Brunei joined in 1984).
79. According to S.D. Muni, India's "Look East" policy was not new and had gone through at least four key phases since Independence. The current thrust, which could in some ways be traced to the Rajiv Gandhi Government, had four key dimensions-greater participation in regional organizations, strengthening bilateral economic ties, efforts to revive old cultural connexions and a clear emphasis on relating to the security situation in the region. See, *The Statesman*, New Delhi, September 28, 1996.
80. The Indian National Congress (I), Election Manifesto 1991, p. 57.
81. Quoted in Ramesh Thakur, *The Politics and Economics of India's Foreign Policy*, (Delhi: OUP, 1994), p. 238.
82. *Hindu Weekly*, March 27, 1993, p. 12.

83. *Times of India,* March 18, 1993.
84. The ARF was launched in Bangkok in July 1994 as a "forum for dialogue" in which members could exchange ideas about the Asia-Pacific region in particular and international polities and defence affairs in general. The invitees included the Foreign Ministers belonging to 18 countries: the six ASEAN states (Vietnam was not yet a member of the ASEAN in that time); ASEAN's seven dialogue partners (Australia, New Zealand, Canada, South Korea, Japan, the US and the European Union); the three observers (Papua New Guinea, Laos and Vietnam); and the two consultative partners (China and Russia).
    India was accepted as a full dialogue partner by ASEAN following the ASEAN Standing Committee meeting of January 29-31, 1996, in Jakarta. This made India eligible to participate for the first time in the ARF.
85. Such views were conveyed to India by the ASEAN member countries. See J.N. Dixit, *op. cit.*, pp. 264-273.
86. Sujit Dutta, "India and ASEAN: A Framework for Comprehensive Engagement" *Strategic Analysis,* Vol. XX, NO. 3, June 1997.
87. See Sridharan Kripa, *The ASEAN Region in India's Foreign Policy,* (Aldershot: Dartmouth, 1996), Table-3, p. 208.
88. Ministry of External Affairs, *Annual Report 1994-95, op. cit.*, p. 17.
89. Sridhran Kripa, *op. cit.*, p. 214.
90. *Hindustan Times,* September 9, 1994.
91. Government of India, Ministry of Commerce, *Annual Report,* Various Issues, (New Delhi: Government of India Press).
92. Ministry of External Affairs, *Annual Report 93-94, op. cit.*, p.12.
93. Ministry of External Affairs, *Annual Report 1995-96, op. cit.*, p. 21.
94. See Ministry of Commerce, *Annual Report 1994-95* and *1995-96, op. cit.*
95. India Investment Centre, New Delhi.
96. J.N. Dixit, *op. cit.*, p.
97. *The Hindu,* January 29, 1992.
98. J.N. Dixit, *op. cit.*, p. 255.
99. *Hindustan Time,* June 24, 1992.
100. J.N. Dixit, *op. cit.*, p. 258.
101. See Ministary of External Affairs, *Annual Report 1993-94, op. cit.*
102. See Ministry of External Affairs, *Annual Report 1994-95, op. cit.*
103. For details, see *Times of India,* January 6, 1995.
104. K.V. Kesavan, "India and Japan", in Foreign Service Institute, *Indian Foreign Policy: Agenda for the 21st Century,* Vol. 2, (New

Delhi: Konark Publishers, 1997), p. 335.

105. J.N. Dixit, *op. cit.*, pp. 255-56.
106. V.P. Dutt, *op. cit.*, p. 326.
107. Quoted in V.P. Dutt, *op. cit.*, p. 326.
108. Takako Hirose, "Role of India in the Post-Cold War Era: A Japanese Perspective" in Nobuo Matsunaga and Jasjit Singh (eds.), *Enhancing Peace and Cooperation in Asia*, (New Delhi, IDSA, 1996), p.172.
109. K.V. Kesavan, *op. cit.*, p. 337.
110. See Ministry of External Affairs, *Annual Report*, Various issues, *op. cit.*
111. Takako Hirose, *op. cit.*, p.177.
112. See *Economic Survey 1995-96, op. cit.*
113. For a detailed study on the relationship between India and South Korea during the Cold War, see Chan-Wahn, Kim, *India and South Korea: Perspectives and Policies*, Unpublished M. A. Dissertation, Department of Political Science, University of Delhi, 1994.
114. Interview with Manmohan Singh, March 6, 1997.
115. B.M. Oza, "India-Korea Relations: Holding Hands Across Asia", *Times of India*, February 26, 1996.
116. John P. Lewis, *India's Political Economy: Governance and Reform*, (Delhi: OUP, 1995), p. 294.
117. Victor D. Cha, "Politics and Democracy under the Kim Young Sam Government: Something Old, Something New", *Asian Survey*, Vol. XXXIII, No. 9, September, 1993, p. 851.
118. Embassy of the Republic of Korea, New Delhi, 1997.
119. *Economic Survey 1995-96, op. cit.*
120. Indian Embassy, Seoul, 1995.
121. *Ibid.*
122. Government of India, Ministry of Industry, *Secretariat for Industrial Approval*, (New Delhi: Government of India Press, 1997).
123. See Chan-Wahn, Kim, *India's Foreign Economic Policy 1984-94*, Unpublished M. Phil. dissertation, Department of Political Science, University of Delhi, 1996.
124. For discussions of the background to SAARC, see Shamsul Haq, "South Asian Regional Cooperation", *Third World Quarterly* 5 May-June 1994 and several articles by Imtiaz H. Bokhari, S.D. Muni, Syedur Rahman, Sridhar K. Khatri and Mohammed Ayoob, in a special issue of *Asian Survey*, 25 April 1985.
125. Ramesh Thakur said that "organisation would be too strong a word" for the SAARC. see Ramesh Thakur, *op. cit.*, p. 200.

126. See Summary of the Study, Regional Trade Arrangements in the IMF Survey, April 13, 1992.
127. V.N. Khanna, *Foreign Policy of India*, (New Delhi: Vikas Publishing House, 1997), p. 215.
128. Nancy Jetly, "India and SAARC: The Political Imperatives", in Kanta Ahuja et al., *Regime Transformations and Global Realignments: Indo-European Dialogues on the Post-Cold War World*, (New Delhi: Sage Publications, 1993), p. 325.
129. See Sumitra Chishti, "Regionalism and Globalization in South Asian Countries", in S.D. Muni (ed.), *Understanding South Asia: Essays in the Memory of Late Professor (Mrs.) Urmila Phadnis*, (New Delhi: South Asian Publishers, 1994).
130. See Takako Hirose, *op. cit.*
131. See *Direction of Trade Statistics Year Book*, Various Issues, (Washington: IMF, Annual).
132. *Ibid.*
133. Ramesh Thakur, *op. cit.*, p. 200.
134. Nancy Jetly, op. cit., p. 320.
135. See Government of India, Ministry of Industry, Handbook of Industrial Policy and Statistics 1996, (New Delhi, Government of *India Press*, 1996).
136. *India Today*, March 31, 1993.
137. The two classic formulations of neofunctionalism are Ernst B. Haas, *The Uniting of Europe: Political, Social and Economic Forces, 1950-57*, (Stanford: Stanford University Press, 1968) and Leon Lindberg, The Political Dynamics of European Economic Integration, (Stanford: Stanford University Press, 1963).
138. Cited in Kanti Bajpai, "Discord and Collaboration: Domestic Politics and Indian Diplomacy in SAARC" in Baladas Ghoshal (ed.), *Diplomacy and Domestic Politics in South Asia*, (New Delhi: Konark Publishers, 1996), p. 78.
139. Takako Hirose, *op. cit.*

Six

Conclusion

This study sought to present an analysis of the relationship between economic liberalization and India's foreign policy during 1990-95. During the period the grave economic situation and subsequent economic liberalization became the dominant concern of India's politics and economics. The need to stem the economic crisis and improve economic growth became imperative. Gradually the interaction and interdependence of foreign and economic policies intensified during the first half of the 1990s. While all foreign policies include significant economic dimensions, the introduction of liberalization and globalisation into a comparatively protected economy like India's had far reaching implications for New Delhi's foreign policy and perspectives. There is a thin line demarcating foreign policy from economic policy. Thus, an analysis of economic liberalization and its impact on the foreign policy perspectives of India during the period becomes both interesting and important.

The study attempted to examine two interrelated hypotheses, namely, that (i) the economic crisis and the subsequent economic liberalization became the major concern of, and, provided a significant guideline to, India's foreign policy; and (ii) the economic liberalization programme of India increased its dependency on foreign capital, while it enhanced the openness of its economy towards the rest of the world.

In addition to this, the study addressed several important issues. One was related to the imperatives of economic reforms in India. It attempted to explore what were the compulsions behind the changes in the economic policy and consequently foreign economic policy. Secondly, the research sought to evaluate how far the economic liberalization was successful in coping with the economic crisis situation, and to what extent, it was able to help the overall economic growth.

The study further analysed the extent to which India's foreign economic policy was impinged by the imperatives of domestic political economy. The work also sought to examine the extent to which economic liberalization could be actually effected in the external and internal sectors; and whether reforms could be implemented in both the sectors to an equal extent. It also examined how successful India was in resisting outside pressure, both bilaterally and multilaterally, during the period of the economic crisis situation and during the subsequent economic liberalization process. A special study of its relations vis-a-vis international economic institutions was pursued.

This study also sought to underline the determining role of economic crisis and subsequent economic liberalization in (a) shaping the direction, scope, nature and objective of India's foreign policy and diplomacy; and (b) the impact it has on India's relations with the major countries and with the significant blocs. These various issues are recapitulated here with the related arguments and their implications.

Chapter-I provided a conceptual basis to study the linkage between economic liberalization and foreign policy. It further briefly summarised the different perspectives with regard to political economy, namely, the liberal, the Marxist and the realist approaches. Though the study did not test any theory, the research used concepts and models from the different approaches to explain the complex relationship between development and foreign policy. The chapter then briefly probed the history of its foreign economic policy, and the evolution of India's policy of liberalization.

The study noted that soon after independence, in order to achieve the objectives of a self-reliant economy, India adopted a policy of diversification and bargaining with major centres of global power. This was carried out with the help of its politics of non-alignment and friendship with all countries which underlined the independent approach in foreign policy. As a result, India could have external assistance from both the blocs during the Cold War era. This enabled the establishment of a firm heavy industrial and agricultural base by the nineteen seventies. This was a significant achievement for India's foreign economic policy. However, it is important to note that it was helped, not by an overt emphasis on the economic aspects of foreign policy, but mainly by the geo-political understanding between India and the two superpowers. Even during the 80s, especially the mid-80s, when India took some partial economic liberalization measures, the economic dimension of foreign policy was less emphasised, except for the short period of the initial Rajiv Gandhi government.

It was observed that during the 1980s, the lack of emphasis on the economic dimension of foreign policy was mainly due to the piecemeal nature of economic reforms. The economic liberalization steps under the Indira Gandhi government (1980-84) were very cautious because of various socio-political factors. Her son, Rajiv Gandhi, opened a new era of economic reform in the mid-1980s. Armed with the ideology of a post-independence generation, Rajiv Gandhi initiated policies which indicated a definite break from the Nehruvian model of development. In this, he was supported both by a massive electoral victory as well as by certain socio-economic classes. The government led by him emphasised export-oriented strategy and industrial deregulation measures. However, Rajiv Gandhi's economic liberalization could not last long mainly due to political challenges from both within his own Congress party and from the opposition parties. As a result, the liberalization programme during the Rajiv Gandhi regime remained an unfinished agenda. In this context, it was observed that as a whole, India's foreign economic policy before 1990s was mainly determined by politics rather than economics.

In searching for the imperatives for change in the direction, nature, scope and objectives of India's foreign economic policy in general and its economic policy in particular during the first half of the 1990s, chapter II analyzed both domestic and global imperatives.

It was observed that among the domestic determinants, political factors were significant. A greater degree of political freedom was enjoyed by the leadership within the ruling party at this juncture. A new ideology of the ruling elite also contributed to the background of economic liberalization. This was possible particularly during 'the honeymoon period' of the Congress government led by P.V. Narasimha Rao, which could blame the previous governments' mismanagement for the ills of the economy.

It was noted in the chapter that when the Congress government launched the economic liberalization programme in the early 1990s, the opposition parties were divided and fragmented on the economic policy to be pursued, in accordance with their ideologies and political interests. In addition to this, the main opposition party, the Bharatiya Janata Party (BJP) supported the initial economic policy of the Rao government. Furthermore, the opposition parties did not want to pull down the Congress minority government because they did not see any benefits in dissolving the Lok Sabha and to have another general elections. This kind of political situation helped the Rao government to carry out the liberalization programme.

Besides that, the chapter underlined the fact that the Prime Minister Rao also enjoyed a degree of political autonomy within his party, combining the post of president of the Congress party as well. Though there were some challenges from his own party members, like Arjun Singh, Rao's robust position within the party and the government could not be marginalised because of the backing of most of the Congress workers who also supported the ideology of a market-oriented economic policy. The chapter further observed that the market-oriented policy was firmly established with the technocratic economic ministers, secretaries and advisors who had a strong confidence in the economic merits of liberalization under the Rao government. On the whole, the new Congress leadership could utilize a considerable degree of political autonomy to carry out a dramatic reform in the economy.

Secondly, it was noted that Rao's economic liberalization policy got significant support from certain socio-economic forces, namely, the industrial bourgeois, the rich farmers and the middle classes- the presumed beneficiaries of the economic policy. In India, these groups could significantly influence the directions of national policies with their strong lobbying capabilities and mobilizing power of electoral supports. Their support for the economic liberalization policy was enhanced by their linkages with the Non-Resident Indians (NRIs) who contributed to the growing globalisation of Indian society. On the other hand, it was observed that the majority of the low income classes, who were not benefitted or were adversely affected by the programme, could not effectively resist the new direction of the economic strategy. This was largely due to their unorganized and marginalized socio-political position.

Thirdly, and without doubt, the economic crisis condition in the year 1990-91 provided a crucial basis for the economic restructuring policy. The economic crisis had directly resulted in the large macro-economic imbalances for a long time, especially during the 80s. In the mid-1991, India's foreign exchange reserves were just $ 1.1 billion which was a mere fortnight's import requirement of the country. It was observed that this situation was largely caused by a steadily growing deficit in the balance of payments, especially during the 80s. By the year of 1990-91, the trade deficit touched Rs. 16,934 crores. The problem of the balance of payments was accentuated by the existing short-term debt and by the decline of non-residents deposits. India's external debt steadily increased in the 80s. It recorded Rs. 66,314 crores by the year of 1990-91. The external liabilities of the Central government constituted 12.5 per cent of the Gross Domestic Product (GDP) level at the end of 1990-91.

The balance of payments situation also deteriorated by the unsustainable high fiscal deficit. The combined fiscal deficit of the Central and State governments, as a proportion of GDP, crossed 11.4 per cent level in 1990-91. The widening gap of fiscal deficit had to be met by borrowing at home. It was noted that this created the internal debt trap which was 53.3 per cent of GDP in 1990-91. This high fiscal deficit accelerated an inflationary spiral in 1990-91. The inflationary spiral continued during the period of 1990-91 and then peaked to 16.3 per cent in September 1991. All these economic conditions along with the political instabilities during the year 1990-91, degraded India's credit rating among the international banking community.

The chapter further explored the interlinkage between the Gulf War and the deepening economic crisis. The persistent inefficiency of the macro-economy of India could not overcome the temporary shock created by the Gulf War of 1990-91. Instead, it led to an unprecedented macro-economic crisis. The Gulf War as an exogenous factor, imposed a tremendous burden of Rs. 5,180 crores on India's balance of payments for the fiscal year 1990-91. Due to the Gulf War, oil prices skyrocketed and India had to pay a high import bill. It also had to pay for the repatriation and rehabilitation of its nationals from the region. To make matters worse, India lost a handsome amount of remittances from the Gulf region besides export markets in the region. As a whole, India had to ask for loans from the international financial institutions which put several conditions with regard to the liberalization of its economy.

The chapter also focused upon another global imperative of India's economic liberalization policy in the 1990s, namely, the post-Cold War and post-Soviet situations. Traditionally, India had enjoyed a strong economic and political relationship with the European socialist bloc led by the Soviet Union. The socialist bloc, which was known as the Rupee Trade Area, had provided an important trading region for India. The former Soviet Union had been one of the main sources of foreign assistance for India. But suddenly, India lost this major economic region due to the end of the Cold War first and but more crucially due to the collapse of the Soviet Union.

More importantly, most of the countries in the region gave up their closed economic strategies and undertook steps towards liberalization and marketization in their economies. Newly independent Russia was strongly drawn towards the Western capitalist countries, especially the United States (US), for its economic interests. These far-reaching changes in an area which had traditionally enjoyed a bargaining position vis-a-vis the West created a vacuum in India's foreign economic relations. These developments also compelled the ruling elite of India to restructure its economic strategy towards a market-oriented economy, without major ideological challenges and counter arguments.

India's position in the world economy together with the changing international economic environment were observed as two further inputs for changes in policy. By the end of the 80s, while India's economic position in the world economy was very marginal, many developing countries, especially East Asian countries which had adopted market-oriented economic strategies much earlier, had emerged as significant players in the world economy. It was also noted that the market-oriented economic strategies were also supported by the international economic institutions like the World Bank, the International Monetary Fund (IMF) and the General Agreement on Tariffs and Trade (GATT), which encouraged the globalisation of economies. There was also a wave of economic regionalism in the post-Cold War era. If India wanted to sail with the new wave of the global economic environment without lagging behind other developing countries, it had to liberalize its economy. Thus, it was observed that the background of India's economic liberalization in the 90s could not be divorced from the global compulsions prevailing in the post-Cold War and post-Soviet environment.

As a whole, it can be concluded that the far-reaching changes in India's economic and foreign economic policies in the early 1990s were not derivative of any exclusive single imperative which was either domestic or global, but occurred from a combination of a variety of the imperatives within both the external and internal domains. In other words, Indian experience showed that a major shift in development strategy in a democratic regime of a developing country is possible when there are politico socio-economic imperatives on the domestic front and the politico-economic compulsions on the global front.

Chapter three sought to analyse the nature of economic liberalization in India during the first half of the 1990s. First, it tried to analyse the reforms in the public sector as an important aspect of internal liberalization. Many of the Public Sector Undertakings (PSUs) in India could not generate adequate resources for sustaining growth which became one of the main causes of the fiscal crisis. It was seen that the PSUs under the planned economy became the victim of overpoliticisation and overbureaucratisation without adequate commercial and economic considerations. In the context of past performance of the public sector, the Congress government led by Narasimha Rao took some positive steps to ease the burden on the exchequer on account of the public sector and to generate profits based on economic viability.

To this end, the Government of India initiated some important policies and strengthened existing ones. It amended the Sick Industrial Companies Act of 1985 to enable restructuring of the loss making PSUs. It also strengthened the Memoranda of Understanding (MOU) system to reduce frequent interference by the government. The government encouraged the PSUs to raise money through issuing fresh equity from the public than from the government in order to finance their expansion. The government also undertook a disinvestment of the PSUs to raise resources and enhance a market-oriented economy.

However, it was revealed that none of these policy changes could be substantially implemented so as to bring about effective functioning of the PSUs. Neither could these measures actually facilitate the closure of loss-making units in the public sector during this period. It was further seen that there was a lack of determination to transfer the ownership of the PSUs to the private entities as part of the liberalization programme. This created a question of sustainability of internal economic liberalization policy. It seemed that the main reasons for this were not ideological or economic, but revolved around the socio-political compulsions of the ruling elite. As a result, there were no concrete steps to amend legislative laws or change administrative arrangements which could facilitate competitive efficiency and reduce political interference in PSUs.

In contrast, the government of India achieved a great deal on the external front with regard to liberalization of foreign trade and foreign investment. The new Congress government in 1991 liberalised India's foreign exchange rate, import procedures, decanalised several import and export products, abolished several licensing categories, and reduced custom tariffs. All these policies greatly encouraged an export-oriented and market-oriented strategy. These policies were also guided by the concerns regarding the globalisation of the economy. Though these policies were limited in their scope of liberalization while compared to the other developing countries, especially the East Asian countries, they were certainly impressive changes compared to India's own past policies.

As a result of these trade liberalization policies, India's trade increased significantly during the period 1990-91 to 1995-96, despite a drastic decline in its volume of trade with the former Soviet bloc. The chapter noted that the share of trade in GDP dramatically increased from the level of around 15 per cent during the 1980s to more than 24 per cent in 1995-96. With the help of an export-oriented policy, India's exports rose about 12 per cent per annum during the first half of the 1990s. This contributed to a reduction in its trade deficit, from 5-6 billion per annum in 1980s to around 2 billion. This helped in saving considerable foreign exchange. Therefore, it was argued that trade liberalization had a positive impact on India's overall economic development.

It was also observed that the trade liberalization policy significantly changed the direction of India's export and import markets. The most notable change with regard to exports was that while the Asian market emerged as a higher growth market for India's exports, the share of the former Soviet bloc in India's total exports, which was one of India's principal markets traditionally, sharply declined. In terms of commodities, several items in the agricultural and allied, diamond cutting and polishing, garments and software, benefited greatly from the trade liberalization policy. With regard to imports, it was observed that with the ongoing process of expansion and modernisation of Indian industries, an increase was also recorded in imports which was around 10 per cent per annum. The new trade policy also changed the direction of imports. While the share of the Organization for Economic Cooperation and Development (OECD) countries declined, the developing countries assumed increasing importance as a source of India's imports.

The chapter further studied the important measures undertaken by the government of India with regard to Foreign Direct Investment (FDI). For instance, India permitted 51 per cent of foreign equity participation as automatic approval for projects in specified industries producing intermediate and capital goods. It even allowed 100 per cent foreign equity participation in certain sectors like energy sector. In addition, it was noted that it reduced bureaucratic interference in foreign technology agreements.

As a result of these liberalization policies, the entire pattern of FDI in India underwent a significant change as reflected in the higher value of approvals and the rising trend in the actual inflows. The total value of FDI approvals went up substantially from Rs 534 crores in 1991 to Rs 30881 crores in 1995. However, the total actual inflows of FDI slowly increased from Rs 351 crores in 1991 to Rs 6370 crores in 1995, which constituted about 20 per cent of the approved investment in the first half of the 1990s. It was seen that the majority of FDI approvals went to priority sectors, namely, power generation, oil refinery, electrical equipment, etc. This indicated that a major motivating factor of FDI in India was to explore India's domestic market.

However, if one were to look at the FDI in India from the global point of view, the liberalization policy upto 1995 had still not led to a substantial improvement, despite its sizeable domestic market. Nevertheless, the liberalization policy helped India to diversify her sources of FDI. For instance, India attracted a handsome FDI from the newly industrialised countries like South Korea and Singapore. This reflected the rising trend of non-conventional sources of FDI in India. One of the interesting features was that while the US companies manifested maximum response to India's FDI liberalization, Japan exhibited much reluctance. However, the liberalization policy was still not perceived by global economic actors as being sufficient to attract more substantive investment. The policy-makers and politicians had to provide policy credibility and ensure continuity of the liberalization process. This was particularly complex within the context of both state elections in 1994 and 1995, and the 1996 general elections.

India also liberalized the guidelines for investments by its enterprises in joint ventures abroad. The study noted that as a consequence, the number of Indian joint ventures abroad increased from 245 at the end of 1991 to 592 at the end of November 1995. Equity participation by Indian firms abroad were also doubled. In terms of regions, East Europe and South East Asia emerged as the major host countries for Indian joint ventures. Another interesting feature was that in the South Asian region Indian joint ventures were restricted to Nepal and Sri Lanka.

The study also noted that while the liberalization programme met with some success in foreign trade and investment, the reform policy as a whole faced several problems and challenges. These impinged on the effectiveness of the programme. One of the outstanding problems that was observed, pertained to the administrative and institutional barriers in the liberalization process. Despite the central government's efforts to reduce bureaucratic interference and red-tapism, there existed a common complaint by both domestic and foreign corporations against the bureaucratic status-quoism and red-tapism, especially at the lower level of bureaucrats both at the central and state levels. Some of these functionaries claimed that they were not aware of the many changes that had been effected in the new policies. Further, there was a lack of coordination at the administrative level, between the central and state governments. Beside this, explanations to the public regarding the importance of the reform programme was also lacking. All these, in turn, affected the image of India's efficiency and the credibility of its liberalization programme. It has been argued that due to bureaucratic hurdles, India lost a considerable amount of FDI, including that of the NRIs. This indicated that a reorientation of the economic policy, in order to attain a level of sustainable growth, has to be accompanied by institutional and administrative efficiency including a speedy decision-making process.

The investigation also revealed that a major challenge for the economic liberalization process was that development of the social sector was neglected. The vital issues of education and health, which form the basic sources of sustainable growth were sidelined. The study showed that there was a decline in the health and education expenditure, especially in the initial process of the economic liberalization programme. This problem became complicated because the bulk of expenditure on social sector was spent by the state governments. The condition of social sector development was particularly pathetic in many poor and large populous states where education and health problems did not generate electoral debate. As a result, the central government could not properly ensure that the vulnerable sections of society would not be harmed by the new policy. This remained one of the major challenges for the process of liberalization. It was observed that high human development activity must accompany the process of economic liberalization in order to achieve real development.

Chapter-IV studied the changed attitudes of India towards the international economic institutions. It also explored the impact of the Final Text of the Uruguay Round negotiations of the GATT and of the loans from the IMF and World Bank on India's economy in general and foreign economic policy in particular.

In the context of the relationship between India and the GATT/ World Trade Organisation (WTO), it was shown that India entered the 1990s with a changed attitude, from that of initial opposition towards the Uruguay Round negotiations of the GATT. This was mainly due to two factors. One was the decline of counter-hegemony efforts by the Third World. The second was part of the pursuit of a 'conscious policy' of its own. This changed attitude, in turn, did have some negative impact. It damaged its credibility in the eyes of the other developing countries. During the early 1990s, India took a low key attitude towards the GATT negotiations. This was explained by the fact that India was under pressure from the US 301 Trade Act and also pressure from the IMF and World Bank. India's precarious economic situation and subsequent economic liberalization policy were instrumental in influencing its attitudes, particularly with regard to renegotiation on issues of interest to her.

In this regard, it was observed that a weak economic position and subsequent economic liberalization supported by the international institutions, made the country's foreign economic policy more vulnerable to external pressure. Despite domestic criticism and fears expressed by many sections of the society, including the opposition parties, India finally authenticated the Final Agreement of the Uruguay Round negotiations. This was in cognition of the realities of new global economic environment. Such a step was also encouraged by some positive results of economic liberalization. The Government of India further found that it was beneficial to ratify the Final Text and become a member of the

WTO rather than remain in isolation in the new world economic system.

It was further seen that with regard to the Final Text there were certainly some advantages for India. For example, the Final Text improved prospects for Indian agricultural and allied products exports. This was a result of the opening of the developed countries markets and the increasing global price of agricultural products. India also had an advantage in the service sector due to greater access for its professional services, like computer software, engineering, etc., to the developed countries. It was also pointed out that the Final Text enhanced the degree of the Indian economic integration with the rest of the world economy.

However, the study revealed that there were equally many disadvantages for India. One of the notable disadvantages was that the majority of the poor and marginal farmers, who were already made vulnerable by the economic liberalization process, would be further negatively affected by the new patent regime of the Trade-Related Intellectual Rights (TRIPs) agreement. Another serious disadvantage was that the degree of dependency on foreign capital and technology would increase as a result of the prospective strengthening of the hegemony of the Multinational Corporations (MNCs), specially under the agreement on the Trade-Related Investment Measures (TRIMs). Yet another serious concern was that India's sovereign rights with regard to policy options in its domestic socio-economic sectors were threatened by the Final Agreement.

As a whole, it was pointed out that the result of the final agreement of the Uruguay Round negotiations of the GATT and the new WTO Act were in favour of the developed countries, especially for their MNCs. Thus, it was held that the new international trade system provided both opportunities and challenges for Indian economy. Since India had already launched the far-reaching economic reforms which aimed to integrate its economy with the world economy, it was considered wise to stay with the new global economic system. But, the study noted that India has to improve its bargaining skills while dealing with new WTO issues.

On the issue of the relationship between India and international financial institutions, it was pointed out that India had to approach these institutions to overcome its crisis in balance of payments during 1990-92. As a result of the Gulf War, India was forced to borrow loans from the IMF in the early 1991. The IMF quickly cleared its loans for India. It was observed that one of the reasons behind the quick approval of the IMF loans to India in early 1991 was the US goodwill to India. The latter had provided refuelling facilities to the US planes during the Gulf War. This, at the same time, discredited India's stand with regard to its non-aligned foreign policy. The loans of early 1991, however, could not stop a grave economic crisis in India. The Chandra Shekhar government was not able to initiate any major policy change due to domestic political instability.

As a result, the new Congress government led by P.V. Narasimha Rao had to again ask for another IMF loan. In October 1991, the IMF approved a stand-by credit for India authorizing drawings upto the equivalent of Special Drawing Rights (SDR) 1656 million in support of the government's economic and financial programmes. The loan was attached with conditionalities. Interestingly, India undertook significant policy reforms prior to signing the agreement with the IMF for the stand-by loans. This certainly contributed to the IMF approval for the loan of SDR 1656 million. The letter of intent sent by the government of India to the IMF President was probably another contributing factor.

The World Bank also approved a policy based loan amounting to $ 12.25 billion. Traditionally, India was reluctant to receive policy based loans due to a preference for retaining its independence in politically sensitive policy options. Therefore, this reflected a significant change in India's foreign economic policy towards the multilateral international institutions. The Bank loan was facilitated after the IMF approved the second drawing of the Compensatory and Contingency Financing Fund (CCFF) in July 1991 and the Finance Minister of India assured the President of the Bank that it would stabilize its economy through an official letter. It seemed that both the IMF and the World Bank were satisfied with the area of the programmes and with the implementation of their conditionalities by the government of India. The IMF provided the final tranche of its loans and the Bank issued $ 300 million in June 1993.

However, there was significant criticism of the loans and the accompanying conditionalities of the IMF and the World Bank. One of the valid censures was that these financial institutions neglected India's social development by framing priorities and objectives of the economic development of the country. The Congress government was further censured for bringing a reforms programme that was dictated by the Fund and the Bank. But, this criticism was perhaps not fully justified by the fact that it was mutual agreement between the Government of India and the international financial institutions. It depicted the will of the leadership of India to accept the conditionalities for its own economic stability. The chapter observed that the loans despite conditionalities, did help in stabilizing India's grave economic situation. They contributed to attracting a handsome amount of foreign investment as well. More importantly, the improved economic condition of India reduced further dependency of the government on the same financial institutions.

Thus, it is not fully correct to say that the economic liberalization of India supported by the financial institutions was anti-national. Instead, it was rather pointed out that one should blame the bad economy, not the external loan itself which was accompanied with conditionalities. It rather proved that lack of external support could further weaken its sovereignty in a continuing economic crisis situation.

The fifth chapter attempted to make a detailed study of the impact of India's economic liberalization on its foreign relations. It was shown that its precarious economic condition and subsequent liberalization programme became the major concern of, and provided a significant guideline to, India's foreign policy during the first half of the 1990s. As a result, the economic aspect of foreign policy was emphasised during the first half of the 1990s. But, was this change in its economic policy and consequently in foreign policy brought about under compelling circumstances, or was it due to a genuine desire of the Indian government to shape its foreign policy in the sole interest of its economic development? It was studied that in order to overcome its economic crisis and achieve substantial growth by liberalising its economy, India had to change both the ideological and the operational terms of reference in its foreign policy. Such a change was also necessary in order to adjust to the post Cold War and post Soviet international environment which brought about globalisation and regionalization of economies. As a result, economics dominated the substance of India's diplomatic relations. In contrast to the pre 1990s period, the political orientation of bilateral interactions was diluted during the period 1990-95.

The study revealed that with a changed outlook, efforts were made to gear up the diplomatic establishment by imparting training and refresher courses to Ambassadors and middle level diplomats. The objective was to familiarize them with the new economic trends so as to maximise the benefits of the globalisation process. The decision making process began to be guided more by economic rather than political considerations and Indian decision-makers were sometimes showing readiness to bend themselves politically to reach their economic goals- a situation that Indian diplomacy had until the 1990s refused to accept.

This was clearly witnessed in India's foreign relations at both bilateral and multilateral levels. There was a change not only in direction but in the focus of India's foreign relations. There appeared a significant reorientation in India's approach towards the capitalist countries. India began to focus on four major capitalist countries and regions- the US, the European Union (EU), East Asia, and the Association of South-East Asian Nations (ASEAN). The Indian Prime Minister and other important leaders visited most of these countries and regions. During their visits, the Indian leaders focused economic issues in their bilateral discussions with various countries without exception. They were eager to sell India's economic reform programme and convince foreign leaders and business communities that India's new economic policy was irreversible. In turn, Indian leaders got support for their economic reform measures from foreign leaders and the business communities. This was certainly an unprecedented move when compared to India's diplomatic history in the past.

India's outward-oriented foreign economic policy certainly enabled it to improve bilateral relations with many capitalist countries and regions. Though both the major capitalist countries and regions had economic compulsions to improve their relations with India in the light of New Delhi's economic liberalization, for India, it was an absolute imperative to enhance the degree of openness of its economy to the capitalist countries. It was particularly crucial at a time when India lost the former Soviet bloc as an important economic partner and tried to overcome its unprecedented economic difficulties.

It was observed that India's external relations, especially economic relations with the capitalist countries, clearly and inevitably received a boost during the period of 1993 and 1994. Around the same time, India's economic liberalization programme also began to show steady results. This was evident from the fact that the leaders of major EU countries visited India primarily to discuss bilateral economic cooperation between them. The US also began to change its approach towards India basing it more on economic and commercial interests. This indicates that the main attraction of the leading capitalist countries during the period was India's economic potentiality in the light of its liberalization policy. In other words, foreign countries, especially the US, were mainly interested in closer relations with India not due to political security reasons but due to economic factors.

One of the outstanding features of India's foreign policy in the economic liberalization years was the new found interest in Asia, namely, its "Look East" policy. Traditionally India's relations with the states of this region were limited mostly by ideological factors, both in political and economic terms, during the Cold War years. There was now an imperative to attract the new industrialising countries in Asia in the wake of India's economic liberalization programme. India pragmatically approached the countries individually and the region as a whole, on the basis of economic and commercial factors. The change was notable, especially with regard to relations with South Korea and Singapore which were traditionally US allies. This reflected a significant change in India's foreign policy perspectives. Thus, it was said that in the post-Cold War and post Soviet era, the economic liberalization programme of India contributed to India's foreign policy becoming more pragmatic, especially in its approach towards capitalist countries. Thus, it was observed that the economic crisis and subsequent liberalization policy established closer relations with capitalist countries.

A significant component of this analysis was whether this improved economic relationship through liberalization of the economy was utilized as a leverage against the capitalist countries, especially the US, on the issue of security. It was observed that India was still not in a position to obtain any substantial concession on security matters. India was not able to utilize its huge size of domestic market potential, with a far-reaching economic liberalization programme, as a leverage against the US position on its Prithvi and Agni missile programmes. It was mentioned that India desperately needed the Western capital, technology and markets, rather more than the Western countries needed India's markets. India's trade relations with them was asymmetric. Moreover, the leading capitalist countries were preoccupied with Eastern Europe, the Russian Federation, China and other emerging industrialising countries in Asia. This was very significant in India's bargaining power capability vis-a-vis the Western countries in the post-Soviet era.

The chapter also underlined that in the era of economic regionalism and in the line of its economic liberalization policy, India wanted to establish a special relationship with important regional economic organisations. It established important linkages with the EU through various channels. Further, due to various problems in the South Asian Association for Regional Cooperation (SAARC), India became interested in wider regional frameworks. These were the Asia-Pacific region and the Indian Ocean region. India made attempts to become a member of the ASEAN and through that of the APEC. India also gave a positive reaction to the creation of a new economic regional group around Indian Ocean, i.e., the Indian Ocean Rim Association for Regional Cooperation (IORARC). Before the 1990s, India was not particularly interested in a wider regional framework, especially that of the ASEAN and Asia Pacific Economic Community (APEC). This reflected another important change in India's foreign policy thinking.

Here a question arose as to whether a specific course in the foreign economic policy of a developing country is sufficient to enable it to become a member of particular regional group. The Indian experience shows the answer to be in the negative. The reason is that the existing regional groups would be prepared to offer membership only if a particular state becomes crucial to their interests, and emerges as a significant factor in their economic, strategic and geo-political considerations. India's economic liberalization policy was not a sufficient condition, but only a necessary condition to be member of ASEAN or APEC though the existing economic groups both collectively and bilaterally favoured New Delhi's new economic policy. Importance also had to be given to India's problems with its own regional countries, especially with Pakistan. A functional approach of India towards Pakistan could not materialize during the period of the first half of the 1990s. The tension between the two countries created a limitation for India's "Look East" policy. This was seen as one of the possible reasons for the ASEAN and APEC countries' reluctance to accept India into their "comfortable" group.

Besides this, India had still not emerged as a significant economic power as a result of its own economic liberalization policy. There was also a considerable difference between India and the countries of these groups, with respect to the pace of decision-making and implementation process of economic measures. These were also part of the reasons that Japanese investors kept a 'wait and watch' attitude towards India. Therefore, it was considered that though India boosted its economic potentiality by liberalising its economy, it could not capitalize on its merits to be used as a leverage to gain a membership of the ASEAN and APEC, and thereby invite more foreign investors into India.

In sum, the economic crisis and the subsequent economic liberalization became the major concern of, and, provided a significant guideline to India's foreign policy. The economic libaration programme of India increased its dependency on foreign capital and markets, while it enhanced the openness of the economy towards the rest of the world.

Bibliography

Primary Sources

AICC(I), 1991 *General Election Manifesto of INC(I),* (New Delhi: AICC, 1991).

AICC(I), *Central Manifesto, 1994 Assembly Elections,* (New Delhi: AICC, 1994).

AICC(I), *Surajkund Session of the INC(I), One-Man-One-Post Resolution,* (New Delhi: AICC, 1993).

AICC(I), *Tirupati Session of INC(I),* Economic Resolution, (New Delhi: AICC, 1992).

Asian Development Bank, *Asian Development Outlook, Various Issues,* (New York: OUP).

BJP, *Humanistic Approach to Economic Development: A Swadesh Alternative,* (New Delhi: BJP, 1992).

BJP, *Speeches on Budget 1991-92,* (New Delhi: BJP, 1992).

Commonwealth Secretariat, *Engendering Adjustment for the 1990s,* Report of a Commonwealth Expert Group on Women and Structural Adjustment, 1989.

European Union, Commission of the European Communities, Communication from the Committee to the Council, *Towards a New Asia Strategy,* Com (94) 314 final, 13 July, 1994.

European Union, Commission of the European Communities, Communication from the Commission, *EU-India Enhanced Partnership,* Com (96) 275 final, Brussels, 26 June, 1996.

GATT Secretariat, *An Analysis of the Proposed Uruguay Round Agreement with Particular Emphasis on Aspects of Interest to Developing Countries,* (Geneva: GATT Secretariat, 1993).

Government of India, Ministry of Commerce, *Annual Report, Various Issues,* (New Delhi: Government of India Press).

Government of India, Ministry of Commerce, The Uruguay Round of Multilateral Trade Negotiations: A Paper for Discussion, Monthly Commentary, July 1992.

Government of India, Ministry of External Affairs, *Annual Report Various Years,* (New Delhi: Government of India Press, 1995 and 1996).

Government of India, Ministry of Finance, *Economic Survey, Various Years,* (New Delhi: Government of India Press).

Government of India, Ministry of Finance, *Export and Import Policy: 1 April 1992 - 31 March 1993,* (New Delhi: Government of India Press).

Government of India, Ministry of Finance, *Interim Report of the Tax Reforms Committee,* (Chairman: Raja Chelliah), New Delhi, 1992.

Government of India, Ministry of Industry, *Secretariat for Industrial Approval,* (New Delhi: Government of India, 1997).

Government of India, Ministry of Industry, *HandBook of Industrial Policy and Statistics 1996,* (New Delhi: Government of India Press, 1996).

Government of India, Ministry of Industry, *Report of the committee on Industrial Sickness and Corporate Restructuring* (Chairman: Omkar Goswami), New Delhi, 1993.

Government of India, Planning Commision, *Towards Social Transformation: Approach to the Eighth Five-Year Plan 1990-1995,* (New Delhi: Government of India Press, 1990).

Government of Japan, Ministry of Foreign Affairs, *Japan's Official Development Assistance 1992,* (Tokyo: Ministry of Foreign Affairs, 1993).

IMF, *Direction of Trade Statistics Year Book, Various Issues,* Washington D.C.

IMF, *The IMF Survey, Various Issues,* Washington D.C.

IMF, *World Economic Outlook 1994,* Washington D.C., 1994.

Public Interest Rechearch Group, *The Great Surrender,* Delhi, 1995.

Public Interest Research Group, *GATT Strophe,* (Delhi: Public Interest Research Group, 1994).

Public Interest Research Group, *The World Bank and India,* (Delhi: Public Interest Research Group, 1995).

Reserve Bank of India, *Annual Report Various Issues,* (Bombay: Reserve Bank of India).

Reserve Bank of India, *Report on Currency and Finance Various Issues,* Vol. I and II, (Bombay: Reserve Bank of India).

The United Nations Development Programme, *Human Development Report 1994,* (New York: OUP, 1994).

United States International Trade Commission, *International Trade Review,* Washington, D.C., June 1995.

US Embassy, *Survey of US Investment in India,* (New Delhi: US Embassy, 1994).

US Embassy, *May 1992 Economic Trends Report,* Cable No. 11319, (New Delhi: US Embassy, 1995).

World Bank, *Annual Report Varous Years,* (Washington D.C.: World Bank).

World Bank, *Economic Developments in India: Achievements and Challenges,* (Washington, D.C., The World Bank, 1995).

World Bank, *India: Structural Loan/Credit,* Washington D.C.: World Bank, 1991).

World Bank, *The World Bank in India,* New Delhi, 1993.

World Bank, *World Development Report,* Various Issues, (New York: OUP).

World Economic Forum (International Management Development Institute), *World Competitiveness Report 1993,* Geneva, 1993.

Secondary Sources

(A) Books

Ahluwalia, Isher Judge and I.M.D. Little, *India's Economic Reforms and Development: Essays for Manmohan Singh,* (Delhi: OUP, 1998).

Ahluwalia, Shashi and Meenakshi Ahluwalia, *Profils of Indian Prime Ministers: Nehru to Narasimha Rao,* (New Delhi: Mittal Publications, 1991).

Ahuja, Kanta et al., *Regime Transformations and Global Realignments: Indo-European Dialogues on the Post-Cold War World,* (New Delhi: Sage Publications, 1993).

Anderfelt, U., *International Patent Legislation and Developing Countries,* (The Hague: Martinus Nijhoffs, 1971).

Appadorai, A and M.S. Rajan, *India's Foreign Policy and Relations,* (New Delhi: South Asian Publishers, 1985).

Appadorai, A., *National Interest And India's Foreign Policy,* (Delhi: Kalinga Publications, 1992).

Arora, Ramesh K and Rajni Goyal, *Indian Public Administration: Institutions and Issues,* 2nd edition, (New Delhi: Wishwa Prakashan, 1996).

Bardhan, Pranab, *The Political Economy of Development in India,* (Delhi: OUP, 1984).

Bardhan, Pranab, *The Political Economy of Development in India,* Expanded Edition with an Epilogue on the Political Economy of Reform in India, (Delhi: OUP, 1998).

Bates, Robert H. and Anne O. Krueger, *Political Economic Interaction in Economic Policy Reforms,* (Oxford: Basil Backwell, 1993).

Batra, G.S. and Narinder Kaur (eds), *GATT: Implications of Dunkel Proposals,* (New Delhi: Anmol Publications, 1994).

Beteille, Andre, *Society and Politics in India: Essays in a Comparative Perspective,* Second Impression, (Delhi: OUP, 1998).

Bhaduri, Amit and Deepak Nayyar, *The Intelligent Person's Guide to Liberalization,* (New Delhi: Penguin Books, 1996).

Bhagwati, Jagdish and T.N. Srinivasan, *India's Economic Reforms,* (New Delhi: Government of India, Ministry of Finance, 1993).

Bhagwati, Jagdish, *India in Transition : Freeing The Economy,* (Delhi: OUP, 1995).

Bhalla, G.S. and Manmohan Agarwal (eds.), *World Economy in Transition,* (Shimla: Indian Institute of Advanced Study, 1992).

Bhalla, V.K., *Foreign Investment and New Economic Policy,* (New Delhi: Anmol Publications, 1994).

Bhambhri, C.P., *Indian Politics Since Independence,* (Delhi: Shipra Publications, 1994).

Bhambhri, C.P., *The Indian State: Fifty Years,* (New Delhi: Shipra Publications, 1997).

Bhorali, D., *GATT Agreement or Dunkel Draft Treaty,* (New Delhi: Mittal Publications, 1994).

Bora, Dalip Kumar S., *India's Foreign Trade With the European*

Economic Community, (Almora: Shri Almora Book Depot, 1994).

Bose, Sugata and Ayesha Jalan (eds.), *Nationalism, Democracy and Development: State and Politics in India,* (Delhi: OUP, 1997).

Brass, Paul R., *The Politics of India since Independence,* (Cambridge: Cambridge University Press, 1990).

Buchanan, M.M., R. Tollison and G. Tullock (Eds.) *Toward a Theory of the Rent-Seeking Society,* (College Station: Texas A and M University Press, 1980).

Byres, Terence J., *The State and Delvelopmet Planning in India,* (Delhi: OUP, 1994).

Cassen, Robert and Associates, *Does Aid Work?: Report to an Intergovernmental Task Force,* (New York: OUP, 1994).

Cassen, Robert and Vijay Joshi (eds.), *India: The Future of Economic Reform,* (New Delhi: OUP, 1995).

Chatterjee, Partha (ed.), *State and Politics in India,* (New Delhi: OUP, 1997).

Chatterjee, Partha (ed.), *Wages of Freedom: Fifty Years of the Indian Nation-State,* (Delhi: OUP, 1998).

Chenery H. and T.N. Srinivasan (eds.), *Handbook of Development Economics,* Vol. 1, (Amsterdam: North Holland, 1988).

Chomsky, N, *Powers and Prospects: Reflections on Human Nature and the Social Order,* (Delhi: Maydhyam Books, 1996).

Chomsky, N., *Profit Over People: Neoliberalism and Global Order,* (Delhi: Madhyam Books, 1999).

Chomsky, N., *Year 501: The Conquest Continues* (Boston: South End Press, 1993).

Chopra, H.S. (ed.), *India and the European Union into the 21st Century,* (New Delhi: Indian Council of World Affairs, 1998).

Cohen, Benjamin J., ed., *American Foreign Economic Policy: Essays and Comments,* (New York: Harper and Row, 1968).

Cohen, Stephen D. and Ronald I. Meltzer, *United States International Economic Policy in Action: Diversity of Decision Making,* (New York: Preager, 1982).

Cohen, Stephen D., *The Making of Unitied States International Economic Policy,* (New York: Preagen Publishers, 1977).

Corbo, Vittorio, Stanley Fischer and Steven B Webb (eds.),

Adjustment Lending Revisited- Policies to Restore Growth, A World Bank Symposium, World Bank, 1992.

Cornia, G., R. Jolly and F Stewart (eds), *Adjustment with a Human Face,* Vol. 1 (New York: OUP, 1987).

Damodaran, A.K., *Jawaharlal Nehru: A Communicator and Democratic Leader,* (New Delhi: Radiant Publications, 1997).

Dandekar, V. M., *The Indian Economy: 1949-92,* Vol. 1, *Agriculture,* (New Delhi: Sage Publications, 1994).

Das, S.K., *Civil Service Reforms and Structural Adjustment,* (Delhi: OUP, 1998).

Dasgupta, Abhijit and Georg Lechner (eds.), *Development Aid Today,* (New Delhi: Mosaic Books, 1995).

Dell, Sidney, *On Being Grandmotherly: The Evolution of IMF Conditionality,* (Princeton: Princeton University, International Finance Section, 1981).

Dixit, J.N., *My South Block Years: Memoirs of a Foreign Secretary,* (New Delhi: UBSPD, 1996).

Dreze, Jean and Amartya Sen, *India: Economic Development and Social Opportunity,* (Delhi: OUP, 1995).

Dubey, Muchkund, *An Unequal Treaty: World Trading Order After GATT,* (New Delhi: New Age International Publishers, 1996).

Dutt, V.P., *India's Foreign Policy in a Changing World,* (New Delhi: Vikas Publishing House, 1999).

Echengreen, Barry and Peter Lindert, (eds.), *The International Debt Crisis in Historical Perspective,* (Cambridge: M.I.T. Press, 1990).

Firansman M. and King K. (eds.), *Technological Capability in the Third World,* (London: Pinter, 1984).

Foreign Service Institute, *Indian Foreign Policy: Agenda for the 21st Century,* Vol. 1, (New Delhi: Konark Publishers, 1997).

Foreign Service Institute, *Indian Foreign Policy: Agenda for the 21st Century,* Vol. 2, (New Delhi: Konark Publishers, 1998).

Frieden, Jeffry A. and David A. Lake, *International Political Economy: Perspectives on Global Power and Wealth,* Third Edition, (New York: St. Martin's Press, 1995).

Gehlot, N.S., *Indian Government and Politics,* (New Delhi: Rawat Publications, 1996).

Ghoshal, Baladas (ed.), *Diplomacy and Domestic Politics in South Asia,* (New Delhi: Konark Publishers, 1996).

Giarini, Orio (ed.), *The Emerging Service Economy,* (Oxford: Pregamon Press, 1986).

Gordon, Sandy, *India's Rise to Power in the Twentieth Century and Beyond,* (New York: Martin's Press, 1995).

Gupta, Bhabani Sen, *India: Problems of Governance,* (New Delhi: Konark Publications, 1996).

Gupta, K.R. (ed.), *GATT Accord and India,* (New Delhi: Atlantic Publishers, 1998).

Gupta, M.G., *Rajiv Gandhi's Foreign Policy: Continuity and Change,* (Agra: M.G. Publishers, 1987).

Gupta, S.P. et al. (eds.), *Trade Policy Reforms,* (New Delhi: Macmillan India, 1994).

Haas, Ernst B., *The Uniting of Europe: Political, Social and Economic Forces, 1950-57,* (Stanford: Stanford University Press, 1968).

Haggard, Stephan and Steven B. Webb (eds.), *Voting for Reform: Democracy Political Liberation, and Economic Adjustment,* (New York: OUP, 1994).

Hardgrave, Robert L. Jr., and Stanley Kochanek, *India: Government and Politics in a Developing Nation,* 4th edition, (New York: Harcourt Brace Jovanovich, 1986).

Iyer, K. V. and L.R. Kumar, *Foreign Collaboration in Industry-Policies And Procedures,* Vol. 1, (New Delhi: Indu Publications, 1985).

Jain, B.M. (ed.), *Reflections on India's Foreign Policy,* (Jaipur: RBSA Publishers, 1989).

Jalan, Bimal (ed.), *The Indian Economy: Problems and Prospects,* (New Delhi: Penguin Books, 1993).

Jalan, Bimal, *India's Economic Crisis: The Way Ahead,* (Delhi: OUP, 1991).

Jalan, Bimal, *India's Economic Crisis: The Way Ahead,* 2nd impression, (Delhi: OUP, 1993).

Jalan, Bimal, *India's Economic Policy: Preparing for the Twenty-First Century,* (New Delhi: Viking, 1996).

Jannuzi, F. Tomasson, *India's Persistent Dilemma: The Political*

Economy of Agrarian Reform, (New Delhi: Orient Longman, 1994).

Jeffrey, Robin, *What's Happening to India?*, Second Edition, (London: The Macmillan Press, 1994).

Jha, Prem Shankar, *India: A Political Economy of Stagnation*, (Bombay: OUP, 1980).

Jilberto, Alex E. Fernandez and Andre' Mommen (eds.), *Liberalisation in the Developing World: Institutional and Economic Change in Latin America, Africa and Asia*, (London: Routledge, Kegan Paul, 1996).

Johnson, Harry G., *On Economics and Society* (Chicago: University of Chicago Press, 1972).

Jones, R.J. Barry (ed.), *The Worlds of Political Economy*, (London: Pinter Publishers, 1988).

Joshi, Vijay and I.M.D. Little, *India: Macroeconomics and Political Economy 1964-91*, (Delhi: OUP, 1994).

Joshi, Vijay and I.M.D. Little, *India's Economic Reforms 1991-2001*, (Delhi: OUP, 1996).

Kahler, Miles, (ed.), *The Politics of International Debt.*, (Ithaca: Cornell University Press, 1986).

Kapila, Uma (ed.), *After 4 Years of Economic Reforms*, (Delhi: Academic Foundation, 1995).

Kapur, Harish, *India's Foreign Policy 1947-1992: Shadows and Substance*, (New Delhi: Sage Publication, 1994).

Karunakaran, K.P., *India in World Affairs 1950-53*, (Calcutta: OUP, 1958).

Karunakaran, K.P., *Modernization of Capitalism, Communism and World Politics*, (Neerut: Meenaksh, 1975).

Kaviraj, Sudipta (ed.), *Politics in India*, Paperbacks, (Delhi: OUP, 1999).

Keohane, R. and J.S. Nye, eds., *Transnational Relations and World Politics*, (Cambridge: Harvard University Press, 1973).

Keohane, Robert O. and Joseph S. Nye, *Power and Interdependence*, second edition (Glenview, Illinois: Scott, Foresman and Company, 1989).

Khanna, V.N., *Foreign Policy of India*, (New Delhi: Vikas Publishing House, 1997).

Khilnani, N.M., *New Dimensions of Indian Foreign Policy*, (New

Delhi: Westvill Publishing House, 1995).

Kim, Chan-Wahn, *India and South Korea: Perspectives and Policies,* Unpublished M. A. Dissertation, Department of Political Science, University of Delhi, 1994.

Kim, Chan-Wahn, *India's Foreign Economic Policy 1984-94,* Unpublished M. Phil. Dissertation, Department of Political Science, University of Delhi, 1996.

Kohli, Atul (ed.), *India's Democracy: An Analysis of Changing State-Society Relations,* (New Delhi: Orient Longman, 1991).

Kohli, Atul, *Democracy and Discontent: India's Growing Crisis of Governability,* (Cambridge: Cambridge University Press, 1991).

Kohli, Atul, *The State and Poverty in India: The Poltics of Reform,* (New Delhi: Orient Longman, 1987).

Komiya, Ryutaro, *The Japanese Economy Trade, Industry and Government,* (Tokyo: University of Tokyo Press, 1990).

Kothari, Rajni, *Politics in India,* (New Delhi: Orient Longman, 1970).

Kripa, Sridharan, *The ASEAN Region in India's Foreign Policy,* (Aldershot: Dartmouth, 1996).

Krommenacker, Raymond J., *World-Traded Services: The Challenge for the 1980s,* (Dedham, Mass.: Artech House, 1984).

Kumar, Ramesh, *Congress and Congressism in Indian Politics,* (New Delhi: Deep and Deep Publications, 1994).

Kurien, C.T., *Economic Reforms and The People,* (Delhi: Public Interest Research Group, 1996).

Kurien, C.T., *Global Capitalism and The Indian Economy,* (New Delhi: Orient Longman, 1994).

Lewis, John P., *India's Political Economy: Governance and Reform,* (Delhi: OUP, 1995).

Lindberg, Leon, *The Political Dynamics of European Economic Integration,* (Stanford: Stanford University Press, 1963).

Lipton, Michael and John Toye, *Does Aid Work in India?: A Country Study of the Impact of Official Development Assistance,* (London: Routledge, 1990).

Lyon, Peter and James Manor (eds.), *Transfer and Transformation: Political Institutions in the New Commonwealth: Essays in Honour of W.H. Morris-Jones,* (New Hampshre: Leicester

University Press, 1983).

Mackinlay, R.D. and R. Little, *Global Problems and World Order*, (London: Frances Pinter, 1986).

Manor, James, *Power, Poverty and Poison: Disaster and Response in an Indian City*, (New Delhi: Sage Publications, 1993).

Mathur, Krishan D. and P.M. Kamath, *Conduct of India's Foreign Policy*, (New Delhi:South Asian Publishers, 1996).

Matsunaga, Nobuo and Jasjit Singh (eds.), *Enhancing Peace and Cooperation in Asia*, (New Delhi, IDSA, 1996).

Mishra, Rajan Kumar, *India and International Relations*, (New Delhi: Kanishka Publishers, 1996).

Mohanty, Bijoyini and S.C. Hazary (eds.), *Political Economy of India: Retrospects and Prospects*, (New Delhi: A.P.H. Publishing Corporation, 1997).

Morgenthau, Hans J. and Kenneth W. Thompson, *Politics Among Nations: The Struggle for Power and Peace*, 6th edn., (New York: McGraw, 1985).

Mosely, Paul, James Harrigan and John Toye, *Aid and Power-the World Bank and Policy-based Lending*, (London: Routledge, 1991).

Mosley, Paul, *Conditionality as Bargaining Process: Structural Adjustment Lending, 1980-86*, (Princeton: Princeton University, International Finance Section, 1987).

Mosley, Paul, James Harrigan and Jone Toye, *Aid and Power- the World Bank and Policy-based Lending*, Volumes 1 and 2, (London: Routledge, 1991).

Mukherjee, Pranab, *Challenges Before the Nation*, (New Delhi: Vikas Publishing House, 1993).

Muni, S.D. (ed.), *Understanding South Asia: Essays in the Memory of Late Professor (Mrs.) Urmila Phadnis*, (New Delhi: South Asian Publishers, 1994).

Muravyov, Andrei, *Soviet Indian Economic Relations: Trends and Prospects*, (New Delhi: Panchsheel Publishers, 1990).

Nagpal C.S. and A.C. Mittal (eds.), *India's Foreign Trade*, (New Delhi: Anmol Publications, 1993).

Narain Veena, *U.S. Financial Aid and India's Economic Growth*, (New Delhi: Commonwealth Publishers, 1988).

Nautiyal, Annpurna, *India and the New World Order,* (New Delhi: South Asian Publishers, 1996).

Nayyar, Deepak, *Economic Liberalization in India: Analytics, Experience and Lessons,* (Calcutta: Orient Longman, 1996).

Nelson, Joan (ed.), *Economic Crisis and Policy Choice,* (Princepton: Princepton University Press, 1990).

Oldenburg, Philip, (ed.), *India Briefing,* (Boulder coll: Westview, 1993).

Oommen, M.A., et al., *Crisis in India,* (New Delhi: Kham Publishers, 1995).

Pandhe, M.K., *Surrender of India's Sovereignty and Self-Reliance,* (New Delhi: Progress Printers, 1991).

Pant, Manoj, *Foreign Direct Investment in India: The Issues Involved* (New Delhi: Lancers Books, 1995).

Parikh, Kirit S., *India Development Report, 1997,* (New Delhi: OUP, 1997).

Pastor, Robert A., *Congress and the Politics of U.S. Foreign Economic Policy: 1929-1976,* (Berkeley: University of California Press, 1980).

Prasad, Bimal (ed.) *India's Foreign Policy: Studies in Continuity and Change,* (New Delhi: Vikas Publisher, 1979).

Prasad, D.N., *Food for Peace: The Story of US Food Production to India,* (Bombay: Asia Publishing House, 1980).

Rajan, M.S., et al. (des.), *The Nonaligned and the United Nations,* (New Delhi: South Asian Publishers, 1987).

Rajan, M.S., *Nonalignment and Nonaligned Movement: Retrospect and Prospect,* (New Delhi: Vikas Publishing House, 1990).

Ramachandriah V. (ed.), *GATT Accord: India's Strategic Response,* (New Delhi: Commonwealth Publishers, 1994).

Ramesh Thakur, *The Politics and Economics of India's Foreign Policy,* (Delhi: OUP, 1994).

Rana, A.P., *Four Decades of Indo-US Relations: A Commemorative Retrospective,* (New Delhi: Har Anand Publications, 1994).

Rana, A.P., *Imperatives of Non-Alignment,* (Delhi: Macmillan, 1976).

Rao, C.H. Hanumantha and Hans Linnemann (des.), *Economic Reforms and Poverty Alleviation in India,* (New Delhi: Sage Publications, 1996).

Rao, V.V. Bhanoji, *India's Economic Future: Government, People and Attitudes,* (New Delhi: Tata MacGraw-Hill, 1993).

Ray, H.N., *The World Bank: A Third World View,* (New Delhi: Indus Publishing Company, 1996).

Ray, Rajat K., *Industrialization in India: Growth and Conflict in the Private Corporat Sector, 1914-47,* (Delhi: OUP, 1979).

Rose, Leo E. and Gonsalves Eric (eds.), *Towards a New World Order: Adjusting India-US Relations,* (Berkelery: Institute of East Asian Studies, 1992).

Roy, P.C., *Indo-US Economic Relaiton,* (New Delhi: Deep and Deep Publicaions, 1986).

Roy, Ramashray and Richard Sission (eds.), *Diversity and Dominance in Indian Politics, Vol. 1: Changing Bases of Congress Support,* (New Delhi: Sage Publications, 1990).

Roy, Subroto and William E. James, *Foundations of India's Political Economy: Towards an Agenda for the 1990s,* (New Delhi: Sage Publications, 1992).

Rudolph, Lloyd I. and Susanne H. Rudolph, *In Pursuit of Lakshmi: The Political Economy of the Indian State,* (New Delhi: Orient Longman, 1987).

Sandy, Gordon, *India's Rise to Power in the Twentieth Century and Beyond,* (New York: Martin's Press, 1995).

Sarvepalli, Gopal, *Jawaharlal Nehru: A Biography, Vol. II, 1947-56,* (London: Jonathan Cape, 1979).

Sathyamurthy, T.V. (ed.), *Social Change and Political Discourse in India, Vol. 1, State and Nation in the Context of Social Change,* (Delhi: OUP, 1994).

Sathyamurthy, T.V. (ed.), *Social Change and Political Discourse in India, Vol. 2, Industry and Agriculture in India since Independence,* (Delhi: OUP, 1995).

Saxena, P.R., *The IMF Loan to India: An Economic Assessment,* (Delhi: Anmol Publications, 1986).

Saxena, Rekha, *Indian Politics Transition: From Dominace to Chaos,* (New Delhi: Deep and Deep Publications, 1994).

Saxena, S.S. and R. K. Pandey, *The Uruguay Round of Multilateral Trade Negotiations Under GATT: Mid-Term Review at Montreal - Main Outcome - an Appraisal,* (New Delhi: Indian Institute of Foreign Trade, 1998).

Shah, Ghanshyam, *Social Movements in India: A Review of the*

Literature, (New Delhi: Sage Publications, 1990).

Sharma, R. K., *The Economics of Soviet Assistance to India,* (New Delhi: Allied Publishers, 1981).

Shaw, Timothy M. and Olajide Aluko (eds.), *The Political Economy of African Foreign Policy: Comparative Analysis,* (Aldeshot: Gower Publishing Company, 1984).

Shelp, Ronald Kent, *Beyond Industrialization: Ascendancy of the Global Service Economy,* (New York: Praeger, 1981).

Sheth, D.L. and Ashis Nandy (eds.), *The Multiverse of Democracy: Essays in Honour of Rajni Kothari,* (New Delhi: Sage Publications, 1996).

Shukla, Vijay, *World Bank and Development SAARC Nations,* (New Delhi: Deep and Deep Publications, 1995).

Singer, H.W. and Sumit Roy, *Economic Progress and Prospects in the Third World,* (Cambridge: Edward Eigar, 1993).

Singer, H.W., et al., (eds.), *Joint Ventures and Collaborations,* (New Delhi: Indus Publishing Company, 1991).

Singer, H.W., et al., (eds.), *Trade Liberalization in the 1990s,* (New Delhi: Indus Publishing Company, 1991).

Singh, Josh Harcharan, *India's Foreign Policy,* (New Delhi: Surjeet Publications, 1989).

Singh, M., *India Export Trends* (London: OUP, 1964).

Singh, M.P. and Himanshu Roy (eds.), *Indian Political System: Structure, Policies, Development,* (New Delhi: Jnanada Prakashan, 1995).

Singh, M.P. and Rekha Saxena (eds.), *India's Political Agenda: Perspectives on the Party System,* (Delhi: Kalinga Publications, 1996).

Singh, Rama Shankar (ed.), *IMF Policies Towards Less Developed Countries (LDCs): With Special Reference to India,* (Delhi: Deep & Deep Publications, 1996).

Singh, Rama Shankar, *Indo-Soviet Cooperation and India's Economic Development,* (New Delhi: Deep and Deep Publications, 1989).

Srinivasan, K. and Abusaleh Shariff, *India: Towards Population and Development Goals* (Delhi: OUP, 1997).

Stubbs, Richard and Geoffrey R.D. Underhill (eds.), *Political Economy and the Changing Global Order,* (London:

Macmillan, 1994).

Stubbs, Richard and Geoffrey R.D. Underhill (eds.), *Political Economy and the Changing Global Order,* (London: Macmillan, 1994).

Suri, Kamla, *India's Economy and The World,* (New Delhi: Vikas Publishing, 1992).

Swamy, Dalip S., *The Political Economy of Industrialisation: From Self-Reliance to Globalisation,* (New Delhi: Sage Publications, 1994).

Taylor, L., *Varieties of Stabilisation Experience* (Oxford: Clarendon Press, 1988).

Thakur, Ramesh, *The Government and Politics of India,* (London: Macmillan Press, 1995).

Thakur, Ramesh, *The Politics and Economics of India's Foreign Policy,* (New Delhi: OUP, 1994).

Tyagi, P.N., *Education for All: A Graphic Presentation,* first edition (New Delhi: National Institute of Educational Planning and Administration, 1993).

Vanaik, Achin, *India in a Changing World,* (New Delhi: Orient Longman, 1995).

Vanik, Achin, *The Painful Transition: Bourgeois Democracy in India,* (London: Verso, 1990).

Varma, M.L., *International trade,* (New Delhi: Vikas Publishing House, 1995).

Varma, Shanta Nedungadi, *Foreign Policy Dynamics: Moscow and India,* (New Delhi: Deep and Deep Publications, 1999).

Varshney, Ashutosh, *Democracy, Development, and the Countryside: Urban-Rural Struggles in India,* (New York: Cambridge University Press, 1995).

Viswanathan, V.N., *Dunkel Draft: Its Implications for India,* (New Delhi: Academic Publishers, 1994).

Vohra, Dewan C., *Economic Relevance of Non-Alignment,* (Delhi: ABC Publishing House, 1983).

Wadhva, Charan D., *Economic Reforms in India and the Market Economy,* (New Delhi: Allied Publishers, 1994).

Weiner, Myron, *The Child and the State In India: Child Labor and Education Policy in Comparative Perspective,* (Delhi: OUP, 1991).

Williamson, John (ed.), *The Political Economy of Policy Reform,* (Institute for International Economics, 1994).

Williamson, Jone (ed), *IMF Conditionality,* (Washington D.C.: Institute for International Economics, 1983).

B. Articles

Agarwal, M., "India and the World Economy", *International Studies,* Vol. 24, No. 4, 1987.

Agarwal, Manmohan, "Implications of Economic Liberalization for India's Foreign Policy", *International Studies,* 30, 2, 1993.

Ahluwalia, M.S., "Balance of Payments Adjustment in India 1970-71 to 1983-84", *World Development,* Vol. 14, No. 8, 1986.

Aksoy, M. A. and F. M. Ettori, "Protection and Industrial Structure in India", Policy Research Working Paper, No. 990, *World Bank,* October 1992.

Bardhan, Pranab and John E. Roemer, "Market Socialism: A Case for Rejuvenation", *Journal of Economic Perspectives,* Vol. 6, No. 3, 1992.

Baru, Sanjay, "No Couse for Woory," *The Sunday Times of India,* New Delhi, November 28, 1993.

Berg, Elliot and Alan Batchelder, "Structural Adjustment Lending: A Critical Review", *World Bank,* CPD 8521, Washington D.C., 1985.

Bhagavan, M.R., "Technological Implications of Structural Adjustment: Case of India", *EPW,* February 18-25, 1995.

Bhatt, M.C., "Joint Ventures and Technology Trade", *Foreign Trade Review,* January-March 1993.

Bhusan, Bharat, "World Bank Comments on Plan Draft Before Parliament Sees It", *Indian Express,* 16 July, 1992.

Bird, Graham, "IMF Lending", Overseas Development Institute Working Paper, *IMF,* London, No. 64, 1993.

Bora, D.K.S. and N.K. Sah, "Indo-EC Relations: Retrospect and Prospects", *India Quarterly,* January-June 1994.

Byres, T.J., "A Chicago View of the Indian State: An Oriental Grin without an Oriental Cat and Political Economy without Classes", *Journal of Commonwealth and Comparative Politics,* November 1988.

Cassen, Robert, Vijay Josh and Michael Lipton, "Stabilization and

Structural Reform in India", *Contemporary South Asia,* 2(2), 1993.

Cha, Victor D., "Politics and Democracy under the Kim Young Sam Government: Something Old, Something New", *Asian Survey,* Vol. XXXIII, No. 9 September, 1993.

Chandhoke, Neera, "Marxian Political Economy as Method: How Political Is Political Economy?", *EPW,* Vol. XXIX, No. 5, January 29, 1994.

Chishti, Sumitra, "India and Global Investment Flows", *World Focus,* November-December 1994.

Chossudovsky, M., "India under IMF Rule", *EPW,* March 6, 1993.

Chossudovsky, M., "Globalisation of Poverty", *Frontline,* March 13, 1992.

Clad, James, "Friends in Need", *Far Eastern Economic Review,* August 9, 1990.

Dasgupta, Biplab, "SAP: Issues and Conditionalities; A Global Review", *EPW,* May 17-24, 1997.

Dasgupta, Rajaram, "Subsidies, Patents and Market Access in Dunkel Draft", *EPW,* May 1993.

Datta, Bhabatosh, "The Central Budget and the New Economic Policy", *EPW,* April 20, 1985.

Drazen, Allan and Vittorio Grilli, "The Benefits of Crisis for Economic Reforms", *American Economic Review,* Vol. 83, No. 3, June 1993.

Dutta, Sujit, "India and ASEAN: A Framework for Comprehensive Engagement" *Strategic Analysis,* Vol. XX, No. 3, June 1997.

Ezhilarasi, M., "The Refuelling Issue, Its Relevance to our Foreign Policy in the Context of the Gulf War", *Indian Journal of Asian Affairs,* Vol. 6, 1993.

Gadgil, D.R., "The Economic Prospect for India", *Pacific Affairs,* Vol. XXII, No. 2, 1994.

Ganesan, A.V., "Uruguay Accord: An Opportunity", *The Hindu,* January 25, 1994.

Ghemawat, Pankaj and Murali Patibandla, "India's exports since the reforms", *EPW,* Vol. XXXIII, May 16-22, 1998.

Ghose, Kamal, "India and Europe, 1992: Possible Effect on Exports", *Frontne India,* December 16, 1990.

Ghosh, Arun, "Eighth Plan: Challenges and Possibilities", *EPW*, February 9, 1991.

Ghosh, Jayati, "Statistical Quibbles", *The Economic Times*, October 10, 1990.

Gidadhubli, R.G. "Indo-Soviet Trade: Compulsions for Status Quo", *EPW*, August 11, 1990.

Gujral, I.K., "Dilemmas of the Third World", *The Hindu*, August 1993.

Gulati, Ashok and Anil Sharma, "Agriculture Under GATT: What It Holds for India", *EPW*, Vol. XXIX, No. 29, July 16, 1994.

Gupta, Anand P., "Political Economy of Privatisation in India", *EPW*, Vol. XXXI, No. 39, September 28, 1996.

H. D. Shourie, "Our Government Offices Lack Work Ethos", *Times of India*, December 31, 1998.

Haq, Shamsul, "South Asian Regional Cooperation", *Third World Quarterly* 5 May-June 1994.

Hooke, A.W., "The IMF-Its Evolution, Organisation and Activities", *The IMF*, Pamphlet, No. 37, Washington, D.C., 1982.

Hushes, J., "The Philosophy of Intellectual Property", *Georgetown Law Journal,* Vol. 77 (2), 1988, pp. 287-366.

Jain, B.M., "Rethinking India's Foreign Policy and Foreign Relations", *Indian Journal of Asian Affairs,* Vol. 3, 1990.

Jha, P.S., "The End of the Tunnel: Return to Sanity in Economic Policy", *Times of India,* August 13, 1982.

Joshi, Vijay and I.M.D. Little, "Indian Macro Economic Policies", *EPW*, Vol. XXII, No. 9, February 28, 1987.

Karunakaran, K.P., "Non-alignment", *Seminar*, March 18, 1961.

Katti, Vijaya, "India's Economic Reforms: An Assessment of the Impact on Industry and FDI", *Foreign Trade Review,* Vol. XXVIII, No. 1, April-June 1993.

Katyal, K.K., "Reforms Will be Speeded Up: Rao", *Hindu Weekly,* July 4, 1992.

Kaushal, Neeraj, "For a Few Dollars More", *India Today,* July 31, 1991.

Khan, M.S. and M.D. Knight, "Fund Supported Adjustment Programmes and Economic Growth", *IMF Occasional Paper,* No. 4, Washington D.C.

Khare, Harish, "India Means Business", *Seminar,* 425 Annual, January 1995.

Khare, Harish, India Means Business, *Seminar,* January 1995.

Killick, Tony, "Continuity and Change in IMF Programme Design 1986-92", *ODI Working Paper,* No. 69, London, 1992.

Kohli, Atul, "Politics of Economic Liberalization in India", *World Development,* Vol. 17, No. 3, 1989.

Kothari, Rajni, "Globalisation and Revival of Tradition: Dual Attack on Model of Democratic National Building", *EPW,* March 15, 1995.

Kumar, Krishna, "Market Economy and Mass Literacy: Revisiting Innis's Economics of Communication", *EPW,* Vol. XXVIII, No. 50, December 11, 1993.

Kumar, Nagesh, "Industrialisation, Liberalisation and Tow Way Flows of Foreign Direct Investments: Case of India", *EPW,* Vol. XXX No. 50, December 16, 1995.

Kumar, Nagesh, "Liberalization and Changing patterns of Foreign Direct Investments: Has India's Relative Attractiveness as a Host of FDI Improved?", *EPW,* Vol. XXXIII No. 22, May 30, 1998.

Kumar, Prem, "Uruguay Round of Trade Negotiations: An Assessment and Overview", *EPW,* December 4, 1993.

McDonald, Hamish, "Looking for Friends", *Far Eastern Economic Review,* September 19, 1991.

Mehta, Balraj, "Changing Pattern of Foreign Aid", *Financial Express,* July 23, 1992.

Menkhaus, Kenneth, J. and Charles W. Kegly, jr., "The Compliant Foreign Policy of the Dependent State Revisited: Empirical Linkages and Lessons from the Case of Somalia", *Comparative Political Studies,* Vol. 21, No. 3, October 1988.

Mukerjee, Dilip, "Challenge to Foreign Policy", *Seminar,* January 1991.

Mukul, "Uttar Pradesh: Workers Challenge Privatisation", *EPW,* Vol.-XXVI, January 4-11, 1992.

Nachane, D.M., "Intellectual Property Rights in the Uruguay Round: An Indian Perspective", *EPW,* Vol. XXX No. 5, February 4, 1995.

Nayyar, Deepak and Abhijit Sen, "International Trade and the Agricultural Sector in India", *EPW*, May 1994.

Nogues, J., "Patents and Pharmaceutical Drugs: Understanding the Pressures on Developing Countries", PRE WP Series No. 502, *The World Bank,* Washington D.C., 1990.

Nuri, Maqsudi Hasan, "Indo-US Relations: The Economic Dimension", *Regional Studies,* Summer 1995.

Omvedt, G., "Three Sides of Every Story", *Down to Earth,* July 31, 1993.

Oza, B.M., "India-Korea Relations: Holding Hands Across Asia", *The Times of India,* 26 February, 1996.

Palkhivala, N.A., "The Union Budget 1995-96: An Election-Oriented Approach", *The Times of India,* March 21, 1995.

Panagariya, Arvind, "India as Scapegoat: US Actions under Super 301", *Times of India,* New Delhi, June 23, 1989.

Paranjape, H.K., "New Lamps for Old!: A Critique of the New Economic Policy", *EPW,* September 7, 1985.

Patnaik, Prabhat and C.P. Chandrasekhar, "Indian Economy under 'Structural Adjustment'", *EPW,* Vol. XXX, No. 47, November 25, 1995.

Patnaik, Prabhat, "International Capital and National Economic Policy: A Critique of India's Economic Reforms", *EPW,* March 19, 1994.

Pedersen, Jorgen Dige, "India and the EC in a New World Order", *Contemporary South Asia,* 2 (3), 1993.

Prakash, Padma, "Changing Priorities in Health Care", *EPW,* Vol. XXIX, March 19, 1994.

Prasad, H. Ashok Chandra, "Foreign Investment in India: Some Basic Facts and Issues", *Foreign Trade Review,* January-March 1994.

Przeworski, Adam and Fernando Limongi, "Political Regimes and Economic Growth", *Journal of Economic Perspectives,* No. 3, Summer, 1993.

Ramachandran, Sushma, "Indo-US ties on Even Keel", *The Hindu,* 21 July 1994.

Ramachandran, V.K., V. Rawal and M. Swaminathan, "Investment Gaps in Primary Education: A Statewise Study", *EPW,* Vol.

XXXII, January 4-11, 1997.

Roy, A.K., "Elections and the Working Class: Puzzling Political Response", *EPW*, Vol. XXXII, No. 14, April 5, 1997.

Ruggie, John Gerald, "Continuity and Transformation in the World Polity: Toward a Neo-Realist Synthesis", *World Politics*, (Baltimore), Vol. 35, January 1983.

Sahai, Suman, "Dunkel Draft is Bad for Agriculture", *EPW*, June 19, 1993.

Sen, Sunanda and Upendra Das R., "Import Liberalization as a Tool of Economic Policy in India since mid-Eighties", *EPW*, March 21, 1992.

Sengupta, Arjun, "Indira Gandhi's Economic Reforms", *Mainstream*, December 9, 1995.

Sheshan, A., "The Burden of Domestic Debt in India", *Reserve Bank of India, Occasional Papers*, Vol. 8, No. 1, 1987.

Shrivastava, B. K., "Indo-American Relations: Search for a New Equation", *International Studies*, 30,(2), 1993.

Singh, S. Nihal, "Tokyo Worry of Red Tape", *Hindustan Times*, April 4, 1991.

Thakur, Ramesh, "India and the United States: A Triumph of Hope over Experience?", *Asian Survey*, Vol. XXXVI, No. 6, June 1996.

Thomas, P., et. al., "Implication for Rural Sector", *EPW*, March 26, 1994.

Vaidhya, Adhya, "US Deplores India's Textile Trade Policy", *Times of India*, New Delhi, April 2, 1994.

Vaidhya, Adhya, "US Official's Visit seen to Boost Trade Ties", *Times of India*, New Delhi, February 3, 1994.

Wadhva, Charan, "Exim 1993: Welcome Modifications", *The Economic Times*, New Delhi, April 22, 1993.

Wadhva, Charan, "New Export Incentives", *The Hindustan Times*, New Delhi, October 16, 1991.

Walter Andersen, "India in 1995: Year of the long Campaign", *Asian Survey*, Vol. XXXVI, No. 2, February 1996.

Newspapers and Periodicals

American Economic Review
Asian Survey
Business India
Business Standard.
Comparative Political Studies
Competition Success Review
Contemporary South Asia
Economic Times.
Euromoney.
Foreign Trade Review
Frontne India
Georgetown Law Journal
Hindu Weekly.
India Today.
Indian Express.
International Studies
Journal of Commonwealth and Comparative Politics
Journal of Economic Perspectives
Mainstream
National Herald.
Pacific Affairs
Regional Studies
Seminar
Strategic Analysis
Sunday Observer.
Sunday.
The Hindu.
The Hindustan Times.
The Indian Journal of Public Administration
The Pioneer.
The Statesman.
Third World Quarterly
World Development
World Politics

Index